# ANCIENT INDIAN TRADITION & MYTHOLOGY



*Translated by*

**A BOARD OF SCHOLARS**

*And Edited by*

**Late Dr. G.P. BHATT**

VOLUME 73

# ANCIENT INDIAN TRADITION AND MYTHOLOGY SERIES

[PURĀṆAS IN TRANSLATION]

*Volumes Released*

ŚIVA 1-4
LIṄGA 5-6
BHĀGAVATA 7-11
GARUḌA 12-14
NĀRADA 15-19
KŪRMA 20-21
BRAHMĀṆḌA 22-26
AGNI 27-30
VARĀHA 31-32
BRAHMA 33-36
VĀYU 37-38
PADMA 39-48
SKANDA, PARTS I-XXII, 49-71
VĀMANA 72-73
GANEŚA 74-75

*Volumes Under Preparation*

BHAVIṢYA
BRAHMAVAIVARTA
DEVĪBHĀGAVATA
KĀLIKĀ
MĀRKAṆḌEYA
MATSYA
VIṢṆU
VIṢṆUDHARMOTTARA

# THE VĀMANA-PURĀṆA

## PART- II

*Translated and annotated by*

DR. R. S. SHIVA GANESHA MURTHY

MOTILAL BANARSIDASS PUBLISHERS
PRIVATE LIMITED • DELHI

*First Edition:* ***Delhi, 2015***



ISBN: 978-81-208-3946-5

MOTILAL BANARSIDASS
41 U.A. Bungalow Road, Jawahar Nagar, Delhi 110 007
8 Mahalaxmi Chamber, 22 Bhulabhai Desai Road, Mumbai 400 026
203 Royapettah High Road, Mylapore, Chennai 600 004
236, 9th Main III Block, Jayanagar, Bengaluru 560 011
Sanas Plaza, 1302 Baji Rao Road, Pune 411 002
8 Camac Street, Kolkata 700 017
Ashok Rajpath, Patna 800 004
Chowk, Varanasi 221 001

UNESCO COLLECTION OF REPRESENTATIVE WORKS—*Indian Series*
*This book has been accepted in the Indian Translation Series of the UNESCO Collection of Representative Works, jointly sponsored by the United Nations Educational, Scientific and Cultural Organization (UNESCO) and the Government of India*

*Printed in India*

by RP Jain at NAB Printing Unit,
A-44, Naraina Industrial Area, Phase I, New Delhi–110028
and published by JP Jain for Motilal Banarsidass Publishers (P) Ltd,
41 U.A. Bungalow Road, Jawahar Nagar, Delhi-110007

# PUBLISHER'S NOTE

The purest gems lie hidden in the bottom of the ocean or in the depth of rocks. One has to dive into the ocean or delve into the rocks to find them out. Similarly, truth lies concealed in the language which with the passage of time has become obsolete. Man has to learn that language before he discovers that truth.

But he has neither the means nor the leisure to embark on that course. We have, therefore, planned to help him acquire knowledge by an easier course. We have started the series of Ancient Indian Tradition and Mythology in English Translation. Our goal is to universalize knowledge through the most popular international medium of expression. The publication of the Purāṇas in English Translation is a step towards that goal.

**Acknowledgement**

It is our pleasant duty to put on record our sincere thanks to Dr. R. N. Dandekar and the UNESCO authorities for their kind encouragement and valuable help in the publication of the volumes in this series.

# CONTENTS

PUBLISHER'S NOTE v

ABBREVIATIONS xi

INTRODUCTION xv

VĀMANA-PURĀṆA
Part- II

| Chapter | Page |
|---|---|
| 46. Sthāṇutīrtha (contd.) | 247 |
| 47. Sthāṇutīrtha: Veṇa Rescued | 251 |
| 48. Sthāṇutīrtha: Veṇa Goes to Heaven | 266 |
| 49. Sthāṇutīrtha: Origin of Caturmukha | 269 |
| 50. Himavān weds Menā | 273 |
| 51. Penance of Umā | 274 |
| 52. Sages Go to Himavān | 281 |
| 53. Wedding of Umā | 287 |
| 54. Birth of Vināyaka | 293 |
| 55. Fall of Caṇḍa and Muṇḍa | 299 |
| 56. Death of Śumbha and Niśumbha | 306 |
| 57. The Birth of Kārttikeya | 313 |
| 58. Killing of Tāraka and Mahiṣa | 320 |
| 59. Episode of Pātālaketu: Andhaka Flees to Pātāla | 329 |
| 60. Birth of Kedāra-tīrtha: Legend of Mura | 334 |
| 61. Killing of Mura | 341 |
| 62. The Legend of Maṅkaṇa | 347 |
| 63. The Story of Daṇḍa | 352 |
| 64. The Story of Suratha and Citrāṅgadā | 358 |
| 65. The Story of Suratha and Citrāṅgadā (contd.) | 364 |
| 66. Setting out of Andhaka's army | 376 |
| 67. Vision of Sadāśiva | 381 |
| 68. The Defeat of Daityas | 385 |

69. Jambha and Kujambha Killed 390
70. Andhaka is Granted Boon 402
71. Birth of Maruts 410
72. Birth of Maruts ( contd.) 414
73. Killing of Kālanemi 419
74. Prahlāda's Advice to Balī 423
75. Jayaśrī Resorts to Balī 427
76. Aditi Offered a Boon 431
77. Bali Admonished 436
78. Defeat of Dhundhu 441
79. The Story of Purūravas 448
80. The Vow of Nakṣatra-Puruṣa 454
81. The Killing of Jalodbhava 457
82. The Story of Śrīdāma 460
83. Prahlāda's Pilgrimage 463
84. Prahlāda's Pilgrimage (contd.) 465
85. The Release of the King-Elephant 469
86. The Sārasvata Hymn 476
87. The Sin-Allaying Hymn-1 485
88. The Sin-Allaying Hymn-2 490
89. The Birth of Vāmana 492
90. The Mention of One's Own Abodes 497
91. Dialogue Between Śukra and Bali 500
92. Bali Restrained 509
93. Brahmā's Hymn 515
94. The Lord Eulogized 519
95. Worship of God Viṣṇu 525
Phalaśruti 530

NOTES 532

## ABBREVIATIONS

Common and self-evident abbreviations such as Ch(s)—Chapter(s), p—page, pp.—pages, v—verse, vv—verses, Ftn—Footnote, Hist. Ind. Philo.—History of Indian Philosophy are not included in this list.

| | |
|---|---|
| ABORI | *Annals of the Bhandarkar Oriental Research Institute,* Poona |
| AGP | S.M. Ali's The Geography of *Purāṇas,* PPH, New Delhi, 1973 |
| AIHT | *Ancient Indian Historical Tradition,* F.E. Pargiter, Motilal Banarsidass (MLBD), Delhi |
| AITM | *Ancient Indian Tradition and Mythology-Series,* MLBD, Delhi |
| AP | *Agni Purāṇa,* Guru Mandal Edition (GM), Calcutta, 1957 |
| Arch. S. Rep. | *Archaeological Survey Report* |
| AV | *Atharva Veda,* Svādhyāya Maṇḍal, Aundh |
| BdP | *Brahmāṇḍa Purāṇa,* MLBD, Delhi 1973 |
| BG | *Bhagavadgītā* |
| BhP | *Bhāgavata Purāṇa,* Bhagavat Vidyapeeth, Ahmedabad |
| Br | *Brāhmaṇa* (preceded by name such as Śatapatha) |
| BsP | *Bhaviṣya Purāṇa,* Vishnu Shastri Bapat, Wai |
| BVP | *Brahma Vaivarta Purāṇa,* GM, 1955-57 |
| CC | *Caturvarga Cintāmaṇi* by Hemādri |
| CVS | *Caraṇa Vyūha Sūtra* by Śaunaka, Commentary by Mahīdāsa |

| | |
|---|---|
| DB | *Devī Bhāgavata, GM,* 1960-57 |
| De or GDAMI | *The Geographical Dictionary of Ancient and Mediaeval India,* N.L. De, Oriental Reprint, Delhi, 1971 |
| DhS | *Dharma Sūtra* (preceded by the author's name such as Gautama) |
| ERE | *Encyclopaedia of Religion and Ethics* by Hastings |
| GP | *Garuḍa Purāṇa,* ed. R.S. Bhattacharya, Chowkhamba, Varanasi, 1964 |
| GS | *Gṛhya Sūtra* (preceded by the name of the author such as Āpastamba) |
| HD | *History of Dharma Śāstra,* P.V. Kane, G.O.S. |
| IA | *The Indian Antiquary* |
| IHQ | *The Indian Historical Quarterly* |
| JP | *Purāṇa* (Journal of the Kashiraj Trust), Varanasi |
| KA | *Kauṭilya Arthaśāstra* |
| KP | *Kūrma Purāṇa,* Veṅkaṭeśvara Press Edn., Bombay; also Kashiraj Trust Edn., Varanasi, 1971 |
| LP | *Liṅga Purāṇa,* GM, 1960; also MLBD, Delhi, 1981 |
| Manu | *Manusmṛti* |
| Mbh | *Mahābhārata,* Gītā Press, Gorakhpur, VS 2014 |
| MkP | *Mārkaṇḍeya Purāṇa* |
| MN | *Mahābhārata Nāmānukramaṇi,* Gita Press, Gorakhpur, VS 2016 |
| MtP | *Matsya Purāṇa,* GM, 1954 |
| MW | Monier Williams' *Sanskrit-English Dictionary,* MLBD, Delhi 1976 |
| NP | *Nāradīya* or *Nārada Purāṇa,* Veṅkaṭeśvara Press, Bombay |

| | |
|---|---|
| PCK | *Bhāratavarṣīya Prācīna Caritrakośa*, Siddheshwar Shastri, Poona, 1968 |
| PdP | *Padma Purāṇa*, GM, 1957-59 |
| PE | *Purāṇic Encyclopaedia*, V. Mani, English version, MLBD, Delhi, 1975 |
| PR or PRHRC | *Puranic Records on Hindu Rites and Customs*, R.C. Hazra, Calcutta, 1948 |
| ṚV | *Ṛg-Veda*, Svādhyāya Maṇḍal, Aundh |
| Śat Br | *Śatapatha Brāhmaṇa* |
| SC or SMC | *Smṛti Candrikā* by Devanna Bhaṭṭa |
| SEP | *Studies in Epics and Purāṇas*, A.D. Psalkar, Bharatiya Vidya Bhavan (BVB), Bombay |
| SkP | *Skanda Purāṇa* |
| SP | *Śiva Purāṇa* |
| VāP | *Vāyu Purāṇa* |
| VR | *Vālmīki Rāmāyaṇa* |
| VdP | *Viṣṇudharmottara Purāṇa* |
| VmP | *Vāmana Purāṇa* |
| VP | *Viṣṇu Purāṇa* |
| VrP | *Varāha Purāṇa* |

# INTRODUCTION

*Vāmana* is assigned fourteenth position in the list of eighteen *Mahāpurāṇas* or major Purāṇic texts, preceded by *Skanda* and succeeded by *Kūrma*. It gets its name after Vāmana or the dwarf incarnation of God Viṣṇu, which is the first human incarnation followed by the "Fish", "Tortoise", "Boar" and "Man-Lion" incarnations that can, by the way, be seen as corresponding to the earlier stages of the evolution of life on the earth, the main purpose of the *Purāṇa* being a description of the legend of the demon Bali, grandson of Prahlāda, the Viṣṇu devotee *par excellence*, suffering a great discomfiture due to a very tactful manoeuvre resorted by God Viṣṇu as the dwarf.

The extant text of *Vāmana* has 95 chapters and approximately 6,000 *ślokas*, though *Bhāgavata* and some other *Purāṇas* state that *Vāmana* had an *Uttarabhāga* also containing four *Saṁhitās* of 1000 *ślokas* each, which, however, has not been discovered so far.

Pulastya and Nārada are the interlocutors of the *Purāṇa*. In the beginning Nārada questions Pulastya about the assumption of the form of Vāmana by Viṣṇu, waging of war by Prahlāda against gods, Satī's agreement to be the wife of Śiva, Satī's self-immolation at the *yajña* of Dakṣa and her being reborn as the daughter of Himālaya with a desire of becoming the spouse of Śaṅkara, the glory of the places of pilgrimage, account of *dāna, vrata, upāsanā,* etc.

As the title indicates, this *Purāṇa* has mainly a Vaiṣṇava theme but Śaiva material also forms an integral part of it, e.g. Śiva's killing of the demon Andhaka, marriage of Śiva and Pārvatī, birth of Gaṇeśa and Kārttikeya, defeat of

Mahiṣāsura by Devī, glorification of *Śivaliṅgas* and their installation.

The legends, stories and episodes included in this *Purāṇa* are generally of the same type as found in other *Purāṇas*. Here we may call attention to some noteworthy features of the *Purāṇa*. One is that it was composed in the Kurukṣetra region of North India, to the glorification of which it gives special attention, particularly to the *tīrthas*, rivers, hills and other geographical features of the area.

Secondly, the *Purāṇa* gives equal prominence to Vaiṣṇavism and Pāśupata Śaiva-sect in its description and exhibits a spirit of tolerance and magnanimity in its treatment of both, as is evidenced in its representation of Śiva as saying, "Even if you cut me into twain, you will find the presence of Viṣṇu in my heart" (67.37), and of Viṣṇu as telling the *Devas*, "Śiva is present here in my heart in the form of *Liṅga* where you may worship him" (62.21-23).

Thirdly, a very much noteworthy feature of this *Purāṇa* is the preponderance of the *asura* motif. No other *Purāṇa* gives the accounts of so many *asura* heroes in so liberal and zestful manner as this *Purāṇa* does. So many *asuras* are represented in an edifying way as following the ideals of *Dharma*, righteousness, e.g. Prahlāda, a great devotee of Viṣṇu and his grandson Bali who, despite the warning given by the preceptor Śukrācārya, prominently exhibits the spirit of a liberal donor and quite unmindful of his personal interest ungrudgingly accepts underworld status to which he is reduced by God Viṣṇu. Perhaps one of the reasons is that the narrator of the *Purāṇa* is Pulastya, the grandfather of demon Rāvaṇa.

As to the date of the *Purāṇa*, it was some time between 5th and 10th centuries CE, probably the first half of the seventh century CE when Harṣavardhana was the king in North and Mahendravarman Pallava in the South, when the assimilative spirit, religious tolerance and the intellectual fertility characterising the Gupta Age permeated the society.

As to the contents of the *Purāṇa*, it is found that in addition to the legends, myths, stories, etc. of the gods, *asuras*, *ṛṣis*, etc. which belong to the *Purāṇas* generally *Vāmana* is rich in the description of pilgrimage centres, i.e. *tīrthas*, in the stotras or eulogies to the gods, geographical materials, description of the mountains, rivers, Janapadas, etc. Here we make a brief survey of more interesting items of the contents—

Chapter 6 mentions four schools of Śaivism, viz. *Śaiva*, *Pāśupata*, *Kāladamana* and *Kāpālika*. The *Kāladamana* sect is better known by the name *Kālāmukha*.

Chapter 7 has a short inset showing the birth of the nymph Urvaśī from the thigh of Nārāyaṇa, the *ṛṣis* who together with another one, Nara, was performing penance in Himālayas.

Chapter 9 describes the vehicles of the different gods as follows:

| | |
|---|---|
| Indra | - White elephant |
| Yama | - Bufallo named Pauṇḍraka |
| Varuṇa | - Śiśumāra |
| Kubera | - Nara |
| Eleven Rudras | - White bulls |
| Candramā | - Haṁsa |
| Twelve Ādityas | - Chariots yoked with horses and camels |
| Eight Vasus | - Elephant |
| Yakṣa | - Nara |
| Kinnara | - Serpent |
| Twin Aśvins | - Horse |
| Maruts | - Antelope |
| Bhṛgus | - Parrot |
| Gandharvas | - Walking on foot |

Twelves kinds of *dharmas* are described in chapter 11 including that of humans in whose case it is self-study of *Vedas*, *Brahmacarya*, *Dāna*, *Yajña*, *compassion*, etc. and devotion to Viṣṇu, Śiva, Sūrya and Devī. The seven continents (*Dvīpas*) of the Earth are also described, the seventh, Puṣkara Dvīpa, contains 21 hells (*narakas*).

Chapter 12 gives a list of bests (*Pravara-sūcī*) in the case of 56 classes of deities, mountains, etc. naming, e.g. *Matsya Purāṇa* as the best among *Purāṇas*, *Kuru-Jāṅgala* as the best of *kṣetras*, Pṛthūdaka as the best of tīrthas, etc.

Chapter 13 gives nine geographical divisions of Bhāratavarṣa, which is the name of what we now call greater India. Eight islands, several *Kula-parvatas, Varṣa-parvatas* and *Viṣkambha-parvatas* and 21 hills are also described. Rivers are classified according to their sources. *Janapadas* (political units) of the seven divisions of the country constitute a long list.

Various *Dharmas* including *Sāmānya* and *Āśrama Dharmas* are discussed in chapter 14. They include rules of health and hygiene, purification, food, clothing, ethical and social conduct, *Śrāddha*, worship of gods, performance of Sandhyā, etc. in daily routine.

In chapter 17 the birth of Mahiṣāsura, that of Raktabīja and of Kātyāyanī Durgā are described. The episode of the Vindhya Mountain, bowing to Ṛṣi Agastya, is also related. The death of Mahiṣāsura is described in chapter 20.

Chapter 21 describes the story of Saṁvaraṇa, son of *Ṛkṣa* who lived in *Kṛtayuga*, and of his marriage with Tapatī, daughter of Sūrya, and of the birth, from their wedlock, of Kuru, the king after whom the place is named as Kurukṣetra. It is also explained why it is called Dharmakṣetra.

Chapter 32 has a description of the Vedic river *Sarasvatī* in Kurukṣetra, its source and *Māhātmya.* Its source is given as *Plakṣa* or *Plakṣa-Prasravaṇa,* i.e., the glacial water-flow of *Plakṣa.*

Chapter 33 describes the source of Sarasvatī in Kurukṣetra. She came to Avantika which was in Pṛthūdaka. After sanctifying Kurukṣetra by her waters she took a westerly course to meet the western sea.

The region between *Sarasvatī* and *Dṛśadvatī*, another great river which forms the southern boundary of Kurukṣetra, was known as *Brahmāvarta.*

Chapter 34 gives the names of seven forests and seven rivers of Kurukṣetra. The forests are: *Kāmyaka Vana, Aditi Vana, Vyāsa Vana, Phalakī Vana, Sūrya Vana, Madhu Vana and Puṇyaśīta Vana.* The rivers are: *Sarasvatī, Vaitaraṇī, Āpagā, Amlu Nadī, Kauśikī, Dṛśadvatī* and *Hiraṇvatī.*

Chapters 35-37 give accounts of various *tīrthas* of Kurukṣetra, their glory and their efficacy. The *tīrtha* named Brahmodumbara is associated with the penances of Brahmā and the seven *ṛṣis.*

Chapter 38 contains the episode of sage Maṅkaṇa, his ecstatic dance on seeing the sap of plants issuing forth from his injured hand, his being humbled by Śiva, etc.

Chapter 40 relates the story of rivalry between Viśvāmitra and Vasiṣṭha, of the water of *Sarasvatī* getting polluted by the curse of the former and of purity restored to it by the water of river *Aruṇā* made to flow into it.

Chapter 46 gives a detailed account of the numerous *Śiva-liṅgas* installed in *Kurukṣetra.*

Chapter 47 gives an account of the heretic activities of king Vena, son of Ikṣvāku, and his being killed by infuriated Ṛṣis and of his son Pṛthu who, by contrast, was a righteous king.

Chapters 52-53 give a detailed account of the marriage of Śiva and Pārvatī and a reference to the amusing interlude of Brahmā's losing his self-control and getting impassioned by the beauty of Pārvatī and the consequent birth of Vālakhilyas.

In chapter 61 subsequent to the narration of a number of interesting episodes of Raktabīja, Ṛtadhvaja, Gālava, Pātālaketu, Madālasā, Viśvāvasu, Andhakāsura, etc. we come across Brahmā's new exposition of 21 hells, each of which comprises one or more moral lapses like calumny, unbelief, deserting one's *dharma,* greediness, etc. All these are collectively named as Puṁnāma Naraka.

Here Sanatkumāra brothers are shown as sons of *dharma* and *ahiṁsā* rather than those of Brahmā whose mental sons (*Mānasa Putras*) they are traditionally known to be.

In chapter 69 demon Andhaka assumes the guise of Śiva to seduce Pārvatī but he fails to get her as Pārvatī soon discovers the fraud and conceals herself in the white flower of *arka* plant. In this chapter Mātali, the charioteer of Indra, is said to have Śamīka as his father.

In chapter 70 the birth of a girl from the perspiration appearing on the forehead of Śiva during his fight with Andhaka is described, who becomes goddess Carcikā, the presiding deity of Mount Hiṅgula in Baluchistan. Andhaka is killed by Śiva and made his Gaṇa and named Bhṛṅgin.

Chapter 73 describes the death of Asura Kālanemi at the hands of Indra and chapter chapter 74 shows *asuras* reorganised under the leadership of Bāṇa who defeats the *Devas* and consequently Bali becomes Indra, Bāṇa becomes Yama, Maya becomes Varuṇa, Rāhu Soma, Ketu Sūrya and Śukra Bṛhaspati. At the request of Bali, Prahlāda expounds the duties of a worthy king, protection of the people being his supreme duty. The *Purāṇa* describes Bali as a perfect model of a king, though an *asura* by race, who established a kingdom of perfect righteousness following the ideals of Bhāgavata *Dharma*. Thereafter we find an account of Prahlāda's *Tīrthayātrā*.

Chapter 82 gives an account of Viṣṇu's weapon *Sudarśana Cakra* which is said to have been given by Śiva, whose twelve spokes are said to represent twelve gods.

Chapters 85-88 contain four *Stotras*, viz. *Gajendramokṣa*, *Sarasvatī-Stotra*, and two *Pāpapraśamana Stotras*—one recited by Śiva to Viṣṇu and another recited by Agastya to Viṣṇu.

Chapter 90 gives a long list of Viṣṇu Pīṭhas, 127 in number, which are designated as *Mahālayas*.

Chapter 93 gives the finale consisting of a *stotra* in prose recited by Brahmā glorifying the Vāmana form of God Viṣṇu.

—G.P. BHATT

# CHAPTER FORTY-SIX

## Sthāṇu-tīrtha (continued)

*Sanatkumāra said:*

1. *Śukla-tīrtha* is described as (located) to the north of *Sthāṇu-vaṭa,* and to the east of *Sthāṇu-vaṭa* is *Vyoma-tīrtha,* O eminent Brāhmaṇas.

2. *Dakṣa-tīrtha* is located to the south of *Sthāṇu-vaṭa* and *Nakula-gaṇa* to the west of *Sthāṇu-vaṭa.*

3. All these are considered holy *Tīrthas.* In the middle is *Sthāṇu-tīrtha.* By the very sight of it, one attains the supreme state.

4-7. One who circumambulates these on the eighth (*Aṣṭamī*) and fourteenth (*Caturdaśī*) days and also Umā, in the form of a *Liṅga,* does not leave the proximity of Hara, obtains superhuman powers.

On the northern side of *Vaṭa* is the great *Liṅga* yielding all wishes, established by venerable *Takṣaka.*

On the eastern side of *Vaṭa* is the west-facing great *Liṅga* installed by Viśvakarmā, by visiting which a man becomes accomplished. Exactly there dwells Sarasvatī in the form of a *Liṅga.*

8-10. With rererence prostrating oneself before her one attains intelligence and wisdom.

By visiting Lord Vaṭeśvara, one attains the supreme state. Then by visiting and circumambulating *Sthāṇu-vaṭa,* one will have circumambulated the earth comprising seven islands.

To the west of *Sthāṇu* is situated *Gaṇa Nakuliśa.*

11. By earnestly worshipping him, one is absolved of all sins. To the south of *Sthāṇu* is located the *Tīrtha Rudrākara.*

12-14. A person who bathes in that *Tīrtha* will have bathed in all *Tīrthas.*

To the north (of *Sthāṇu*) is the excellent *Liṅga Gokarṇa* by name installed by the eminent Rāvaṇa. A person who bathes and keeps fast on the fourteenth day of dark half of *Āṣāḍha,* becomes absolved of all blemishes.

There is also the *Liṅga* bestowing all powers installed by Meghanāda.

15. By ardently worshipping (this *Liṅga*), one obtains profuse wealth.

To the west (of *Sthāṇu*) is (found the *Liṅga*) worshipped by Kumbhakarṇa.

16. Listen to the merit accrued to a person who resides (there) with faith keeping fast on the eighth day of the bright half of *Jyeṣṭha* month.

17-20. At every step the person obtains the merit of sacrifices; there is no doubt. These are ardently frequented by ascetics, *Sādhyas, Ādityas, Vasus, Maruts,* and *Vahnis.* Even any other being that enters (the region of) the excellent *Sthāṇus* all beings absolved of sins reach the supreme state.

The *Liṅga* that is found close to (the *Liṅga* of) the Trident-wielding Lord of lords is Umā in the form of *Liṅga;* she does not leave close proximity of Hara.

He who visits *Gokarṇa* accrues (great) merit.

21. By worshipping Hara, a person will be absolved of all the sins accumulated knowingly or unknowingly.

22. The merit that men acquire through *Brahmacarya,* during childhood, that merit (is acquired) by one who worships Śiva, Śaṅkara, on that eighth day (*Aṣṭamī)*

23. If one desires extraordinary beauty, prosperity or wealth, that can be accomplished by the greatness of *Kumāreśvara.* There is no doubt about this.

24. Having worshipped the Liṅga on the north of it (*Sthāṇu*), Vibhīṣaṇa became ageless and immortal.

25. By worshipping on the eighth day of the bright half of *Āṣāḍha* and by keeping fast, one attains immortality.

26. O best of Brāhmaṇas ! In that place is the *Liṅga, Pūrṇa,* established to the east. By worshipping the *Liṅga* with zeal, all desires of a person are fulfilled.

27. Even Dūṣaṇa and Triśiras having gladly worshipped Maheśvara there, obtained their desired objects.

28. To the person who worships there during the bright half of *Caitra,* the two wish-yielding gods fulfill his wishes.

29. To the east of *Sthāṇu-vaṭa* is situated *Hastipādeśvara* Śiva. By visiting the *Liṅga* one is absolved of sins incurred in other births.

30. To the south of it (*Sthāṇu-vaṭa*) is the *Liṅga* of the sage Hārīta, by earnestly prostrating before which, a man attains accomplishment.

31. On its right side is the *Śiva-liṅga* of the eminent *Vāpīta,* known in all the three worlds and destroying all sins.

32. It is the exalted *Liṅga* established by the venerable Rudra of the form of skeleton and is the destroyer of all evils.

33. It is spoken of as the giver of enjoyment of salvation and the remover of all blemishes. By visiting only the *Liṅga,* one obtains the merit (of the performance of) *Agniṣṭoma.*

34. To the west of it is the *Liṅga* established by *Siddhas,* famous as Siddheśvara who bestows all accomplishments.

35. To its south is the *Liṅga* established by the exalted Mṛkaṇḍu, by visiting which one is bestowed with all accomplishments.

36. To its east is the excellent *Liṅga* able to destroy all sins and established by the exalted Āditya.

37. The *Gandharva* Citrāṅgada and the best of the *Apsarās,* Rambhā, were mutually in love and were desirous of visiting *Sthāṇu.*

38. Having come, they visited and worshipped *Sthāṇu.* The two who were attached to each other, installed god Maheśvara.

39. O Brāhmaṇa ! Having visited *Citrāṅgadeśvara* as well as *Rambheśvara,* a person will have birth in a decent family and becomes prosperous and handsome.

40. To the south of it, is the *Liṅga* installed by the Wielder of thunderbolt (*Indra*) in the past. By its grace, the fruit cherished by one's mind is obtained.

41. So also excellent poetic gift was acquired by sage Parāśara by visiting Śaṅkara.

42. Having propitiated Parameśvara, Sage Vedavyāsa obtained omniscience and the knowledge of Brahman by the grace of the god.

43. To the west of Sthāṇu is installed the *Liṅga Himavateśvara* which grants all accomplishments to the meritorious.

44. To the west of this is the sin-destroying *Liṅga* installed by *Kārtavīrya*, by visiting which, one is absolved of sins instantly.

45. To the north of this is the *Liṅga* installed by Supārśva, propitiating which Hanumān became accomplished by the grace of the Lord.

46. In a place to the east of this, the all-powerful Viṣṇu by propitiating the wish-granting Lord in the middle of the wheel (obtained) *Sudarśana*(*-cakra*).

47. To the east of this are the two excellent *Liṅgas* fulfilling all desire, installed by Indra and Varuṇa.

48-49. All these are capable of destroying every sin and are zealously frequented by sages, *Sādhyas*, *Ādityas* and *Vasus*: the *Liṅgas*, the self-existing *Sthāṇu* and those installed by sages knowing truth—their number, however, is unlimited.

50. To the north up to the river Oghavatī and to the west of the *Lord*, are one thousand one *Liṅgas*.

51. And to the east of the god upto *Sannihita* pond, there are millions of Rudras installed by the exalted *Vālakhilyas*.

52. To the south of the god are the *Liṅgas* which are countless in number, installed by *Gandharvas*, *Yakṣas* and *Kinnaras*.

53. Vāyu spoke of thirty-five million *Liṅgas*. There are thousands of uncounted *Liṅgas* which are found in the region of Rudra (*Sthāṇu*).

54. Having known this, one must resort with faith to *Sthāṇu-liṅga* by whose grace one obtains cherished things.

55. Having entered the temple of *Sthāṇu*, a person with or without any desire, reaches the highest state being absolved of dreadful sins.

56-57. On the most holy thirteenth day of *Caitra* (dark fortnight) when there is conjunction of Venus, Moon and Sun associated with an auspicious star, *Sthāṇu-liṅga* was installed by Brahmā, the supporter of the universe; it is being worshipped for eternal years by sages and groups of gods.

58. Those people who with faith and fasting worship Śiva on such a day, reach the highest state.

59. Those who having known the *Liṅga* established there, perform circumambulation, will have circumambulated the earth comprised of the seven *Dvīpas*.

## CHAPTER FORTY-SEVEN

### Sthāṇu-tīrtha: Vena rescued

*Mārkaṇḍeya said:*

1. O sage ! I like to hear the efficacy of *Sthāṇu-tīrtha*. Who has obtained power here that destroys the fear of all sins ?

*Sanatkumāra said:*

2. Listen to the complete excellent glory of *Sthāṇu-tīrtha* by hearing which people become free from all sins.

3. When the Universe of both moveable and immoveable things was lost in one indistinguishable watery mass, the Grandsire of the entire world was born (in the lotus that emerged from) the navel of Viṣṇu.

4. Marīci was born of him. His son was Kaśyapa. From Kaśyapa was born Bhāsvān (sun) from whom Manu was born.

5. When Manu sneezed, his son emerged from his mouth. He became the protector of all earth bound by the four oceans and of righteousness (*Dharma*).

6. His wife was the dreadful one, Bhayā by name, born of Death, the daughter of Time.

7. To her was born Vena, the wicked despiser of *Veda.* King Kṣuta having seen his son's face, retired to forest.

8. There he performed a severe penance covering both heaven and earth with righteousness and attained that highest abode from which there is no return (to human existence).

9-12a. Vena became the king of the whole of earth. Vena, the son of the daughter of *Kāla,* was wicked and despiser of *Veda.* He, due to the (inherited) bad nature of the maternal grandfather, proclaimed in the city: "There shall be no gifts, no sacrifices and never any oblations to fire (in the name of god). I am the only one who is ever to be saluted and honoured by you. You being under my protection, live happily. For, there is no deity other than myself, who would be your resort."

12b-15. Having heard this, all the sages came together and said this to the king: "The *Veda* is the authority for *Dharma* and by that *Yajña* is established. The deities residing in the heaven are not pleased without sacrifices and if they are not pleased, they do not give (rain) for the growth of vegetation. Therefore, the world of moveables and immoveables is sustained by sacrifices and deities."

15b-19. Having heard this, Vena repeatedly said with an angry look, "No sacrifice; no charity" and he became extemely furious. All those sages got enraged and struck him with *Kuśa* grass purified by incantation and endowed with *Vajra.* As there was anarchy then in the world and as it was enveloped by gloom, the people, distressed by robbers, resorted to those sages. Then the sages churned his (Vena's) left hand and from it sprang a man of short stature. All the sages said to him: "You please be seated."

20. From him were born Niṣādas produced by the sins of Vena. Then the sages churned the right hand.

21. As that hand was churned, there was born another man resembling a lofty mountain and having auspicious marks.

22-23. His hands had marks of bow, arrow, discus and banner. Having seen him come into being, all the gods with Indra consecreted him in this world as the king, the protector of the earth. Thereupon, he delighted the world with righteousness.

24. The people who were distressed by his father were well protected by him. Then he got the name '*rājā*' because he delighted (rañjana) the world.

25-26a. King Vainya, having got the kingdom, thought: "My father was unrighteous and an obstructor of sacrifice. How should the obsequies (*śrāddha*) that bring about happiness to him in the other world be performed?"

Even as he was thinking so, Nārada came to him.

26b-28. Having given him a seat and after saluting him, Vainya asked him: "Venerable Sir, you know the good and the bad of all people. My father was wicked, despiser of deities and Brāhmaṇas. He deserted the righteous path and has attained the other world, O Brāhmaṇa !"

29. Comprehending with his divine insight, Nārada told him: "He is born among *Mlecchas* and is afflicted with consumption and leprosy."

30. Having heard the words of the noble Nārada, he (Vainya) was grief-stricken and pondered: "How should I act?"

31. A thought occured to that noble soul who was thus considering: "In this world, he is called a son who rescues the fathers from the fear (of hell)." So thinking, he then asked the sage:

*Nārada said:*

32. You go to the great *Tīrtha*, the pond *Sannihita*, and having taken bath, cleanse his body in all *Tīrthas*.

33. Having heard these words of venerable Nārada, the king found out that country and went there too.

34-37. Having gone to the northern region, he spotted him (Vena) among the *Mlecchas.* Having seen him afflicted with leprosy and consumption, he (Vainya) being deeply distressed by grief, said these words: "O *Mlecchas*! I bow down to this man and I take him to my house. There I will make him cured of the disease, if you agree." "Be it so, do as you deem fit", said the *Mlecchas* bowing with all their limbs to the compassionate person (Vainya), then he brought men able to carry a palanquin.

38-39. Offering double the wages, he asked them to take the twice-born safely. Then at the words of the compassionate king, they quickly carried the palanquin through Kurukṣetra. Having taken him to *Sthāṇu-tīrtha,* they made him alight and went (on their way).

40. Then at noon, the king arranged to get him bathed. At that moment, Vāyu spoke thus in the sky —

41-42. "My boy, do not act thoughtlessly; safeguard the *Tīrtha* carefully. This person is deeply entwined with very serious sin. Despising *Veda* is a serious crime for which there is no redemption at all. If he takes ablution (here), he at once destroys this sacred pond."

43-44. Having heard the words of Vāyu, he was afflicted with deep sorrow. Being very much aggrieved and agonised by his (father's) suffering, he said: "He is (no doubt) entwined by dreadful sin. But I will perform the expiation as directed by the deities."

44b-48. Then all the deities told thus: "You take bath and pour water (of the *Tīrtha*) over (him). You do this on the bank of Sarasvatī (river) till the blemish is cleansed. A person endowed with faith attains salvation by taking ablution. But this man was interested in nourishing himself and engaged in reviling the deities. And he has been spurned by Brāhmaṇas. He never gets purified. Therefore, with devotion you take bath on his behalf in the *Tīrthas* and pour (*Tīrtha*) water over him. By that he becomes purified."

48b-50. Having heard these words, he constructed a cottage for him. Then the king proceeded on a pilgrimage for the sake of his father. Day after day without fail he took ablution in the *Tīrthas* and poured water of the *Tīrtha* over his father. In the meanwhile there came a dog.

51. (The dog was in its previous birth) the chief of the *Kaulas* and custodian of the property of the deity in the temple of *Sthāṇu*. He was ever looking after the property in his possession.

52. He was liked by all people and was intent on the duties towards the deity. He was carrying on thus in pious path.

53. In course of time, his mind changed to destroy the temple property. With the commitment of such impious act, he went to the other world.

54. Having seen him, Yama pronounced the sentence: "Be born as a dog before long." Immediately after his sentence, he was born as a dog in *Saugandhika* forest.

55. As time went by, he was surrounded by a large pack of hounds. He was despised and was very much distressed.

56-57. Having left *Dvaitavana*, he came to the holy *Sannihita* pond. Immediately on his entry, due to the grace of *Sthāṇu* only, he felt too thirsty and plunged into Sarasvatī river. With his body being splashed (with water) in the river, he was absolved of all sins.

58-61. The dog, then, entered the *Kula Maṭha* desirous of food. Seeing the dog entering and frightened, he patted it and plunged into *Sthāṇu-tīrtha.*

The fallen one bathed with drops of water in earlier *Tīrthas,* was sprinkled with sprays of water thrown by the body of that dog. Afterwards, he, the one self-controlled with a mind free from attachment, was rescued by the killing (*Kṣaṇena*) of the dog and by his son and due to the efficacy of *Sthāṇu-tīrtha.* In a moment, he was endowed with a divine body. Having prostrated to *Sthāṇu,* he (Vena) began a eulogy (obscure).

*Vena said:*

62. I resort to you, O Deva Īśāna ! The birthless, moon-ornamented, great god, the exalted one, the Lord of the entire universe.

63. Salutation to you, O lord of gods ! O destroyer of all foes ! O master of gods ! O restrainer of Bali ! O one adored by *Devas* and *Daityas* !

64. O one of deformed eyes ! O thousand-eyed one ! O three-eyed one ! O one liked by the lord of *Yakṣas* ! You, O one having hands and feet everywhere ! O one having eyes, head and face on all sides !

65. O one having ears everywhere ! You stand in the world encompassing everything. O spike-eared one ! O large-eared one ! O pot-eared one ! O ocean-dweller !

66. O elephant-eared one ! O cow-eared one ! O palm-eared one ! Salutations to you. O hundred-tongued one! Oone having hundred locks of hair ! O hundred-bellied one ! O hundred-faced one !

67. Singers sing (about) you. Reciters recite (the praise of you), the adorable ! They indeed consider you as Brahmā superior to Indra.

68. O vast-bodied one ! In your body, there are the seas and the earth as well; all deities are here like cows in a pen.

69. In your body, I see Moon, Fire, the Water-lord (Jaleśvara), Nārāyaṇa as well as Sun, Brahmā and Bṛhaspati.

70. O Venerable one ! That (your body) is the cause, the effect, the cause of an action, the creation and the dissolution, the existent and the non-existent and the god-head.

71. Salutation to Bhava (the Existence), to Śarva (the Injurer), to the benefactor, to one of ferocious form! Salutation to the destroyer of Andhaka, to the Lord of beings.

72. Salutation to the triple-tufted one, to the triple-headed one, to one whose hand is wielding the Trident, to the triple-faced one, to the triple-eyed one, O killer of triple city ! Salutation to you.

73. Salutation to Daṇḍa (the Sceptre), to the terrific one, to the egg, the cause of creation, to the one whose hand is busy with *Diṇḍima* drum! Salutation to you, O Daṇḍimuṇḍa!

74. Salutation to one having erect hairs and protruding teeth, to the white one, to the unchanging one, to one of deep red and black hue. Salutation to you, the blue-necked one.

75. Salutation to one of matchless form, to the deformed one, to the auspicious one, to one having garland of Suns, to the Sun, to one having garland of banners of one's own form.

76. Salutation to one diversely delightful. Salutation to the more dexterous. Salutation to the Lord of *Gaṇa*-chiefs, to one having shoulders of a bull, to the archer!

77. (Salutation) to the roarer, to the violent, to one having a leafy cup (*parṇadhārapṛtāya*). Salutation to one of golden hue, to one of golden lustre.

78. Salutation to the lauded one, to the laudable one; salutation to you, to one abiding in laudation, to the all, to the all-eating one, to the body of all beings.

79. Salutation to the reciter (*Hotṛ*), to the slayer, to the one having lofty white flag. Salutation to obeisance, to *Mantra* and salutation to a *Kaṭakaṭa*.

80. Salutation to the enjoyer of pearls, to the lying one, to the vigilant one, to the existent, to the essence of energy, to the shaven-headed one and to the crooked one.

81. Salutation to one engaged in dancing, to one having an instrument to keep musical time, to one covetous of gift of dancing, to one having mouth instrument.

82. Salutation to the seniormost one, to the most worthy, to the vanquisher of the strong and the stronger, to the destroyer of Time (Death), to the (embodiment of) Time, to the one having the form of annihilation of the cycle (of birth and death).

83. Salutation to you, the Lord of Himavān's daughter, to Bhairava (the terrible). Salutation ever to the ferocious. Salutation to the ten-armed one.

84. (Salutation) to the one fond of pyre-ashes, to one holding a skull in hand, to the frightening one, to the dreadful one, to the observer of the vow of snow (*himavratadharāya*).

85. Salutation to one having deformed face, to one having ferocious sight at the corner of the face, to one greedy of cooked and raw flesh, to one fond of *Tumbī-viṇā*.

86. Salutation to the one showering (boons) on the pious. Salutations to you, to the owner of cattle, to Kaṭakaṭa, to the formidable one, salutation to Pacapaca.

87. Salutation to the worthiest one of all, to the chosen one, to the benefactor. Salutation to the one of dispassionate face, to the creative faculty, to the wearer of string of Rudrākṣa beads.

88. (Salutation) to the one beyond varieties and differences, to the shade, to the scorcher, to the one who is both benevolent and malevolent in form to the one who is more violent than the violent.

89. Salutation to the auspicious one. Salutation to the peaceful one, to the most peaceful one (of all), to the one with many eyes and skulls. Salutation to you, O one of a single form.

90. Salutation to the lowly, to the greedy, to the one fond of sacrificial share, to the king of Pañcāla (country), to the white-bodied one. Salutation to the restrainer of Yama.

91. Salutation to the possessor of large wonderful bell, to one having series of bells and gongs, to one having millions of bells, to the one adorned by string of bells.

92. Salutation to the (sound of the) bell that unites the animals, to the one fond of *kila-kila* (sound), to the one of the form of the sound *hum hum*, to the ultimate one, to the syllable *hum*, to the favourite.

93. Salutation to the one who ever resides in houses and trees equally, to the jackal (fond of the) embryo-flesh, to the helmsman, to the ferry.

94. Salutation to the sacrifice, to the sacrificer, to one to whom offering is made, to the offering, to the carrier of sacrifice, to the oblation, to one fit to be burnt, to the Sun.

95. Salutation to the mouth, to the one worthy of mouth. Salutation to the lord of mouths, to the food-giver, to the master of food. Salutation to the consumer of diverse food.

96. Salutation to the one of thousand heads and feet, to the one having thousand raised shears, to the one with thousand ornaments.

97. (Salutation) to the protector of innocent followers and cattle, to the enjoyer of child's play. Salutation to the young, to the old, to the agitated, to the agitator.

98. Salutation to the one whose hair is dishevelled by Gaṅgā, to the one having *muñja* like hair. Salutation to the one pleased with six-fold duties, to the one engaged in three-fold duties.

99. (Salutation) to the one of uncultivated sense-organs, to the violent one, to the emaciated, to the one busting forth, to the one worthy of being spoken by and speaking about (human values): *dharma, artha, kāma* and *mokṣa.*

100. (Salutation) to *Sāṅkhya* (philosophy), to the chief of *Sāṅkhya* (philosophers), and to the lead into *Sāṅkhya* and *Yoga.* Salutation to the carriage-less cart-horse, and to the one having carriage (moving) on the cross-roads.

101. Salutation to you, the one with black buck skin as upper garment, to the tawny-haired one, to the three-eyed lord of Ambikā, to the manifest and yet unmanifest, to the creator.

102. O desire ! O giver of wishes ! O suppresser of desire! (salutation to you) to the one discriminating the satiated and the unsatiated. Salutation (to you), O one giving up all compassion to you who moves in the twilight of deluge !

103. O magnanimous one ! O one of strong arms ! O mighty one ! Salutation to you. O one shining like a large cloud and earth ! O Time Supreme ! O most lustrous one (Salutation to you) !

104. O cause of cycle of clouds ! O cause of cycle of *Yuga* to the lord of Sun and Moon ! Salutation to you. You are the food, the consumer of food, the consumer of the cooked food, the purifier, the fire.

105. Salutation to you, the viviparous, the oviparous, the sweat born, the plants. O supreme god of gods ! You are the four-fold group of living beings.

106. (You are) the creator, the sustainer as well as the destroyer of this moveable and immoveable (world). The learned ones speak of you as Brahma, the goal of the knowers of the supreme Brahman.

107. You are the supreme enlightener of the mind and also the lustre of all lights, the swan, the tree, the honey-bee; (so) the expounders of the *Veda* characterise you.

108. The sages say that you are the bricks of the (altar of) sacrifice, the holy-place *Śreṣṭhaka.* You are ever lauded in hymns by the host of the esoteric parts of the *Veda.*

109. Brāhmaṇas, Kṣatriyas, Vaiśyas, Śūdras and those of the lower order- are all you. You are indeed the cluster of clouds, the lightning and the bang of the thunderbolt.

110. You are the year, the seasons, the months and the fortnight; (you are) the *Yugas,* the *Nimiṣas,* the *Kāṣṭhas,* the stars, the planets and the *Balas.*

111. You are the *Kakubha* (tree) among trees; among mountains, the Himālaya; tiger among the beasts; *Garuḍa* among birds and *Ananta* among hooded serpents.

112. You are the Milk-ocean among oceans, bow among mechanical devices; *Vajra* among the throwing weapons, the (vow of) truth among vows.

113. You are hatred, desire, attachment, deliverance, forbearance and impatience, industry, steadfastness, greed, lust, anger, success and failure.

114. You are the wielder of arrow, of mace, of *Khaṭvāṅga,* of bow. You are the chopper, the breaker, the striker; you are the thinker, and the ageless leader.

115. You are *Dharma* with its ten characteristics, Artha as well as *Kāma*. You are the seas, the rivers, Gaṅgā, the mountains and the ponds.

116. You are the climber and the creeping (plants), the grass and the herbs, the animals, the wild beasts and birds. You are the source of the numerous actions and qualities. You are the time, the giver of flowers and fruits.

117. You are the beginning and the end of the *Vedas*; you are *Gāyatrī*, and *Oṁkāra* as well. You are the red (colour), the green, the blue, the black, the yellow as well as the white (colour).

118. You are the tawny, the brown, the gray, the smoky as well as the dark-blue (colour). You are the coloured, yet the colourless. You are indeed the doer and the destroyer.

119. You are Indra, Yama, Varuṇa, Kubera, Vāyu. You are the calamity, the *Citrabhānu*, *Svarbhānu* and the Sun.

120. You are the disciples, the office of *Hotṛ*, the three *Suparṇa* hymns, the *Śatarudrīya* (section) of *Yajus* (*Saṁhitā*). You are sanctifying of the sanctifiers and auspicious of the auspicious.

121. (You are) the *Tinduka* tree grown on mountains. You are the green gram, the life of all animals. You are *Sattva*, *Rajas* as well as *Tamas*, the Lord of intellect.

122. (You are) *Prāṇa*, *Apāna*, *Samāna*, *Udāna* and *Vyān*. (You are) the closing and the opening (of eyes), the sneeze and the yawn.

123. (You are) immanent in blood; you are the vision, the large-faced one, the big-bellied one, the bright-haired one, the tawny-bearded one, the one with hairs raised up and you are the mobile and the immobile.

124. You are the one versed in song, (musical) instruments and dance, the lover of music and (musical instruments). You are the fish, the net, the leech, the one who sports with time, the hero in arts.

125. (You are) the inopportune time, the adverse time, the bad time, and the Time. (You are) the Death, and the

one causing death. (You are) the sacrifice and the menace to sacrifice.

126. (You are) *Saṁvartaka,* the destroyer. (You are) *Saṁvartaka,* the cloud. (You are) the bell, the bell-bearer, the bearer of large bell, the wanderer, the wearer of garland and (you are) Mātali (inspirer).

127. (You are) the ruler of Brahmā, Kāla, Yama and Agn. (You are) the one of (tonsured) head. (You are) the three-headed one. (You are) the four ages, the four *Vedas* and the promulgator of *Cāturhotra.*

128. (You are) the leader of the system of four stages of life. (You are) the ordainer of the four-fold (*Varṇa*) division of society. (You are) the one fond of goal always, the one of tangible form, the chief of the *Gaṇa,* and the Lord of the *Gaṇa.*

129. (You are) the wearer of red garlands and garments, the one belonging to mountain, the one fond of mountain-born ones. (You are) the artisan, the best of artisans, the promoter of all arts.

130. (You are) the spike to *Bhaga*'s eyes, *Śambhu,* the feller of *Pūṣan*'s teeth ! (You are) the utterances—*Svāhā, Svadhā, Vaṣaṭkāra, Namas* and *Namo-namas.*

131. (You are) the one of secret vows, the one of secret austerity, the saviour, the one studded with stars, the creator (of the universe), the dispenser (of fruits of actions of people), the unifier, the one engaged in supporting the earth.

132. (You are) Brahma, austerity, truth, performance of vows, as well as straightforwardness. (You are) the self of all beings, the creator of the great elements, the prosperity, the source of past, present and future.

133. (You are) *Bhūḥ, Bhuvaḥ, Svaḥ,* and the cosmic order. (You are) the one perpetually pure, O great lord ! (You are) the consecrated one, the non-consecrated one, the lovely one, the unrestrainable, the one born of the restrained.

134. (You are) the one who causes the cycle of moon, the one causing the year turn round, the *Saṁvarta* (cloud of deluge), the inspirer. (You are) the subtle one, the desire, the atom, the gross one, the one fond of garland of *Karṇikāra* flowers.

135. (You are) one of gay countenance, of dreadful face, the one favourable and the one unfavourable. (You are) the Golden Embryo, the bird, the lord of great serpents, the transcendent.

136. (You are) the destroyer of vice (adharma), the great god, the wielder of sceptre, the one much attached to *Gaṇa*, the one roaring like a bull, the bearer of cattle, the one having the chief of excellent bulls as vehicle.

137. (You are) the guardian of the three worlds, the chief herdsman, the one who has the ways of cattle, the path, the eternal one, the most superior one, the firm one, the one angerless, the anger.

138. (You are) the uncontrollable one, the insurmountable one, the unbearable one, the unsurpassable one, the unassailable one, the unrevealable one, the invisible one, the unconquerable one, the victory.

139. (You are) moon, fire, cold, heat, hunger, thirst, old age, ill-health, mental afflictions, bodily diseases, remover of mental ill-health, eradicator of diseases.

140. (You are) the multitude as well as the non-multitude, the annihilater, the eternal god, the tufted one, the one with lotus-like eyes, the one dwelling in a lotus grove.

141. (You are) the triple-eyed one, the bearer of sceptre, the sharp-tusked one, the one who uproots *Kula*, the one who has the most severe poison, the eminent celestial, you are the drinker of *Soma*, O master of *Maruts* !

142. (You are) the partaker of ambrosia, the protector of Universe, the supreme lord of the hosts of *Vedas* and *Devas*, the consumer of fire of poison, the drinker of *Soma*, the drinker of milk, the drinker of *ājya*.

143. (You are) the drinker of honey from those shedding honey, you are the one having Brahma (knowledge), O

power of Ghṛta ! You are enjoyer of all the world, O Grandsire of entire Universe !

144. (You are) the one having golden vitality. You are the only Puruṣa. You are the female, you the male and indeed neuter. (You are) the child, the youth, the old with wornout teeth, the swallower at the end, the maker of the Universe, the designer of the Universe.

145. You are creator, the adorable to the creator of the Universe ! (They) with their (body) bent down, worship you always. Sun and Moon are your eyes, you are *Bhavānī*, fire and the Grandsire too. (You are) Sarasvatī, the source of vocal strength. (You are) the day and night, the cause of closing and opening of eyes.

146. Neither Brahmā nor Govinda nor those ancient sages are able to comprehend your eminence in its reality, O Śaṅkara !

147. Beyond the thick 'darkness' which is surrounding hundreds of beings, you are always the guardian and the thinker.

148. To that lustre, the *Yogātman*, visualised by the persons in *Yoga* who being in *Sattva*, sleepless controlling their breath, with their senses conquered, salutation.

149. As a father of his own son, you ever protect me, with those of your subtle bodies which cannot be pointed out.

150. O sinless ! Protect me this myself who am to be protected by you. Salutation to you. O one venerable and compassionate to devotees ! I am always devoted to you.

151. Salutation always to the one of matted hair, to the bearer of sceptre, O pot-bellied one ! O sacrifice ! O long-tongued one ! O one with large tusks ! To you such a Rudra, salutation.

152. In whose hair are found the clouds, and rivers in all bodies joint, and the four seas in the stomach, to such one of water-form, salutation !

153. When the end of an epoch is there, he who reclines on water after consuming all beings, to that reposer on water, I resort.

154. (You are the one) who swallows the Moon, at night having entered the mouth of *Rāhu* and *Svarbhānu* seizing the Sun, is protected by your power.

155. Those offsprings following the saviour son, O Rudra! (to them) salutation. *Svadhā, Svāhā* and those getting your pleasure, (salutation to them).

156. May those thumb-sized *Puruṣas* dwelling in the bodies of good beings, protect the bodies! May this always comfort me !

157-160. Those who are in rivers, in seas, in mountains, in caves, at the foot of trees, in pens, and depth of forests, at road-crosses, in streets, in courtyards, in assemblies, in stables of elephants, horses and chariots, in deserted parks and abodes, those who are in the five great elements, in the main and the intermediate quarters, those who are in between the Sun and the Moon and in the rays of the Sun and of the Moon; those who are in *Rasātala* and those who are beyond it—to them salutation, salutation to them, and salutation to them always.

161. Salutation always to them for whom there is no (limit of) number, quantity or form, and to those countless *Gaṇas* of Rudra.

162. Please do favour me. May there be auspiciousness to you and to me devoted to you! May my heart be in you, O god ! My intellect be in you and my mind be in you !

163. Having lauded the supreme god thus the best of the twice-born stopped.

# CHAPTER FORTY-EIGHT

## Sthāṇu-tīrtha: Vena goes to heaven

*Sanatkumāra said:*

1. Then God Bhava, the lord of the three worlds and the knower of speech, said these fine encouraging words to him.

*Śiva said:*

2. O King of best vows! I am pleased with this your eulogy. Why speak more? You will reside close to me.

3. Having lived for a long time, you will spring out of my body again and will become an *Asura* by name Andhaka killing heavenly beings.

4-5. You will be born in the house of Hiraṇyākṣa, and will obtain prosperity. When you, due to the past terrible *Adharma* caused by censuring the *Veda*, entertain love for the Mother of the Universe, I will fell your body killing it with the trident, in same way as Arbuda.

6. Having been cleansed of sin there also and regarding me again with devotion, you will become a famous leader of *Gaṇas* and known by the name Bhṛṅgiriṭi.

7-11. By my company, you will then attain perfection. He who recites this eulogy composed by Vena or listens to it, will never come by evil and will attain long life. Just as among gods, venerable Śiva is pre-eminent, so this eulogy composed by Vena is most excellent of all eulogies. Those who are desirous of fame, kingdom, happiness, prosperity, wealth, honour and (other) things and specially the seekers of learning should listen (to this) with devotion. The one afflicted with disease, the miserable one, the needy, or the one apprehending fear from thieves or king and the one dismissed from government job—(all) will be relieved of the great fear. The person attains superiority over the *Varṇas* with that very body.

12-16. The person becomes pure and becomes endowed with lustre and fame. Neither *Rākṣasas*, nor *Piśācas*, nor *Bhūtas* nor *Vināyakas* will cause any obstacle in the house, where this eulogy is recited. A woman who after obtaining permission from her husband, listens to this eulogy becomes honourable like a goddess in both the maternal side and the paternal side. All the endeavours of the person who recites or hears this divine hymn with attention, meet with success at all times. Whatever is thought in the mind and whatever is spoken vocally by a person all that become realised by recitation of this eulogy. The sins committed mentally, physically or vocally, get destroyed.

Choose a boon which is cherished by your mind. May you be happy !

*Vena said:*

17. Indeed because of the magnanimity of this *Liṅga* as well as by the visit to the *Liṅga* and by seeing you, I am absolved of all sins.

18-19. If you are pleased, O god of gods ! If you are to grant me a boon, then, O Śaṅkara ! you will also kindly do favour to this your servant born as dog due to devouring god's property. I was felled into the middle of the lake by (dog) life of this.

20. I had been warded off by the gods from bathing in this *Tīrtha* earlier. He has done me a good turn and I beseech you on his behalf.

21-23. Having listened to his words, Śaṅkara who was pleased said: "He too shall be absolved of sins, there is no doubt.

O mighty one ! He will go to the abode of Śiva by my favour. So also he having heard this eulogy gets absolved of all sins.

O Lord of earth ! Having heard the excellence of Kurukṣetra and of this lake as well to the origin of my *Liṅga*, one is cleansed of sins.

*Sanatkumāra said:*

24. Having said so the venerable one prostrated by all people disappeared there only, in the presence of everyone.

25. That dog at that very moment remembering his past birth, assumed a divine form and attended on that king.

26. Then Vainya, having bathed and desirous of seeing him father, found the cottage in *Sthāṇu-tīrtha* vacant and was sorrowful.

27-29a. (Vena) having seen (him) said the words in great joy: "My boy, by you a worthy son, I have been rescued from the ocean of hell. Everyday water was poured by you on me who was lying on the sandy bank of the *Tīrtha.* By the favour of this pious one and by the sight of god *Sthāṇu,* I, relieved of sins, will proceed to heaven where Śiva resides."

29b-30. Having said so to the king and having set up Maheśvara, he (Vena) liberated by his son, attained perfection in *Sthāṇu-tīrtha.* And that dog (attained) the highest perfection by the grace of *Sthāṇu-tīrtha.*

31-33. (And) being absolved of all sins, he went to the abode of Bhava. The king (Vainya) relieved of his obligation towards the father, having protected the earth, obtaining sons as per *Dharma,* performing sacrifice without any impediment, granting the *Vipras* their desires, enjoying varieties of enjoyments, making the friends endowed with wealth, satisfying the women with their aspirations, coronating his son in the kingdom, proceeded to Kurukṣetra.

34. Having performed severe austerities there and worshipping Śaṅkara, he reached the highest abode abandoning his body at his own will.

35. This is the efficacy of the *Tīrtha* of *Sthāṇu.* A person who hears this, reaches the highest abode being absolved of all sins.

# CHAPTER FORTY-NINE

## Sthāṇu-tīrtha: Origin of Caturmukha

*Mārkaṇḍeya said:*

1. O sinless one ! I have a desire to hear in detail the origin of the Four-faced One and of the kings.

*Sanatkumāra said:*

2. O sinless one ! Listen. I will narrate to you all in detail about what happened to the lotus-born Brahmā who desired to create.

3. Venerable Brahmā, the grandsire of the world, even as he was born, created all beings, immobile and mobile.

4. Again as he was musing about creation, a pretty damsel as darkish as a blue lotus petal, of thin waist, and of beautiful eyes, was born.

5. Having seen that lovable one, Brahmā invited her for copulation. Because of this very serious sin, the head of Brahmā shattered.

6. With that shattered head, he proceeded to the holy *Tīrtha, Sānnihatya* lake, well-known in the three worlds and able to cleanse all sins.

7-8. Then in the holy *Sthāṇu-tīrtha* resorted to by sages and *Siddhas,* the Four-faced One established (a *Liṅga*) on the northern bank of Sarasvatī and worshipped everyday with pleasing sandalpaste and fragrant fumes, presents as well as the charming Rudra hymns.

9. Venerable lord of blue-red complexion himself appeared before him who was thus devoted and engaged in the worship of Śiva.

10. Brahmā, grandsire of the world, having seen Lord Śiva appear before him, lowered his head to the ground and eulogized him.

*Brahmā said:*

11. Salutation to you, O great god ! O basis of past, present and future! Salutation to you, O ever praise-worthy one ! Salutation to the fosterer of the three worlds.

12. Salutation to the one of sanctified body, to the eradicator of all blemishes, O one venerated by the mobile and the immobile (world) ! O revealer of the secret of secrets!

13. O extirpator of all diseases (of even) those not cured with medicines ! O one clad in the skin of Ruru deer ! O discarder of sorrow ! Salutation to you.

14. O one calming down the great intellect agitated as if by the waves of water! O god ! Those who repeat your name too are not subject to the (cycle of worldly) existence.

15. Salutation to you, O eternal one of the eternals ! Salutation to you, the annihilator of the three worlds, to Śaṅkara, to the inconceivable one and the curer of diseases.

16. (Salutation) to the highest one who cannot be gauged, to one who likes all beings, to the master of *Yoga*, to the god who washes away all sins.

17. Salutation to the famous *Sthāṇu*, to the one extolled by *Siddhas* and *bards*, to the one who cannot be reached by the cycle of birth and death of the beings, to the omniformed one.

18. Salutation to one whose eminence is recounted by the Lord of Serpents, to one who wears the shoulder-ornament of the best of snakes, to one who wears the grand necklace of the chief of snakes, to Bhāskara, salutation.

19. Eulogized thus the great Lord Śaṅkara said to Brahmā: "Never should you feel worried in a matter that has to happen.

20. "In the past, in the *Varāha-kalpa*, I had nipped one of your heads and you became four-faced one and there is no time when it does not remain so.

21. "By installing my *Liṅgas* in this *Sannihita-tīrtha* with devotion, you shall become absolved of all sins.

22. "Because I was inspired by you desirous of creating, saying "so be it" to you, I became visible to the beings.

23. "Performing austerities for a long time, I remained sunk in the Sannihita (lake). Then you remained waiting for me for a long time.

24-26. "I was imagined by you mentally as the creator of all beings. Then he told you spotting me immersed in water.

'If there is no elderly person other than these, then we will create the beings.' You said: 'There is no elderly person other than you. This *Sthāṇu* immersed in water, is unable to do anything. You do me a favour.' He created all beings and Dakṣa and other Prajāpatis.

27-28. "Even as they were created, all those hungry beings at once went after Prajāpati who fashioned all this four-fold group of beings, to eat. Then he being pinched, ran to the Grandsire seeking protection.

29-30. "(He said:) "Enough subsistence be arranged for these beings." Food was given to them by you: the great herbs (as food) of immovables and weak movable beings (as food) of the strong ones. Their food being fixed, all the beings went back as they came.

31-36. "All of them then, prospered with mutual affection. When the host of beings prospered and you the master of the Universe were satisfied, I, emerging from the water (of the pond), surveyed the beings. Then seeing those beings settled, I threw the *Liṅga* uprooted with my own effulgence, in great anger. When that (*Liṅga*) thrown thus stood in the middle of the pond upright, then onwards, it was well-known in this world as *Sthāṇu*.

A person being absolved of all sins by a mere visit (to the *Liṅga*) attains the highest salvation from which there is no return again. One who stays with a composed mind in this *Tīrtha* on the eighth day of the dark fortnight, shall be cleansed of all sins caused by having intercourse with forbidden ones."

So saying the venerable god disappeared there only.

37. Brahmā cleared of sins, worshipped the Four-faced god. He installed the *Liṅgas* of the god of gods in the middle of water.

38. The first one is *Brahmasaras* installed beside Hari. The second one, *Brahmasadana*, was installed in his own hermitage.

39. To the east of it was installed the third one. The fourth *Liṅga* of Brahmā stands on the bank of Sarasvatī.

40. These *Tīrthas* have been made holy and able to purify. Those who visit (them) without taking food, go to the highest abode.

41-42. During the Kṛta (age), it was by the side of Hari; during Tretā, in the hermitage of Brahmā; to the east of it during Dvāpara, and on the bank of Sarasvatī during Kali (age). People who visit and worship there, with devotion, they reach the highest goal being cleansed of all sins.

43. Maheśvara who was worshipped on the north bank of Sarasvatī by the venerable one at the time of creation, is widely known as the Four-faced One.

44. One of controlled senses having worshipped with perseverence keeping fast, is relieved of stains (caused) by association with the forbidden (etc.). There is no doubt about this.

45. Then at the approach of Tretā age, the eminent *Liṅga*, also the four-faced one, near god Sthāṇu, is to be worshipped.

46. Bowing down with faith to that *Liṅga* and to Līlā-Śaṅkara-sambhūta as well as Bhānuśaṅkara, one is relieved of all sins.

47. In the same way, as the Dvāpara age approaches, (by worshipping) Prācya-Śaṅkara in Svāśrama, one gets cleansed of *Rājasa* attitude caused by intermixture of *Varṇas.*

48. Then a person worshipping on the fourteenth day of dark fortnight, becomes absolved of all sins caused by eating prohibited food.

49. As the Kali age advances, one going to *Vasiṣṭhāśrama* and establishing the four-faced one, attains supreme Siddhi.

50. Particularly, those who fasting with restrained senses worship Mahādeva with faith, go to the highest abode.

51. Thus the greatness of *Sthāṇu-tīrtha* has been related to you. Having listened to it, a person becomes absolved of all sins.

## CHAPTER FIFTY

### Himavān weds Menā

*Sanatkumāra said:*

1. Then the superior god told the *Tīrtha*: "Because you are going alone, your name will be Pṛthūdaka only, and you will be a superior *Tīrtha* on the earth."

2. O Celestials ! Such is the holy Pṛthūdaka destroying fear of sin. You go to that eminent *Tīrtha*. Locate it after enquiry.

3. When the Sun, Moon and Jupiter are in *Mṛgaśiras* asterism, that *Tithi* (lunar day) called *Akṣayā*, is the foremost.

4. Therefore, O Chiefs of celestials ! Go there where Prācī-Sarasvatī is. There you devotedly attend on *Pitṛs* with *śrāddha.*

5. Having heard the words of Murāri, the celestials together with Indra, came over to the holy *Pṛthūdaka-Tīrtha* in Kurukṣetra.

6-8a. The celestials having taken bath there urged Bṛhaspati: "O Effulgent one ! O Venerable one ! This is asterism Mṛgaśiras. See that holy Tithi cleansing sin, comes about. This your time has come. The Sun is moving towards it and the Moon too is entering it. The purpose of celestials depends on you. O Guru ! Therefore,.you do your (job)."

8b. So told by celestials the preceptor of celestials said this —

9. "O Celestials ! If I am going to be the lord of the year, then I shall proceed." All the celestials said, "Very well." Then he occupied *Mṛgaśiras*.

10-11. In *Āṣāḍha* month on a *Tithi* with *Mṛgaśirā* star during the dark fortnight, the delighted Purandara (Indra) with devotion offered to *Pitṛs*, the *Piṇḍa* of rice fit for oblation mixed with sesamum and honey. Then the pleased *Pitṛs* spoke about that lady (Menā) as their own daughter.

12. And the celestials gave Menā to the mountain Himavān. Having obtained that Menā, Himavān was pleased with the celestials and sported with pleasure to his heart's content.

13. Then Himavān enjoying with the daughter of *Pitṛs* all pleasures, as per his wish. She gave birth to three divine damsels endowed with beautiful form as daughters.

## CHAPTER FIFTY-ONE

### Penance of Umā

*Pulastya said:*

1. Three daughters endowed with beauty and virtues and a fourth (child) a son well-known as Sunābha were born of Menā.

2. O Sage ! The eldest daughter, Rāgiṇī by name, born of Menā had a reddish body, red eyes and was clad in red garments.

3. The next one, Kuṭilā by name, had auspicious body with eyes like a lotus petal, with black curly hairs and was clad in white garments and wearing white flowers.

4. The youngest daughter of Menā, Kālī by name, (had a body) like a mass of collyrium, with dark eyes like blue lily and was of matchless beauty.

5. O Sage ! These daughters before completing six years from their birth, proceeded to perform austerities and the celestials observed those auspicious ones.

6. Then Kuṭilā radiant like the Moon, engaged in penance was taken away to *Brahmaloka* by all the Ādityas and Vasus.

7. Then all the celestials said: "Brahmaṇa, you please tell us if this (lady) gives birth to a son, who kills Mahiṣa."

8. Then the Lord of celestials said: "This poor one is not capable of bearing the semen of *Śarva.* Leave this pitiable one."

9-11. O Nārada ! Kuṭilā was angry at that and told Brahmā: " O venerable one ! I will try so that I will bear Śiva's semen which is not easy to bear. So also listen, O most pious one ! Propitiating Janārdana through well-performed austerity, I will do in such way, O Grandsire ! That I will bend down the head of Hara. What I said, O god !iIs true and verily so."

*Pulastya said:*

12. O Great sage ! Then the angry Grandsire, the venerable Creator and master of everything told the harsh Kuṭilā.

*Brahmā said:*

13. O Kuṭilā ! Because you could not forbear my words, you will be burnt by my curse and you will all become water.

14. So cursed by Brahmā, the daughter of Himavān immediately turned into water and flooded *Brahmaloka,* O sage !

15. The Grandsire seeing her violent water, bound her on all sides with bonds of *Ṛk, Sāma, Atharva* and *Yajus.*

16. That Daughter of Mountain of water-form being bound remained there only, O Brahmaṇa ! Flooding the pure abode of Brahmā.

17. That one (daughter of Himavān) Rāgavatī by name, was also led to heaven by the celestials and was presented before Brahmā. Prajāpati told (the same) about her also.

18. She too, got angry and said to him, "I will perform such severe penance that the killer of Mahiṣa will be associated with my name."

19. Brahmā then cursed her: "You who are per force transgressing my words which cannot be transgressed even by celestials, shall become twilight light."

20. "O best of sages ! That Rāgavatī, Daughter of Mountain, then became really twilight assuming a stony form near *Kṛttikā* asterism.

21. Poor Menā learning about the two daughters gone, dissuaded, (the third) from going for penance. She indeed said: "U-mā."

22. The auspicious mother gave that only, Umā, as her daughter's name with the permission of her father. (But) she went to penance grove.

23. She then performed an arduous austerity firmly placing god Rudra, trident-bearer and bull-bannered, in her mind.

24. Then Brahmā said to the celestials, "You go and bring here that Kālī, daughter of Himavān practising austerity in the Himālaya."

25. Then the celestials came and saw the Daughter of Mountain. They, however, were overpowered by her effulgence and were unable to approach her.

26. Indra along with the troops of Maruts being shaken by her splendour returned and reported that her splendour excelled that of Brahmā.

27-28. Then Brahmā told celestials: "She is definitely the consort of Śaṅkara. You endowed with splendour were indeed knocked down lustreless. Therefore, you go back to your places without any anxiety. You can as well take that Mahiṣa along with Tāraka is killed in the battle."

29. So told by the divine Brahmā, the celestials along with Indra, free from affliction, went immediately to their abodes.

30. Himavān, the Lord of mountains, along with his wife brought home Umā who was practising penance, after retracting her from austerity.

31. The god (Śiva) of great intellect taking upon himself the rigorous *Nirāśraya* (abode-less) vow, roamed on mountains as excellent as Meru.

32. Once he came over to the great mountain Himavān. Being honoured by him with devotion, Hara stayed there for the night.

33. On the second day, Mahādeva was invited by the Lord of mountains, "O Lord ! please stay here only for practising austerity."

34-35. So said by the Mountain, Hara made up his mind accordingly. As the Trident-bearer God of gods was residing resorting to a hermitage and giving up his (vow of) *nirāśrama* (not being in any particular place), Kālī the handsome daughter of the King of mountains came to that place.

36. Having seen her as beloved Satī reborn coming, he honoured her with a welcome and sat absorbed in *Yoga.*

37. That charming damsel having approached him, folded her hands and bowed down to his feet along with her companions.

38. Then after a long time Śarva saw the daughter of Mountain (still there) and saying, "It is not proper", he disappeared along with his *Gaṇa.*

39. At the harsh words of Śarva, Pārvatī, though burning inside with grief, wise as she was, told her father—

40. "O Father ! I shall go into thick forest to practise a very arduous austerity to please god Śaṅkara, wielder of Pināka."

41. "Be it so", said her father. And on his (Himālaya's) wide slopes, she by the name Lalitā, practised penance desirous of propitiating Hara.

42. Her companions then served the lady by collecting fuel, *Darbha* grass, fruits and roots and so on.

43. A fine and shining figure of the Wielder of Trident was made of earth for amusement of Pārvatī. She said, "May I have (this) Rudra."

44. She worshipped that (figure) only gazing it at time and again. The Vanquisher of Triple City was gratified by her faith.

45-46. Assuming the form of a student he (Hara) smearing his whole body with ash, clad in deer skin, wearing *Muñja* girdle and *Yajñopavīta,* holding a staff and an umbrella, sporting a *Kamaṇḍalu* (water pot carried by ascetics and *Brahmacārins*) in hand and wandering through every hermitage came to the *Āśrama* of Kālī.

47. O Nārada ! Kālī got up with her companions and worshipping him as per procedure, asked him thus—

*Umā said:*

48. O Mendicant ! From where are you coming? In which place is your *Āśrama*? Why are you on a journey? Please tell me fast.

*The Mendicant said:*

49. O Young lady ! My *Āśrama* is located in Vārāṇasī. Well, I shall go to Pṛthūdaka on a pilgrimage, O lady of pure vows!

*Devī said:*

50. O best of Vipras ! What merit is there in Pṛthūdaka that you are going there? What fruit have you earned by taking ablutions on your way and in which (*Tīrthas* did you bathe)?

*The Mendicant said:*

51-53. First of all, I took ablution in Prayāga, O pretty lady! then in the *Tīrthas* at Kubjāmra, Jayanta, Caṇḍikeśvara, Bandhuvṛnda, Karkandha, Kanakhala, Sarasvatī, Koṭitīrtha, and Takṣaka. And I came to your *Āśrama.* I took ablution (in the *Tīrthas*) without any desire in view.

54. After talking to you who are here, I shall go to Pṛthūdaka. I ask you (a question) at which you should not get annoyed.

55. O lovely maiden ! If I am wasting myself with a restrained body in young age through austerities, it is only commendable for the twice-born ones.

56. Why is it you? O damsel ! Being in the prime of your life, who have taken up this severe penance? A doubt occurs to me.

57. O lovely maiden ! For women time passes in enjoying pleasures along with their husbands in the prime of life.

58. O Daughter of Mountain ! All beings–mobile and immobile–here seek beauty, exalted family and prosperity through austerity and you have these in ample.

59. Then why is it that you are having this matted hair discarding ornaments? Why is it that you are wearing bark garments leaving aside silk cloth ?

*Pulastya said:*

60. Then Somaprabhā, a companion of Devī and senior in penance, told the fact about her to the mendicant.

*Somaprabhā said:*

61. O best of the twice-born ! Listen to the purpose for which penance has been undertaken by Pārvatī while Mahākālī desires Hara as her husband.

*Pulastya said:*

62. Having heard the words of Somaprabhā, the mendicant nodded his head. Bursting into loud laughter, he said these words—

*The Mendicant said:*

63. O Pārvatī ! I tell you this. Who gave this idea to you ? How does your hand as tender as sprout go with Śarva's hand coiled around by serpent ?

64. So also you are having silken garments, Rudra is clad in lion's skin. You are used to sandal (paste); he is adorned with ash. This does not appear to me proper.

*Pulastya said:*

65. O best Vipra ! When the mendicant said so, Pārvatī told him: "O Mendicant ! Do not speak like this. Hara excels on all counts.

66. "The Lord of celestials may be calm or ferocious, opulent or penniless, adorned or unadorned (with ornaments) !

67. "Or he may be of the sort he is. He shall be my lord. O Śaśiprabhā ! This mendicant with quivering lips desires to speak (further); stop him. A despiser is not such a big sinner as a hearer (of despise)."

*Pulastya said:*

68. So saying, the maiden girl desired to get up. Then Bhava abandoned his form of mendicant and assumed his own form.

69. Doing so, Hara said, "Dear, you go (now) to your own father's house. I will send the great sages to the house of Himavān for your sake.

70. "This earthen figure of Īśvara you made here while seeking Rudra, will be known all over the world as Bhadreśvara.

71. "*Devas, Dānavas, Gandharvas, Yakṣas, Kiṁpuruṣas,* reptiles and human beings wishing to obtain welfare, will always worship (Bhadreśvara)."

72. O Sage ! The Daughter of Mountain so told by *Deva,* went to her own father's house taking to aerial (path).

73. The effulgent Śaṅkara too after sending away the Daughter of Mountain, proceeded to Pṛthūdaka and took ablution as per precepts.

74. The foremost *Deva* Maheśvara being cleansed of his blemishes after a bath in Pṛthūdaka, came to the great mountain Mandara along with his vehicle *Nandī* and the *Gaṇas.*

75. When the vanquisher of triple city came along with the *Gaṇas,* the great Mountain (Mandara) was pleased at

heart and shone with all his seven peaks having horripulation. The Mountain offered worship with delicious fruits, clean water, roots and kanda and so on to the Three-eyed Lord along with all his *Gaṇa* chiefs.

## CHAPTER FIFTY-TWO

### Sages go to Himavān

*Pulastya said:*

1. Then Rudra, on being worshipped by the Mountain, was pleased. He remembered the great sages together with Arundhatī.

2. Remembered by the great Śaṅkara, the sages came to the great mountain Mandara of charming caves.

3. Having seen them arriving, the Lord, the destroyer of triple city, got up and receiving them with honour said thi—

4. "Blessed is this great Mountain; it is fit to be praised and respected by the gods; it has become one with sins thrashed out because of (the touch of) your lotus-feet.

5. "Please take your seat on the lotus-coloured stone slabs which are very smooth and soft in the holy mountain plateau which is charming, wide and even."

*Pulastya said:*

6. So told by god Śaṅkara, the great sages together with Arundhatī entered the tableland of the mountain.

7. As the sages took their seats, *Nandī*, the leader of the *Devagaṇa* worshipped them with *Arghya* and so on and stood with pious mind.

8. Then the Lord of celestials said the words that were just and favourable to the celestials, for enhancing his own fame to the Seven Sages endowed with restraint.

*Hara said:*

9. Kaśyapa, Atri, Vasiṣṭha (son of Varuṇa), Viśvāmitra (son of Gādhi), Gautama, please listen; Bharadvāja, please listen; Aṅgiras, you also please listen.

10. My beloved was Satī, daughter of Dakṣa. Long ago, you know, she gave up her life through *Yoga* because of Dakṣa's anger.

11. She is now born again as Umā, the daughter of Lord of mountains. O great Brāhmaṇas ! She may please be solicited from the Lord of mountains for me.

*Pulastya said:*

12. The Seven Sages so told, replied, "Very well" and started towards Himavān uttering, "Om, Obeisance to Śaṅkara."

13. Then Śarva told Arundhatī also: "O lovely one ! You (also) please go. Indeed women alone know the custom of women."

14. When told so, Arundhatī unable to transgress the popular custom, went with her husband, uttering, "Obeisance to you, Rudra."

15. Going to Oṣadhiprastha on the peak of Himālaya, they saw (the city) of the King of mountains, which was like the city of Purandara (Indra).

16-17. Then being worshipped with honour by the folks of the mountains and by alert mountains Sunābha and others as well as by *Gandharvas*, *Kinnaras*, *Yakṣas* and their other followers, they entered the attractive mansion of Himālaya shining like gold.

18. Then, approaching the main door, those magnanimous ones whose blemishes were cleansed by penance, stopped because there was a doorkeeper.

19. However, mountain Gandhamādana who was at the door, immediately came there himself, holding a big staff of ruby in hand.

20. Then the sages said, "Go to the blessed Lord of mountains and report that we have come here. We are on an important mission."

21. So told by the sages, the leading mountain Gandhamādana went to the place where the Mountain Lord was sitting surrounded by other mountains.

22. Kneeling on the ground with the staff under his arm and holding the hands against the mouth he said these word—

*Gandhamādana said:*

23. O Mountain Lord ! These sages who have arrived at your abode are standing at the door; they have (some) errand and look forward to meet you.

*Pulastya said:*

24. Hearing the words of the doorkeeper, the Mountain Lord stood up and himself went to the door taking the best materials of *Arghya.*

25. Worshipping them with *Arghya* and other things, the Mountain led them to the assembly hall and after they took their seats, he, the knower of speech, said these words—

*Himavān said:*

26. Is this a shower without clouds or a fruit without flower? This your arrival is indeed unexpected and unconceivable.

27-28. From today I am blessed; O exalted ones ! I am king of mountains. Today only I am of a body pure completely. For you O best of the twice-born ! have cleared my abode from the association of evil; it was cleansed by sight and by stepping like *Sarasvatī-tīrtha.*

29. O Vipras ! I am your servant. Indeed I have earned merit because you are in need (of me). So you will do well to command me.

30. I, the indisputable king, along with my wife, children and dependents, are your servant and stand at your command. So please speak.

*Pulastya said:*

31. Hearing the words of the Mountain Lord, the sages of accomplished vows asked elderly Aṅgiras: "Please present the matter before the Mountain."

32. So urged by Kaśyapa and all other sages, that Aṅgiras spoke to the Mountain the excellent words—

*Aṅgiras said:*

33. O best of Mountains ! Please listen to the purpose for which we have come along with Arundhatī, to your house, O Mountain !

34-36. We have been sent to approach you, O Mountain ! By him who is magnanimous, soul of all, destroyer of Dakṣa's sacrifice, giver of peace, wielder of trident, Śarva, three-eyed, having bull as vehicle, cloud-bannered, subduer of foes, enjoyer of sacrifice, lord by himself, whom some call Īśvara, (some) Śiva, (others) Sthāṇu the best, Hara, Bhīma, Ugra, Maheśāna, Mahādeva and Paśupati.

37. This your daughter Kālī is the (most) beautiful in all the worlds. The Lord of *Devas* solicits her and you will do well to give her (in marriage to Śiva).

38. O best of Mountains ! That father is indeed blessed whose daughter gets a husband who is a proper (match) for her in beauty, family and wealth.

39. Whatsoever mobile and immobile and four types of beings are there, to all of them. O Mountain ! This lady (will be) the mother, for, Hara is regarded as the father.

40. Having prostrated to Śaṅkara, let the celestials prostrate to your daughter; let her foot covered with ashes be placed on the heads of (your) foes.

41. We are the solicitors, Śarva is the bride-groom, you are the giver, and Umā the mother of Universe is the bride. (In the circumstances) do what is propitious for you.

*Pulastya said:*

42. Listening to those words of Aṅgiras, Kālī stood with her head lowered with joy but immediately she felt dejected.

43. Then the King of Mountains said to Gandhamādana, "Go and inviting all Mountains, bring here."

44. The agile Mountain (Gandhamādana) went fast from house to house. He invited Meru and other most propitious Mountains around.

45-47. They too arrived in haste thinking the matter to be very important. They entered (the assembly hall) with curiosity. Udaya, Hemakūṭa, Ramyaka, Mandara, Uddālaka, Varuṇa, Varāha, Garuḍāsana, Śuktimān, Vegasānu, Dṛḍhasṛṅga, Śṛṅgavan, Citrakūṭa, Trikūṭa, and other smaller mountains—all these sat on golden seats in the assembly hall after bowing down to those sages.

48. Then the Lord of Mountains himself invited his wife, Menā: "Blessed lady, please come along with your son."

49. At that she entered with her son after bowing down to the feet of the sages and exchanging wishes with all relatives.

50. Nārada ! After the mountains took their seats, the great Mountain, an expert in speaking, said these words in a pleasant voice after wishing them good—

*Himavān said:*

51. Here are the Seven Holy Sages soliciting my daughter for Mahādeva. That I should inform you.

52. So tell me what is proper. You only are my relatives. I do not give her in marriage passing over you. Therefore you will do well to speak what is appropriate (now).

*Pulastya said:*

53. Hearing the words of Himavān every one of those great mountains, Meru and others, sitting in their seats, spoke—

54. "O Mountain ! Solicitors are the sages; bridegroom is Hara the destroyer of triple city; this Kālī be given (to Hara). The son-in-law is agreeable to us."

55. Menā then said to her husband, "O Mountain-chief ! Listen to my words: "A daughter was granted to me by *Pitṛs* only for this purpose.

56. The son who will be born from her (Kālī) by the Lord of beings, shall kill the *Daitya*-chief (Mahiṣa) and also Tāraka."

57. So told by Menā, the Lord of Mountains said to his daughter, "O Child ! You have been now given (in marriage) to Śarva."

58. He said to the sages: "(O Sages)! Rich in penance, daughter Kālī wife of Śaṅkara makes obeisance to you bending low with devotion."

59. Then Arundhatī placing the bashful Kālī on her lap, cheered her with compliments pleasing with appropriate names of Hara.

60-62. Then the Seven Sages said: "O Mountain-King ! Listen to the very auspicious holy lunar day having well aspected seventh house. O Himavān ! On the third day (from today) the Moon will have conjunction with *Uttarāphalgunī* (asterism). This period is called Caitra. On that day, Hara will ceremoniously hold the hand of your daughter. Now we are going. You will better permit us."

63. The Mountain King took leave of the bulls-among-sages after worshipping each of them according to custom with auspicious fruits and roots.

64. They too returned faster taking to sky and reaching Mandara mountain, they met Śaṅkara again.

65. Bowing down to Maheśvara, they said: "You are the bridegroom, the daughter of the Mountain is the bride. The

three worlds together with Brahmā will see you the cloud-borne one."

66. Then the pleased Hara Maheśvara offered homage in accordance with the custom, to all the sages along with Arundhatī in due order.

67. The honoured sages then went to invite the *Devas.* They—Brahmā, Viṣṇu, Indra and Sun-too came over to visit— Hara.

68. O Great sage ! They, having approached (the abode) of Maheśvara, entered there after bowing down. (Maheśvara) recalled *Nandī* and all others. They came to Venerable Hara and sat.

69. The Lord of *Gaṇa* (Śiva) with dishevelled matted hair surrounded by *Devas* and *Gaṇas,* shone like a large banyan tree among *Sarjas* and *Kadambas* in a forest.

## CHAPTER FIFTY-THREE

### Wedding of Umā

*Pulastya said:*

1. Seeing the *Devas* arrive, Nandī informed the omnipresent Lord. Then (he) got up and cordially embraced Hari.

2. That Śaṅkara welcomed Brahmā by bowing down his head, Indra by greeting and other groups of celestials by casting glance at them.

3. The *Gaṇas* led by Vīrabhadra, the Pāśupata and other *Śaivas* entered Mandara mountain exclaiming 'Victory to the Lord'.

4. Then adorable Śarva along with the *Devas* went from there to the great Mountain Kailāsa to perform matrimonial rites.

5. At that time the blessed Mother of *Devas* Aditi, Surabhi, Suramā and other (ladies) eagerly made decorations on the great mountain.

6-7. With Mahāsthi on the crest, with charming forehead mark of *rocanā*, with lion's skin (as cloth), with ear-rings of jet black serpents, with bracelet, necklace, armlet and anklet—all made of great serpents, with raised matted hair and riding on a bull, Hara appeared fine.

8. Ahead of him went the *Gaṇas* riding on their respective vehicles. The celestials led by Agni went behind.

9. Janārdana with Lakṣmī riding on *Vainateya* proceeded on a side of the Lord and the Grandsire on the *swan* (on the other side).

10. Thousand-eyed Indra with Indrāṇī riding on the elephant held a wide umbrella of white cloth.

11. Yamunā, the best among the rivers, holding in hand a white chowrie went along sitting on a tortoise.

12. The great river Sarasvatī riding on an elephant held an exquisite chowrie shining like *swan, jasmin* and moon.

13. The six seasons moving as they wished, proceeded taking sweet-scented flowers of fine colours for the sake of Maheśa.

14. Pṛthūdaka carrying unguents went fast on an elephant in rut resembling *Airāvata.*

15. *Gandharvas* led by Tumburu followed Mahādeva singing in sweet voice and *Kinnaras* playing on musical instruments.

16. The dancing *Apsarās*, the sages reciting hymns and the *Gandharvas* followed that Three-eyed Lord of the *Devas*, the wielder of trident.

17. There proceeded the groups of one hundred and ten million (eleven crores) of *Rudras*, one hundred twenty million (twelve crores) of *Ādityas*, and eighty million (8 crores) of *Vasus.*

18. Exalted sages, six hundred seventy million (sixty-seven crores) sages, two hundred forty million (twenty four crores) celibates (saints) went along.

19. Innumerable troops of the much excited *Yakṣas*, *Kinnaras* and *Rākṣasas* followed Maheśāna for the marriage.

20. In a moment, then, the Lord of *Devas* reached the place of the Lord of mountains. The mountains on elephant back came from all sides (to welcome him).

21. Then the venerable Three-eyed Lord bowed down to the King of Mountains. The (other) Mountains prostrated to Īśvara, at which he was happy.

22. Together with celestials and courtiers, the Bull-bannered One entered the large city of the King of Mountains, by the path shown by Nandī.

23. "The Cloud-bannered One has arrived", so saying the women of the city gave up their chores and were eager to see him.

24. A lady went towards Śaṅkara with flower wreath in one hand and her braid of hair in another.

25. Another lady of anxious eyes applying lac dye to a foot (hurriedly) came over with the other foot undyed.

26. Learning that the dreadful one had arrived, yet another lady with only one eye having collyrium literally ran holding in hand the rod with collyrium.

27. Another pretty lady curious to see Hara came naked as if mad, holding the garment and the belt in hand.

28. Learning that Īśvara had gone further, a thin-waisted young lady, slow because of full breasts, censured her breasts and her youth.

29. Thus causing excitement in the women of the city, Hara riding on the bull went to the wonderful house of the father-in-law.

30. Then closely observing Śambhu, the women in the mansion of the Mountain-chief, were speaking: "The very severe austerity of Ambikā was rightly performed, indeed, for, this celestial Śambhu is great."

31. "This is he by whom the flower-weaponed One called Kandarpa, was made bodiless, he who destroyed the sacrifice, ruined Dakṣa and blotted out Bhaga's eye, the trident-wielder and Pināka-owner.

32. O Śaṅkara ! O trident-wielder ! O one clad in lion's skin ! O subduer of Kāla ! Salutation (to you). Salutation to one who has the necklace of great serpents and graceful ear-rings. Salutation to the beloved of Pārvatī."

33. Being thus eulogized, Śambhu having bracelets of serpents and charmingly smeared with ashes, with the umbrella held over by the celestial chief (Indra) and saluted by the *Siddhas* of his own side, with the First born One (Brahmā) in front and followed by Viṣṇu of gladdened heart, ascended the auspicious marriage platform on which fire had been set.

34. As the Vanquisher of Triple City arrived along with his followers and with the Seven Sages, as the people in the mansion .of the King of mountains were absorbed in decorating the bride, the mountains got agitated and the deities moved by the honour and so on. Generally friends and relatives engaged in the marriage of (a maiden) become agitated.

35. Then the ladies having adorned Devī Girijā whose slim body was clad in white silk, brought her near Śaṅkara after her brother Sunābha had made celebrations.

36. Then the celestials sitting on the well-made golden upper storey, saw the movements of Śaṅkara and Kālī. The Lord along with the slim-bodied (Kālī) underwent procedures accepted popularly.

37. There were varieties of pleasures, flower-laden trees, devices for sprinkling of drops of water. The ground was sparsely covered with highly fragrant powder. They struck profusely with strings of pearls for the sport of Hara and the Daughter of Mountain. Later they (two) made the ground red with a thick spread of a mass of sindūra.

38. Thus sporting with the Daughter of Mountain, Hara came to the compact southern platform where the sages were sitting.

39. Then came Himavān in haste finely clad in white garments, with *Durba* in hand and holding *Madhuparka*.

40. The Three-eyed God having taken his seat facing east and the Mountain-Chief sat well facing the Seven Sages.

41. The prosperous Mountain folding his hands spoke to Śarva who was seated comfortably, these words as a means of earning virtue for himself—

*Himavān said:*

42. O venerable one ! Please accept this Kālī, my daughter, grand-daughter of the elder brother of Pulaha and grand-daughter (daughter's daughter) of *Pitṛs*-being offered by me.

*Pulastya said:*

43. Having said thus, the Mountain-chief uttering loudly "O venerable one ! Please accept this" gave away uniting the hand (of Kālī) with the hand (of Hara).

*Hara said:*

44. I have no mother nor father, no paternal nor maternal relatives and others. I having no abode (of my own), reside on (some) mountain peak. (Such a one), I accept your daughter, O Mountain-king !

45. So saying the wish-granting Hara held fast the hand of the Daughter of Mountain, with his hand. O divine sage ! She too feeling the touch of Śambhu was immensely joyful.

46. Then the wish-granter ascended the platform along with the Daughter of Mountain after partaking *Madhuparka*. Then Brahmā giving the white parched rice grain (ajā) to the Daughter of Mountain, told her—

47. "O Kālī ! Look at the pretty face of the Lord shining like the moon, with unsullied eyes and being steady, perform circumambulation to Agni."

48. When Ambikā looked at the face of Hara, she became cool like the earth scortched by the rays of the Sun (feels) getting rains.

49. The Grandsire told her once again: " Look at the face of the omnipresent Lord." "I see", she said slowly out of bashfulness to Brahmā.

50. The fire was circumambulated thrice by him along with the Daughter of Mountain and parched rice was offered into fire together with *Havis.*

51. At that time, Mālinī held the feet of Hara for a gift. Hara said, "I shall give you what you ask for; leave (my foot)."

52. Mālinī said to Śaṅkara: "Please confer on my companion that grandeur which belongs to your lineage (*Gotra*). Then will you get released."

53-54. At that Mahādeva said: "O Mālinī ! It is conferred; now leave me. I will tell you about the grandeur of my own lineage which is now hers; listen. Here is this Madhusūdana clad in yellow robes, holding conch; it is his grandeur conferred; it is my own *Gotra.*"

55. Having been said so, Mālinī crowned by excellent virtue of her own *Gotra,* released the Bull-bannered One.

56. When the holy feet of Hara were held by Mālinī, then Brahmā saw Kālī's face brighter than moon.

57. Seeing (such a face), he (Brahmā) became passionate and his semen got ejected. With fear he spread (i.e. covered) the semen in sand.

58. Then Hara said, "O Brahmā ! It is not proper to kill *Dvijas.* These are the blessed great sages—Vālakhilyas, O Grandsire !"

59. Following the words of Maheśa, eighty thousand ascetics stood up. They are known as Vālakhilyas.

60. As the marriage (ceremony) concluded, Hara entered *nuptial* (room). He enjoyed the night in the company of Umā and got up in the morning.

61. Securing the Daughter of Mountain, Śambhu was glad as well as all *Bhūta-Gaṇas.* He speedily returned to his abode after being honoured by the King of Mountain.

62. The Deva of eight forms prostrating or honouring the celestials, chiefs of whom were Brahmā, Hari and Indra,

according to their status and bidding farewell, dwelt on the Mandara mountain along with the *Bhūtas.*

## CHAPTER FIFTY-FOUR

### Birth of Vināyaka

*Pulastya said:*

1. O Sage ! Dwelling on the mountain and moving about at will, Rudra, one day, called Viśvakarma and told him, "Build a house for me."

2. (Viśvakarma) then built for Śarva a golden Svastika type of house, 64 *yojanas* in dimension.

3. The front arch and the projections were made of ivory; (it was) bright with pearl-latticed windows; steps were made of pure crystals; the decorative designs were made of chrysoberyl.

4. (It was) quite wide with seven apartments having all the requisites. Then the Lord of *Devas* performed sacrifice that characterized householdship.

5-6. Śaṅkara was only following that earlier course of action. O Sage ! For the Three-eyed One who was like that and sporting with Pārvatī, a long time passed. Once she was addressed 'Kālī' in connection with (some) worship by Bhava, the Lord of the universe intent on piety.

7. Pārvatī enraged at it told Śaṅkara, "A tree struck by an arrow or cut by an axe, regrows. But the offensive words uttered are cruel; a wound caused by (such) speech does not heal up.

8-9. Darts of speech emerge out of the mouth; one hit by them suffers days and nights. (Therefore), a wise man should not release them. But today, the right course of action was made futile by you. Therefore, I am leaving, O Lord of *Devas*!

for practising best austerity. I will try in such a way that you will no more address me as 'Kālī'."

10. So saying, the Daughter of Mountain bowed down to Mahādeva and being permitted by the Three-eyed One, flew into the sky.

11-12. Flying fast and after descending on a peaceful peak of Himālaya which appeared as if created by carefully chiselling it, she remembered *Jayā, Vijayā, Jayantī* of great virtue and the fourth *Aparājitā.*

13. Those deities being remembered by Kālī came to meet her. And the auspicious ones took up service of the Devī with her permission.

14. As Pārvatī was engaged in austerity, a tiger having teeth and nails as weapon, arrived at the spot from the Himālaya forest.

15. As the Devī was standing on one leg, the tiger thought: "When she falls down unconscious, I will carry her away."

16. So pondering, the lord of beasts, looking only at her face had his eyes fixed on her alone.

17. The Devī, however, remained in austerity for one hundred years, extolling the feet of Brahmā. Then Brahmā, the overlord of the three worlds, arrived there.

18. And the Grandsire said to the Devī, "O Eternal one ! I am pleased. Your sins are all cleansed by austerity. Choose a boon you aspire for."

19. At this, Kālī said, "O Lotus-born ! Please confer a boon on the tiger. I will be immensely happy by that."

20. Then Brahmā conferred a boon on the tiger of admirable action: He granted to him the leadership of the *Gaṇas,* devotion to the omnipresent Lord, invincibility and righteousness.

21. After conferring such a boon on the tiger, he spoke to the beloved of Śiva, "O Ambikā ! Choose a boon without any hesitation; I will grant the boon."

22. Then the Devī, the Daughter of Mountain, prayed to the Grandsire, "O Brahmaṇa ! Please grant me the boon of complexion resembling gold."

23. Saying, "Be it so", Brahmā went away. Pārvatī too, casting off the black sheath, became (one having complexion) resembling the filament of lotus.

24. O Sage ! From that sheath she was born again as Kātyāyanī. Approaching her, the Thousand-eyed (Indra) accepted her *Dakṣiṇā.* The Celestial Indra spoke to the Daughter of Mountain, these words for the sake of heaven—

*Indra said:*

25. May this lady be presented to me. Kauśikī will be my sister. She, born of your sheath (*kośa*), is Kauśikī, and this (myself) is Kauśikā.

26. Hearing this, she presented Kauśikī endowed with beauty (to Indra). The Thousand-eyed (Indra) taking her with him speedily went to the Vindhya mountain.

27. Having gone there, he said (to her), "You please stay on this great mountain being adored by the celestials and well-known by the name *Vindhya-vāsinī.*"

28. Hari (Indra) having established the Devī there, presented to her with a lion as vehicle. Saying, "Also be the killer of the enemies of celestial" he went back to Heaven.

29. Umā too having obtained the boon, returned to her house. O Sage ! She bowing down to Maheśvara, stood with modesty.

30. O Sage ! Then the glorious Lord of celestials, the imperishable one stayed for a thousand years in sexual infatuation with Pārvatī.

31. As Rudra was engrossed in sexual enjoyment, the world shook severely; the seven oceans got agitated and the celestials were terror-stricken.

32. The celestials with Indra, went to the abode of Brahmā. They prostrated and asked the great Lord, "Why is the world so agitated ?"

33. He said to them, "Verily, Bhava is engrossed in sexual sport. These worlds, being overcome by it, are uncontrollably agitated."

34-35. Having said this, he became silent. Then the celestials told Hari (Indra), "O Śakra ! Come along, we will go before it is ended. (For,) once the sexual sport is completed, the baby-boy that is going to be born will be imperishable; he will certainly take away Indra-hood of the King of celestials."

36. Then the wisdom of Indra, unfelled by the dweller in heaven and vanquisher of Bala was obscured by the words of the celestials and by fear and by the instigation of the future events.

37-38. O eminent one ! The Thousand-eyed Śakra, then went to Mandara mountain along with Fire and (other) celestials. They were all unable to enter that house of Bhava among its peaks. Pondering (over it) for a long time, they sent Fire.

39. That eminent celestial approaching (the abode) saw Nandī at the door. Finding it impossible to enter (without his knowledge), Fire was in deep thought.

40. While immersed in the ocean of worry, he saw a large flock of swans emerging from the mansion of Śambhu.

41. Saying (to himself), "This is the way-out", Fire got into the abode of Hara in the guise of a swan, fooling the door-keeper.

42. Entering in subtle form, Fire (standing) on the head side of Kapardin said with a smile but seriously, "The celestials are standing at the door."

43. O Nārada ! Śarva hearing this, immediately got up and leaving behind the Daughter of Mountain, went out of the abode together with Fire.

44. As the Lord of celestials came out, the celestials along with Indra, Sun, Moon and Fire, glad at heart touched the ground with their heads.

45. Then Śiva affectionately told the celestials, "You quickly tell me what is to be done. You have prostrated, (so) I will offer you the best boon."

46. The celestials said, "If you are pleased and if you like to confer a boon on the celestials, then, Īśvara, may this great love-sport be given up anon."

*Īśvara said:*

47. Be it so, O eminent celestials ! I give up this disposition. (But) someone should receive this my upsurging semen.

*Pulastya said:*

48. So told by Śambhu, the celestials including Indra, Moon and Sun sank down like cows caught in a mire.

49. As the celestials were dejected thus, Fire approaching Śaṅkara said, "Śaṅkara, release your semen, I will receive it."

50-51. Then the Venerable One released the trickling semen. After the semen of Śarva was gulped down by celestial Fire as a thirsty one (would drink) water or one desirous of drinking (drinks) a drink of oil, the relieved celestials taking leave of Hara, went to heaven.

52. After the celestials departed, Hara too going into his abode told it to Mahādevī—

53. "Devī, the celestials having come here and sending Fire with great effort, urged me. They prohibit me begetting a son from your womb."

54. Hearing the words of her husband, Śiva's spouse who was refused giving birth to a son, got, indeed, enraged with reddened corners of eyes and cursed the celestials—

55. "Because these wicked ones do not want my son to be born of my bosom, they too will not beget sons in their wives."

56. Having cursed the celestials thus, Gaurī went into bathroom. O ascetic ! She called Mālinī and desired to take bath.

57. The good Mālinī of golden hue taking perfumed and soft scourer scoured with her hands the body of Devī.

58-59. Pārvatī did not mind that cleansing because of the quality of insect (?). Having scoured Pārvatī with a good scourer, Mālinī went home in haste for bathing. After she went away, the Daughter of Mountain created an elephant-faced (figure) out of the scourings.

60. Having made a male figure with four arms and stout chest, and endowed with all lucky markings, (Pārvatī) left it on the ground and sat again in *Bhadrāsana* (posture).

61. Then Mālinī cleansed her head with a smile. Seeing her smiling, (Pārvatī) asked Mālini, O Nārada !

62-64. "O fair one ! Why is it that you are smiling continuously?" She then said, "I am smiling simply. Nandī the *Gaṇa*-chief was told that you will have a son. Hearing that, O pretty one ! I am much amused today, for, you long for a child, but Śaṅkara is prohibited." Having heard this, the Devī took bath as per precepts.

65-67. After bath, and devotedly worshipping Śaṅkara, she came into her abode. Then Śambhu having come took bath in that *Bhadrāsana.* That scourings-person was then covered by his (Śaṅkara's scourings). Umā's sweat and Bhava's sweat mixed with water and earth stood up at his (Śaṅkara's) contact hissing with his trunk. And the Lord of the Universe knowing him to be his offspring, was happy.

68-70. Lifting him up, Hara who blotted Bhaga's eye, told Nandī (about the child). Rudra after taking bath worshipped the divinities and others and *Agni* and *Pitṛs* with water. After reciting the Thousand Names of Viṣṇu, he came near Umā. Approaching Devī, Śaṅkara the wielder of trident, told with a smile, "O Mountain-born one ! You see your son endowed with (fine) qualities. The Daughter of Mountain so told by him, went near and saw the marvel.

71. "(Here is) the divine boy of elephant face created out of scourings of your body." Then the joyous Daughter of Mountain embraced her son.

72-74. Then Śarva smelling his (son's) head, said to Umā "Because this son was born even without me, the Nāyaka (male partner). O Devī ! He shall be known as Vināyaka. He will destroy thousands of obstacles of celestials and others. Devi, not only celestials but also the mobile and immobile worlds will honour him." So saying, he gave the son to the Devī.

75-76. The foremost of the *Gaṇas*, well-known by the name Ghaṭodara as well as *Gaṇas* of female deities, the ferocious *Bhūtas* and those who cause impediment—all these were provided as company (to him) by Parameśvara due to his love for the Devī. Seeing him (with company), the Devī too felt immensely happy.

77. Afterwards, she enjoyed (life) with Śambhu in the Mandāra mountain which had charming caves. Thus this Kātyāyanī who killed earlier the tremendous *Daityas*, Śumbha and Niśumbha, became Devī of the omnipresent Lord.

78. This holy narrative of the birth of Mṛḍānī from the Mountain was related to you. This episode of the Daughter of Mountain leads to heaven and fame, removes sin and gives strength.

# CHAPTER FIFTY-FIVE

## Fall of Caṇḍa and Muṇḍa

*Pulastya said:*

1. O eminent Dvija ! Kaśyapa's wife was Danu by name. She had three sons whose strength was superior to that of the Thousand-eyed (Indra).

2. The eldest *Asura* was known as Śumbha, the other one was Niśumbha and the third was Namuci by name endowed with enormous strength.

3. Hari (Indra) holding *Vajra* desired to kill that *Asura* known as Namuci, son of Danu.

4. Then seeing the Lord of Heaven come (to attack), Namuci out of fear entered the chariot of Sun. So the imperishable (Indra) could not (kill him).

5. So, O Nārada ! The intelligent Śakra forged a treaty with him. He conferred on him invincibility from both weapons and missiles.

6. O Nārada ! Then knowing invincibility from weapons and missiles (granted), he went down to *Pātāla* leaving the chariot of Sun.

7. Even while sinking down in water, the *Dānava*-chief saw the fine foam of the sea. Holding it he said thus (to himself)—

8-9. "Whatever was uttered by Vāsava (Indra), the king of celestials, let it be so. Let this foam touch me." The *Dānava* taking it in his hand filled, at will, his mouth, nose, ears and so on. Indra, the master, placed *Vajra* hidden in it.

10. His (Namuci's) nose and mouth being gagged by that he fell down and died. Because he died according to the agreement, Hari (Indra) was stained with *Brāhmiṇicide.*

11-12. He, however, resorting to this *Tīrtha* bathed (there) and was absolved of the sin. Then his brave brothers, Śumbha and Niśumbha, got enraged and making profuse preparation came to attack the celestials. The celestials too keeping Indra in front went out (for battle).

13-14. They along with their army and with their followers on foot, were conquered by the *Daityas* overpowering (them) and taking away the elephant of Indra, the bison of Yama, the jewel and the umbrella of Varuṇa, the mace of Mādhava (Viṣṇu). The *Nidhis, Śaṅkha* and *Padma* and others were captured and taken away.

15-19. O Nārada ! The three worlds were under the control of the two *Daityas.* They came to earth and met the great *Asura,* Raktabīja. They asked him, "Who are you?" He replied, "Lord, I am a *Daitya,* a counsellor of Mahiṣa. I am well known as Raktabīja of great prowess and of massive shoulders. The two bright and brave officers (of Mahiṣa) were known as Caṇḍa and Muṇḍa. The two mighty ones (are hiding themselves) immersed in water due to fear from the Devī. That *Dānava* who was a King by name Mahiṣa was killed by Mahādevī on the extensive Vindhyā mountain."

"Whose sons are you ? By which names are you known ? How brave are you ? What influence can you wield? You would better speak."

*Śumbha and Niśumbha said:*

20. I am known as Śumbha, the son of Danu, born of her. This is Niśumbha, my younger brother who has deprived Indra of his pride.

21. By him, the celestials including Indra, Rudra and Sun and other warriors more powerful, have been attacked and vanquished several times.

22. So you please tell us how *Daitya* Mahiṣāsura was killed, so that we may kill them (that killed Mahiṣa) surrounded by our army.

23. O Nārada ! Hearing them speak thus on the banks of Narmadā – the *Dānavas* : Caṇḍa and Muṇḍa – emerged from under-water stay.

24. Then, the two eminent *Asuras* came near and joined Raktabīja, and gently asked, "Who is this in front of you?"

25-26. He told the *Daityas*, "This is Śumbha, subduer of celestials. The other one is his younger brother Niśumbha. Under their aegis, I will without doubt marry that wicked killer of Mahiṣa, who is a jewel in the three worlds."

*Caṇḍa said:*

27. You have not spoken properly, you are not worthy of the jewel now. He who is a monarch, deserves the jewel. Therefore, unite (marry) her to Śumbha.

28. Then he spoke to Śumbha and Niśumbha about Kauśikī who had again appeared in the same form as Kauśikī endowed with beauty.

29. Then Śumbha despatched his emissar, a *Dānava* Sugrīva by name, to meet Vindhyavāsinī.

30. The great *Asura* went and having heard the Devī's reply, returned and said, with resentment, to Śumbha and Niṣumbha—

*Sugrīva said:*

31. O *Daitya* leaders ! The Devī was told as per your orders. I went to her today only and told thus—

32-34. "Śumbha is widely known as the pre-eminent one among the *Dānavas* as well. He tells you: O Noble lady ! I am the monarch in the three worlds. Pretty lady, whatever jewels are in heaven, on the face of earth and in nether world, they are all in my mansion permanently. O Fair lady ! you are described as a jewel by Caṇḍa and Muṇḍa. Therefore, you resort to me or to my brother Niśumbha.

35-36. "She, however, said with a laugh, O Sugrīva ! Listen to my words. You have told just the right. This Śumbha is the overlord of the three worlds and certainly worthy of (all) jewels. But obstinate as I am, there is a wish in my heart: That great *Asura* who defeats me in a duel shall be my husband.'

37. "She was told by me: 'You are arrogant. How will he who conquers celestials and *Asuras*, not conquer you? So come on now, O young lady !'

38. "She then said, 'What can we do now that the wish was contemplated without consideration. Well, go and report to Śumbha.'

39. "O Great Asura ! Being told so by her, I have come to you. You do what is appropriate, knowing her to be as effulgent as ten million Fires."

Śumbha, however, said this to *Dānava* Dhūmralocana, (another) emissary—

*Śumbha said:*

40. O Dhūmrākṣa ! You go and bring here quickly that wicked one making her distressed and dragging by hair, like a guilty slave girl.

41. If there be any mighty one on her side, he shall be killed without hesitation even if he may be the Grandsire.

42. So commanded by Śumbha, mighty Dhūmrākṣa marched towards Vindhya mountain accompanied by an army of six hundred *Akṣauhiṇīs*.

43. Seeing Durgā there, he said with his eyes rolling: "Come, O foolish Kauśikī ! Accept Śumbha as your husband. If not, I will forcibly take you (there) distressed by being dragged by hair."

*Śrīdevī said:*

44. You have been sent here by Śumbha to carry me forcibly, is it not? Then what can I, a feeble one (woman), do? Do as you like.

*Pulastya said:*

45. The mighty Dhūmrākṣa was told so by Vibhāvarī. (But) merely with her hum sound, Ambikā reduced him to ashes.

46. Then there was loud wailing in the mobile and immobile universe: By (merely) looking at the *Dānava*, (he and) his army was reduced to ashes by Kauśikī.

47-50. Śumbha too heard that loud noise raised. Afterwards, he ordered the great *Asuras* Caṇḍa and Muṇḍa and Ruru the best of the mighty. They all marched with delight. Their matchless army thronged with elephants, horses and chariots, came presently to the place where the Lady Born-of-Sheath was. Then observing the on-coming enemy army, one thousand million at least, the lion shaking his manes (went on) tearing down the *Dānavas* in battle, some by hitting with the paw, some with the mouth easily.

51-54. And (the lion killed) some others by attacking with claws; killed yet others with the chest. They being killed by the lion dwelling in the mountain cave and by the *Bhūtas*, the retinue of the Devī, resorted to Caṇḍa and Muṇḍa. Seeing their army afflicted, they with their lips quivering in rage fell on Durgā like moths on fire. Observing the two dreadful ones rushing, Parameśvarī knit her eyebrows with three crests in a row. Immediately from the Devī's forehead, wavy due to frown, emerged benign Kālī, a *Yoginī* of terrible countenance.

55. (Kālī) with an emaciated body (was) holding the dreadful *Khaṭvāṅga* in one hand, the sharp sabre (drawn) out of sheath and as terrible as Death (in the other); the body was splashed with blood and was wearing a garland of skulls of the best of men.

56. (She) severed down some with the sabre and others by the *Khaṭvāṅga*. She very much enraged, massacred the enemies and elephants together with chariots.

57. Ambikā flung into her mouth the (weapons)—shield, goad, club and bow with bells as well as elephant with chain.

58. Ambikā flinging the chariot along with wheel, pole, driver and horses and with soldiers into her mouth, chewed.

59. She held one by hair, another by neck; holding the other by feet and she despatched (them) to Death.

60. Then seeing the army with the troop-leader devoured by the Devī, Ruru assailed (her) and Caṇḍa too saw him.

61. She struck the mighty *Asura* on the head with the *Khaṭvāṅga*. He fell down dead on the ground like a tree cut at the root.

62. Then seeing him fallen down, Vibhāvarī cut open his body from hand to feet.

63. With the (severed) body, she tied her nice braids. One braid could not be tied; plucking it out, she threw it on the ground.

64. That braid was born assuming her (Vibhāvarī's) own form, half black and half white, utterly terrible with her hairs anointed with oil.

65. She said, "I shall kill one chosen great *Asura*." The Devī named her, then, Caṇḍamārī which is well-known.

66. (Devī) said: "O lucky one ! You go and bring Caṇḍa and Muṇḍa here. I shall myself kill them. You would do better to bring them."

67. Hearing the words of the Devī, she chased them who afflicted by fear ran away to the southern direction.

68. Then she abandoning her clothings and riding on an ass of great speed comparable to *Garuḍa*, ran after them fast.

69. Wherever those *Daityas* went, there Śivā (Caṇḍamārī) followed them. Then she saw *Pauṇḍra*, the male buffalo of Yama.

70. She pulled out its horns bent like a serpent. Holding it in her hand, she pursued the *Dānavas* speedily.

71. Then they left earth, and flew into sky. Maheśvarī too pursued them on the ass swiftly.

72. She then saw *Garuḍa*, best of poison-eating birds, and *Karkoṭaka*. He at the very sight had his hairs raised upwards.

73. Oppressed by fear, *Garuḍa* appeared like a lump of flesh. The dreadful feathers of that bird dropped down.

74. Collecting the feathers of the chief of birds and taking hold of the serpent *Karkoṭaka*, the Devī swiftly moved (chasing) Caṇḍa and Muṇḍa weak with fright.

75. Then the great *Asuras*, Caṇḍa and Muṇḍa, were caught by the Devī and were tied by Karkoṭaka only. Having tied them, she came back to Vindhya (with them).

76-77. After reporting to Kauśikī, she took hold of the terrible sheath and making a matchless garland of heads of the great *Dānavas* and nice feathers of Garuḍa, she offered it to Caṇḍikā. Also she presented Ghagharā made of lion's skin.

78. Tying on her head another garland of feathers of *Garuḍa*, she drank by herself wine and blood in (the midst of) *Dānavas*.

79. Furious Durgā holding the great chieftains of *Asuras*, severed their heads.

80. A head ornament with their heads only was made by the Devī. Doing (so), she along with Śarva went near Kauśikī.

81. Having approached, she said, "Devī, please accept this eminent head-ornament made of the two heads of the *Daityas* and bound by King-serpent."

82-83. Taking that big crown, Śivā fixed it on the head of Cāmuṇḍā and said to her: "You have executed a formidable act. Because you have worn the nice crown (made of heads of) Caṇḍa and Muṇḍa, your fame as Cāmuṇḍā will (spread) in the world."

84. After saying thus, she being confident told the Three-eyed One, who was wearing (crest-) garland of (heads of) Caṇḍa and Muṇḍa and was naked: "Slay these enemy armies."

85. She, being told so, moved about then, slaying the ferocious enemy army with the point of the horn as well as with the bow (issuing arrows) swiftly and devouring the other *Asuras*.

86. After Caṇḍa and Muṇḍa (were killed), those heroic *Dānavas* being felled by Mārī, the lion and the troops of *Bhūtas*, resorted to *Kakudmin*, lion of Ambikā.

## CHAPTER FIFTY-SIX

### Death of Śumbha and Niśumbha

*Pulastya said:*

1-3. Seeing Caṇḍa and Muṇḍa killed and the army retreated, he (Śumbha) ordered the mighty great *Asura*, Raktabīja, accompanied by three hundred million (thirty crores) *Akṣauhiṇī* (army).

As soon as Caṇḍikā sighted that marching *Daitya* army, Māheśvarī along with Kālī raised a war cry. Then, from the roaring face of the Devī, Brahmāṇī emerged.

4-11. She was in an aerial car drawn by swans and was holding a rosary and a pitcher. Immediately appeared, ferocious Māheśvarī having three eyes, riding a bull, holding a trident, having bracelets of great serpents and ear-rings. O divine sage ! Then, Kaumārī emerged (adorned) with peacock feathers, holding a spear and riding a peacock.

From the arms emerged beautiful Vaiṣṇavī sitting on Garuḍa and holding a *conch, discus, mace, sword, Śārṅga* (bow) and *arrows*. From the back, rose terrible Vārāhī with a large frightful pestle, digging up the earth with the tusks and sitting on Śeṣanāga. From the heart came out ruthless Nārasiṁhī with claws and hitting the planets, asterisms and stars with a toss of the manes. Surveying the *Asura* army being felled by them, the dauntless Caṇḍikā again issued war cries (against) the foes. Hearing that tremendous noise filling the three worlds, the Three-eyed Lord of gods, the wielder of trident, arrived. Having approached Ambikā, he bowed down to her and said thus—

12-17. "O Durgā ! I have come; please command me; I am at your service." Śivā, who emerged from the body of the Devī simultaneously with the utterance, told the Lord of gods: "O Śaṅkara ! Go as an emissary; tell Śumbha and Niśumbha, If you want to live, then, O you wicked ones ! Go to the seventh *Rasātala*; let Vāsava (Indra) get the heaven and let the celestials be free from misery; let these Brāhmaṇas and other *Varṇas* perform sacrifices now; if not, if you, being proud of your strength, desire to fight, then you come without being ruffled; here I shall kill you."

O Nārada ! Because Mahādevī engaged Śiva as her messenger, she got the name Śivadūtī (one whose messenger is Śiva).

Hearing the words of Śiva, full of arrogance, they roaring with anger rushed to that place where Kātyāyanī was.

18. Then, the two great *Daityas* attacked Sarasvatī with a shower of arrows, *pikes*, excellent goads, hatchets, spears, *Bhuṣuṇḍis, paṭṭiśas*, sharp darts (*prāsa*), large clubs with iron tips (*parigha*).

19-22. That Māheśvarī of impetuous valour in battle too, severed the missiles together with their arms, with the arrows discharged by the best bows and with hundreds of arrows killed the other great *Asuras*. Mārī killed others with the trident; Kauśikī (killed) yet others with Khaṭvāṅga; by sprinkling holy water, Brāhmī made (a few) other Asuras lose their strength; Māheśvarī made (the *Asuras*) have their chests rent by her pike; Vaiṣṇavī made others burnt; Kaumārī killed with the spear; Caṇḍī with Vajra; Vārāhi with her snout and discus; Nārasiṁhī made (the *Asuras*) torn by nails; Rudradūtī (felled them) with her loud laughter; so also Rudra (killed) with the trident, and Vināyaka with the hatchet.

23. Those bold sons of Danu being thus felled by the numerous forms of Devī, fell on the ground and being devoured by the *Bhūtas*, died.

24-25. Those great *Asuras* being killed by the gods and agitated by the Mother(-*goddesses*), took refuge in Raktabīja, with their hair dishevelled and eyes tremulous due to fear. That Raktạbīja, taking the best weapon, arrived immediately and entered with his lips quivering due to fury into the circle of mother(-*goddesses*), chasing away the groups of *Bhūtas* all round.

26-27. Seeing him attack, the Mother-goddesses showered sharp-tipped weapons on the Son of Diti. A drop of blood that fell on the ground, stood up as another (*Asura*) of the same stature. Then, Ambikā, Mārī herself said: "May (the *Asura*) be killed now. (So) O Caṇḍī ! Spreading your mouth like marine-fire, drink the blood of the enemy."

28-30. That Varadāmbikā, Carmamuṇḍā, immediately stood up, spreading her fierce mouth, making the satiated mouth, touch the heaven and earth. Then, Ambikā, making the enemy distressed by the seizure of his hair, threw him into her mouth and rent his chest with spear. The other (*Asuras*) born of blood also fell into her mouth. Then, the blood became desiccated. With the loss of blood, the *Asura* lost his strength and she reduced the vigourless one into hundreds of pieces by the discus decorated with gold.

31. When the commander of the army of Danu was killed, the *Dānavas* cried piteously saying, "Alas father ! Alas brother! Where are you going? Stop; come (here) for a while."

32. Other *Daityas* being felled on the ground by Mṛḍānī, raced towards the mountain with their bodies bare and hair dishevelled, carrying shattered shields and ornaments.

33-34. Niśumbha, the Lord of *Dānavas*, observing that army with shields, weapons and ornaments shattered and (himself) in a chariot with broken wheel and axle, angrily approached Mṛḍānī. Holding a sword and a shining shield and seeing her beauty, he shook his head (in admiration). Restraining astonishment, but being afflicted with fever (of lust), he stood as if painted in a picture.

35. Seeing the foe of celestials standing in front stupefied, the Devī said thus with a laugh: "By this valour the celestials were conquered by you and by this strength you ask me to marry you !"

36-39. Hearing the words of Kauśikī, the *Dānava*, an adept among speakers, spoke after deliberating for a long time: "O damsel ! You are of a body, so delicate that by the mere falling of my weapon on you, you will be minced as an unbaked earthen vessel (dissolves) in water. Considering this fact, O lovely one ! I do not think of hurting you. Therefore, O lady of wide eyes ! You resort to me. Even Indra is not capable of withstanding the blow of my sword. Turn away your mind from the battle; become my wife forthwith."

40-41. O sage ! Having heard this uttered by Niśumbha, Yogeśvarī laughed and told Niśumbha these words pregnant with meaning: "O valorous one ! Without being conquered in a battle, I shall not be the wife of anyone. If you want me to be your wife, then win me over in a duel."

42-45. O Nārada ! When this was said, the *Dānava*, whirled the sword and flung it with force towards Kauśikī. She cut down the oncoming sword as well as the shield (in his hand) with six arrows moving fast due to the feathers; that was indeed a wonder. As the sword along with the shield was cut down in the duel, the great *Asura*, grasping a mace, rushed with the speed of wind towards the Devī, born of sheath. Even as he was rushing on the battle-ground, Ambikā, at once, severed his strong arms, raised and grasping the mace, with a crescent-tipped arrow (*Kṣurapra*).

46-48. When the ferocious and dreadful enemy of the celestials was felled, Caṇḍī and other Mother-goddesses made shouts of joy. As the enemy was beaten, the joyous *Devas* led by Indra standing in the sky said: "O Vijayā ! Be victorious!" Then, the trumpets were sounded all round by the groups of *Bhūtas*; the celestials showered a rain of flowers over Kātyāyanī.

49. O noble sage ! Seeing Niśumbha beaten, Śumbha arrived, angrily holding a spear and riding on the elephant, Vṛndāraka.

50-54. Then, seeing the oncoming Lord of *Dānavas* on the elephant, the Devī took out four arrows, the (tips of which) shone like the crescent moon. That Ambikā, with a laugh, sportively severed the two legs of the elephant at the same time with two *Kṣurapras* and with two (others) she hit its temples. As the leg was severed, the elephant sank down of its own accord, like the peak of a tall mountain struck by the bolt of Indra. Śivā severed with an arrow, the head of Śumbha bedecked with ear-rings, whose elephant was subdued and who was jumping up. As the head was severed, the *Daitya*-chief fell down along with the elephant, like the *Krauñca* (which fell) together with the bison, struck by Mahāsena (Kumārasvāmi).

55. Having heard that the (two) enemies of celestials were killed by Mṛḍānī, the celestials including Indra, Sūrya, *Maruts, Aśvins* and *chief vasus,* came to that great mountain and humbly bending down, recited (the hymn) pleasing to the ears of the Devī.

*The Devas said:*

56-63. Om. Salutation to you, O venerable one ! O destroyer of sins ! Salutations to you, O shatterer of the pride of the foe of celestials ! Salutation to you, O bestower of sovereignty to Hari and Hara ! Salutation to you who accomplished the task of the partakers of sacrifice. Salutation to you who annihilated the enemies of celestials. Salutation to you whose feet are worshipped by Indra. Salutation to you who destroyed Mahiṣa. Salutation to you, glorified by Sun having green horses ! Salutation to you having eighteen arms. Salutation to you, O killer of Śumbha and Niśumbha ! Salutation to you, O remover of misery ! O wielder of trident! Salutation, O Nārāyaṇī ! O bearer of discus ! Salutation, O Vārāhī ! ever-carrying the earth ! To you, O Nārasiṁhī ! We bow down. Salutation to you; salutation to you, O wielder of bolt ! O elephant-bannered one ! Salutation, O Kaumārī ! O peacock-vehicled one ! Salutation, O one riding on the swan of the Grandsire ! Salutation, O one bedecked with garland ! O one with fine hair ! Salutation to you, O one riding on the back of the donkey ! Salutation, O remover of all miseries ! O one encompassing the universe ! Salutation to you, O one supreme in the universe ! Please protect the universe; put down the enemy of the twice-born ones and of Devas ! Salutation to you, O one of all-form ! O one of triple eyes ! Salutation, salutation to you, O bestower of boons! Please be gracious; you are Brahmāṇī; you are Mṛḍānī (Māheśvarī); you are Kaumārī, riding on the excellent peacock and holding the spear; you are Vārāhī; you are Vaiṣṇavī of fair face, moving on the lord of birds and endowed with *Śārṅga*; you are ferocious Nārasiṁhī, making roaring sounds; you are Aindrī, endowed with *Vajra*; you are Mārī, Carmamuṇḍā, delighted in moving on corpses and *Yoginī*, perfect in *Yoga*. Om. Salutation to you, O three-eyed one ! O venerable one ! There is never inauspicious-ness, never to those who do not abandon your feet but are humble, bowing down their heads everyday and to those who always glorify (you) and have flower offerings in their hands.

64-65. Being glorified thus by the excellent celestials, the destroyer of the foes of celestials told the celestials, *Siddhas* and the honourable great sages, with a smile: "This most wonderful victory over the foes of celestials, by crushing them on the battle-front, has been achieved by me through your grace. The evil dreams will disappear undoubtedly, in case of the righteous (devoted) persons who repeat this hymn recited by you. So too, you choose another boon you desire."

*The Devas said:*

66. If you yourself are to bestow a boon on the celestials, then, please attend to the welfare of the children of the twice-born ones and of cattle. Again you burn down, O one having fire-like body, the other enemies of gods !

*The Devī said:*

67-70. Born of Yaśodā in the house of Nanda, I will again slay the great foe of celestials. Having incarnated there, (I will kill) Lavaṇa and also the different (other) Śumbha and Niśumbha by striking them with my teeth. Again in *Kaliyuga*, seeing the celestials without food, I will incarnate as Mārī in the house of Indra and along with Devī Saptadhāmā, I shall maintain the celestials with varieties of vegetables. Once again, O Devas ! I will be born in Vindhya to destroy the enemies and to protect the sages. Having killed the *Daityas* of evil conduct and action, I will again have victory, O Devas ! When the great *Asura*, Aruṇākṣa is going (to do harm), I will be there for the welfare (of you all), O Devas ! After taking away his life in the form of a large bee, I will return to Heaven.

*Pulastya said:*

71. Having said thus and having bowed down to the excellent *Dvijas*, the giver of boons to the celestials, the Devī, left the *Bhūta-Gaṇas* and departed to the sky, followed by the groups of *Siddhas*.

72. This ancient history of the victory of the Devī is most holy and brings fortune to the people. This destroys the

*Rākṣasas* and should always be listened to with attention; so said the venerable Lord.

## CHAPTER FIFTY-SEVEN

### The birth of Kārttikeya

*Nārada said:*

1. O sage of auspicious vows ! How did Skanda kill Krauñca along with Mahiṣa ? O Brāhmaṇa of unlimited glow ! Please tell me this in detail.

*Pulastya said:*

2. O Nārada ! Listen. I will tell you the ancient holy story, enhancing the fame of Kumāra Kārttikeya.

3-6. O Brāhmaṇa ! By that semen ejected by the Wielder of Pināka and sucked by Fire, he (Fire) was overcome and became subdued in power. Then, he, of unlimited glow, approached the *Devas* and being sent by them, he went immediately to the abode of Brahmā. While going, Fire saw Kuṭilā Devī on the way. Seeing her, he said: "O Kuṭilā ! This semen indeed cannot be borne. (If left anywhere else) this, ejected by Maheśvara, can burn down all the worlds. Therefore, please receive; this virtuous son will be yours."

7-8ab. So (told) by Agni, that Kuṭilā, the mighty river, remembering her noble desire, told Agni: "Throw (the semen) into my waters." Then, the (river-) goddess bore the semen of Śiva and nurtured it.

8cd-10. (Earlier) the venerable Fire bore (the semen) for five thousand years, wandering at will. His muscles, bones, blood, fat, marrow, hair, beard, eyes and hair on head—all turned golden. Therefore, Fire is spoken of as *Hiraṇyaretas* in the worlds.

11. Kuṭilā, carrying the fire-like foetus for five thousand years, then, came to the abode of Brahmā.

12. The Lotus-born saw that eminent river afflicted. Seeing (her), he asked: "By whom were you impregnated?"

13-14. She said: "That semen of Śaṅkara, sucked by Agni, was thrown into me by him unable to bear it, O noblest one! O Grandsire ! It is (almost) five thousand years since I carried the foetus; (perhaps) there is yet time; it does not (appear) to fall anywhere."

15-16. Having heard it, the venerable one said: "You go to Udayagiri. There is a wide wild growth of reeds extending a hundred *yojanas*. There, on the wide slope of the mountain, O lovely one ! Cast this (foetus). On the completion of ten thousand years, a baby boy will be born."

17-18. Having heard the words of Brahmā, she came to the mountain in human form. The Daughter of the Mountain, having come, abandoned the foetus there through her mouth. She, having left that baby boy, immediately came to Brahmā. She, who had the water form, became auspicious Kuṭilā because of the incantation.

19. That wild (growth) of reeds as also the other trees, animals and birds that inhabited the place (became) golden because of the energy of Śarva.

20-25. Then, as ten hundred autumns elapsed, a boy of lotus-like eyes and glowing like the early morning sun was born. The venerable one, lying on his back on the divine reeds, but keeping his toe in the mouth, cried like a large cloud. At the same time, the six divine *Kṛttikās* of great effulgence, who were moving at will, saw the boy lying among the reeds. Taking pity, they came (to the spot) where Skanda was lying. "I shall be the first (to give) him breast-milk", "I shall be the first" they shouted. Seeing them quarrelling, he became one with six faces. All those *Kṛttikās*, nourished the child.with affection. O sage ! Being nourished by them, the boy grew up. He became famous as Kārttikeya, being the pre-eminent among the mighty.

26. O Brāhmaṇa ! In the meanwhile, the Lotus-born asked the Fire: "How old is your son Guha now?"

27. Having heard his words, Fire, though he knew about his son, replied to the Lord of Devas: "I do not know who is this Guha."

28. The pleased venerable one told him: "The semen of Tryambaka sucked by you is born in the reeds as a boy, the Lord of the three worlds."

29. Having heard the words of the Grandsire, Fire went, hastily riding on a swift ram and Kuṭilā saw him.

30. Then, Kuṭilā questioned (him): "O Kavi ! Where are you going hurriedly?" He said: "(I am going) to see my son, the child born on the thick reeds."

31. She said: "He is my son." Fire said: "(He is) mine." Then, Janārdana, who was moving at will, saw them arguing.

32-33. He asked them as to why they were quarelling there. They said: "About our son, if he is born of the semen of Rudra", god Hari told them, "you go to the Vanquisher of the Three Cities. You do what the Lord of *Devas* tells you. There can be no doubt."

34. O Nārada ! So told by Vāsudeva, Kuṭilā and Fire going near Hara, said: "Whose son is he really?"

35. Hearing those words, Rudra with his heart full of joy, told Pārvatī with horripilation, "Good! Good!"

36. Then, Ambikā said to Hara: "O Lord ! Let us go and ask the child. He will be the son of the person whom he resorts to."

37. Saying, "Very well", the venerable Bull-bannered One, got up along with Umā, Kuṭilā and the wise Fire.

38-41. Hara, Umā, Kuṭilā and Agni arrived in *Śaravaṇa,* the thickest of reeds, and saw the child lying on the lap of the Kṛttikās. Then, the boy Saṇmukha (Six-faced one), considering their thought with respect, became one with four bodies through his mystic power even in childhood. Kumāra went over to Śaṅkara; Viśākha to Pārvatī; Śākha to Kuṭilā and Naigameya to Agni. Then, Rudra became pleased.

Umā as well as Kuṭilā and Agni, the leader of gods, were greatly pleased.

42-46. Then, the *Kṛttikās* said: "Is Ṣaṇmukha son of Hara?" Hara then told them with joy, these specific words, O sage: "Let this be your son with the name Kārttikeya; may he be the imperishable son of Kuṭilā as Kumāra; let him, well-known as Skanda, be the son of Gaurī; as my son, he will be known by the name Guha only; as the son of Fire, he will be known as Mahāsena; as the son of Śaravaṇa, he will be known as Sārasvata. Thus this great *Yogī* gets fame on the earth. Because of his six aspects, this mighty person will be spoken of as Saṇmukha."

47. Having said so, the venerable Śūlapāṇi remembered the Grandsire along with the *Devas* and they came there in haste.

48-49. Having bowed down to Śiva and to Umā, the daughter of the Mountain and after meeting Fire, Kuṭilā and the Kṛttikās with affection, the celestials saw the boy Saṇmukha, extremely brilliant like the sun, who appeared to dazzle the eyes of Devas with his own brilliance.

50-52. All these excellent celestials overwhelmed with wonder, said thus: "O Lord ! The task of the *Devas* has been accomplished by you and then by the divine Fire; so please get up; let us now go to the imperishable *Aujasa-tīrtha* in Kurukṣetra; let us coronate Saṇmukha in Sarasvatī. O Devas! *Gandharvas* and *Kinnaras*, my this (Saṇmukha) be the commander of (our) army; let him kill Mahiṣa and the most ruthless Tāraka."

53-56. "Very well", said Śarva and the celestials got up. Then they, together with Kumāra went to Kurukṣetra that bestows great merits. There, the *Devas* including Indra, Rudra, Brahmā and Janārdana, along with the groups of sages, put forth efforts for his coronation. Then, Hara, *Acyuta* and others consecrated him with the waters of rivers that flow to the seven seas, which gives great merit and with plants and herbs of a thousand kind. When Kumāra of divine form was coronated as the commander of the army, *Gandharvas* and sages sang (his praise) and groups of *Apsarās* danced.

57-59. The Daughter of Mountain (Pārvatī), seeing Kumāra coronated, affectionately placed him on her lap and sniffed his head again and again. The Daughter of Mountain sniffing Kārttikeya's face, wet with consecrated water, shone like Aditi, the mother of gods, sniffing the face of Indra earlier. Then, seeing the son consecrated, Śarva was happy; so also Fire, Kṛttikās and the glorious Kuṭilā.

60-61. Then, Hara gave four *Pramatha* groups equal in prowess to Indra; to Guha who was installed as the commander of the army—Ghaṇṭākarṇa, Lohitākṣa, the violent Naṇdiṣeṇa and the fourth, Kumudamālin, well-known as the foremost of the mighty.

62. O Nārada ! Seeing the *Gaṇas* given by Hara to Skanda, all the gods led by Brahmā also gave their respective *Pramathas*.

63-72. Brahmā gave Sthāṇu-*gaṇa*, Viṣṇu gave three *Gaṇas*: Saṅkrama, Vikrama and the third Parākrama; Indra (gave) Utkleśa and Paṅkaja, Sun (gave) Daṇḍa and Kapiñjala; Moon (gave) Maṇi and Vasumaṇi; Aśvins (gave) Vatsa and Nandin; Fire gave Jyotis, Jvalajjihva and Pura; Dhātā gave three followers: Kunda, Mukunda and Kusuma; Tvaṣṭā (gave) Cakra and Anucakra; Vedhā (gave) Nisthira and Susthira; Pūṣā gave the mighty Pāṇityaja and Kālika; Himavān (gave) the eminent *Pramathas*: Svarṇamāla and Ghanāhva; the lofty Vindhya gave Atikṛṣṇa and Pārṣada; Varuṇa gave Suvarcasa, Ativarcasa, Saṅgraha and Vigraha; Nāgas gave Jaya and Parājaya; Ambikā (gave) Unmāda, Śaṅkukarṇa and Puṣpadanta; Vāyu gave two followers: Ghasa and Atighasa; Aṁśumān gave to Saṇmukha, the five *Pramathas*: Parigha, Vaṭaka, Bhīma, Dāha and Atidahana; Yama gave six followers: Pramatha, Unmātha, Kālasena, Mahāmukha, Tālapatra and Kālajaṅgha; Dhātā gave two *Gaṇa*-chiefs: Suprabha and Śubhakarma; O chief of the twice-born one ! Mitra gave Suvrata and Satyasandha.

73-74. The fifteen *Gaṇas* given by *Yakṣas* to Guha were: Ananta, Saṅkupīṭha, Nikumbha, Kumuda, Ambuja, Ekākṣa, Kunaṭī, Cakṣus, Kirīṭī, Kalaśodara, Sūcīvaktra, Kokanada, Prahāsa, Priyaka and Acyuta.

75-83. Kalakanda was given by Kālindī; Raṇotkaṭa by Narmadā; Siddhayātra by Godāvarī; Adri and Kampaka by Tamasā; Sahasrabāhu by Śīta; Smitodara by Vañjulā; Gandha by Mandākinī; Priyaṅkara by Vipāśa; Caturdaṁṣṭra by Airāvatī; Ṣoḍaśa by Vitastā; Kauśikī gave Mājari; and Gautamī (gave) Kratha and Krauñca; Bāhudā (gave) Śataśīrṣa; Vāhā (gave) Gonanda and Nandika; Bhīmarathī gave Bhīma; Sarayū gave Vegāri; Kālī gave Aṣṭabāhu; and Gaṇḍakī (gave) Subāhu; Mahānadī (gave) Citradeva; Śiprā gave Citraratha; Kuhū gave Kuvalaya; Madhūdakā gave Madhuvarṇa; Dhūtapāpā (gave) Jambūka; and Vetrā gave Śvetānana; Varṇā (gave) Stuta and Prathama; Revā (gave) Sāgaravegi; Prabhāva gave Arthasaha; Kāñcanā (gave) Kanakekṣaṇa; Vimalā (gave) Gṛdhravaktra; Manoharā gave Cārupatra; Dhūtapāpā (gave) Mahārāva; Karṇā (gave) Vidrumasannibha; Oghavatī gave Suprasāda, Suveṇu and Jiṣṇu; Viśālā (gave) Yajñabāhu. Thus the Sarasvatīs (i.e. rivers) gave their *Gaṇas*.

84-87. Kuṭilā gave to her son thirty *Gaṇas* as powerful as Indra; Jaṭādhara gave Karāḷa, Sitakeśa and Kṛṣṇakeśa as well as Meghanāda, Caturdaṁṣṭra, Vidyujjihva, Daśānana, Somāpyāyana and the fierce Devayāji; the Kṛttikās gave to their son these five (*Gaṇas*): Haṁsāsya, Kuṇḍajaṭhara, Mudgagrīva, Hayānana and Kūrmagrīva; the sages gave to Skanda these five (*Gaṇas*): Sthāṇujaṅgha, Kumbhavaktra, Lohajaṅgha, Mahānana and Piṇḍākara.

88-93. Pṛthūdaka-tīrtha gave Nāgajihva, Candrabhāsa, Pāṇikūrma, Aśikṣaka, Cāṣavaktra and Jambūka; Cakra-tīrtha (gave the Gaṇa) Sucakra by name; Gayāśiras (gave the *Gaṇa*) by name Makara; Kanakhala gave his Gaṇa called Pañcaśiva; Ajiśirā (gave) Bandhudatta, Puṣkara and Bāhuśāla; Mānasa (gave) Sarvaujasa, Mahīṣaka as well as Piṅgala; Auśanasa gave Rudra; Mātṛs gave other (*Gaṇas*); Soma-tīrtha gave

Vasudāma; and Prabhāsa (gave) Nandinī; Indra-tīrtha (gave) Viśokā; and Udapāna (gave) Ghanasvanā; Sapta-sārasvata gave the marvellous four (*Gaṇas*) of Mātṛs: Gītapriyā, Mādhavī, Tīrthanemi and Smitānana; Nāga-tīrtha gave Ekacūḍa, Kurukṣetra (gave) Phalāspada.

94-104. Brahmayoni (gave) Caṇḍaśitā; Bhadrakālī (gave) Triviṣṭapa; Dviradapāvana gave Roṇḍī, Seṇḍī and Poṣabheḍī; Mahī (Earth) gave Mopalīyā; Mānasa pond (gave) Śālīkā; Śatānandā (gave) Śataghaṇṭā as well as Ulūkhalamekhalā; Badarikāśrama gave Padmāvatī and Mādhavī; Devī (gave) Suṣama, Ekacūḍā and Dhamadhamā; Utkrāthanī (gave) Vedamantrā and Kedāra (gave) Mātṛs; Raudra Mahālaya gave Sunakṣatra, Kalūlā, Suprabhāta, Sumaṅgala, Devamitrā and Citrasenā; Prayāga Mātṛs gave Koṭarā, Ūrdhvaveṇī, Śrīmatī, Bāhuputrikā, Patitā and Kamalākṣī; Sarvapāpavimocana gave Suyamā, Madhupiṅgā, Kṣānti, the great Dahadahā and another Kheṭakarā; Sudāma (gave) Santānikā, Vikalā, Kramukāmbaravāsinī, Jaleśvarī, Karkuṭikā and Lohamekhalā; Vapuṣmatī (gave) Ulmukākṣī; the one named Koka (gave) Mahāsanī; Raudra (gave) Karkaṭikā and Śveta-tīrtha gave Tuṇḍa.

Seeing the *Bhūtas, Gaṇas* and *Mātṛs*, the noble son of Vinatā gave his son, *Mayūra* (peacock) of great speed; so also Aruṇa gave his son, *Tāmracūḍa* (cock). Fire (gave) *Śakti* (spear); the Daughter of Mountain (Pārvatī) gave cloth; Guru (gave) a staff; Kuṭilā gave a *Kamaṇḍalu;* Viṣṇu gave a garland; the Wielder of Trident (Śiva) gave a banner and Indra (gave) a necklace from his bosom.

Surrounded by the *Gaṇas,* followed by the *Mātṛs,* sitting on the peacock, holding the excellent *Śakti* in hand and installed as the commander of the army by Bhava (Śiva), he of great physique, shone like the sun.

# CHAPTER FIFTY-EIGHT

## Killing of Tāraka and Mahiṣa

*Pulastya said:*

1-2. Kumāra, installed as the commander of the army by the gods, said this, after devotedly prostrating himself before Bhāva (Śiva), Girijā (Pārvatī) as well as the resplendent Fire, bowing to the six *Kṛttikās* as also to the affectionate Kuṭilā and saluting Brahmā:

*Kumāra said:*

3-4. Salutations to the venerable Devī. Om. Salutations to you, O sages rich in penance ! By your grace, I will conquer the enemies, Mahiṣa and Tāraka. I am a child; I do not know what to say, O gods ! Now along with Brahmā you please permit me.

5. When the eminent Kumāra said thus, every one seeing his face (felt) free from panic.

6. Śaṅkara with affection for his son, getting up, led the Lord of beings (Brahmā), holding him in his right hand, towards Skanda.

7. Then, Umā told her son: "Come on, O my boy ! O killer of foes ! Come; bow down to Viṣṇu's charming feet, venerated by all the worlds."

8. Then, Guha asked with a smile: "O mother ! Tell me who is this (Viṣṇu), for, he is respectfully saluted by persons like us."

9-10. The mother replied to him: "After the accomplishment of your task, the Lotus-born (Brahmā) will tell you who this eminent Garuḍa-bannered One is. Your father Śaṅkara has informed me this much only; there is no one superior to this; we and other embodied ones are next to him."

11. When Pārvatī said (thus), Skanda stood with his hands held in suppliance, after prostrating himself before Janārdana and begged permission of Acyuta.

12. Then, the venerable one, the promoter of beings (Viṣṇu), after reciting benediction to ward off the evils to Skanda who held his hands in suppliance, gave permission to proceed.

*Nārada said:*

13. O sage among Brāhmaṇās ! You please expound what benediction Garuḍadhvaja (Viṣṇu) recited to ward off evil to the Peacock-bannered (Skanda).

*Pulastya said:*

14-25. Listen to the holy benediction to ward off evil that was recited by the venerable Hari, for the victory of Skanda and the destruction of Mahiṣa: "Om. May Brahma, the Lotus-born, having *Rājasa-guṇa* grant you welfare; may Viṣṇu, the birthless, having hands holding discus, grant you welfare; may Śaṅkara, the bull-bannered along with his spouse (bestow) welfare with devotion; may Fire confer welfare on you, O Skanda (peacock-vehicled) ! May the Sun grant you welfare always; may the Moon along with Mars and Mercury as well as Jupiter (do so); may Venus bestow welfare on you always; may Saturn bring to you welfare; may those Seven Great Sages stationed in Heaven–Marīci, Atri, Pulaha, Pulastya, Kratu, Vasiṣṭha, Bhṛgu and Aṅgiras–as well as Budha favour you with well-being; may Viśvedevas, Aśvins, Sādhyas, group of Maruts, Agni, Ādityas, Māheśvaras wielding lances, *Yakṣas, Piśācas, Vasus,* as well as *Kinnaras*–all these being ever vigilant, bring to you welfare; may Nāgas, Suparṇas, rivers, lakes, *Tīrthas* (holy spots), meritorious ponds, seas, groups of *Bhūtas* of immense strength, *Gaṇa*-chiefs–all these being ever vigilant, bring to you welfare; may there be harmlessness from bipeds and from the quadrupeds as well; may there be harmlessness from the multipeds and may there be no harm from the feetless beings; may Indra protect the eastern direction and Yama, the southern; may Varunṇa guard the western and *Yakṣas*, the northern direction; may Agni (protect) the south-east and Kubera, the south-west; Vāyu, the north-west and Śiva, the north-east; may Dhruva look after (the region) above and Dharādhara below; may Musalī, Lāṅgalī, Vajrī and Dhanuṣmān protect in-between; may Varāha protect in waters and Nṛsiṁha in a fort; may Mādhava the virtuous and the voice of Sāmaveda protect you all round."

*Pulastya said:*

26-28. So given benediction, the leader Guha, wielding a spear, soared into the sky from earth, after prostrating himself before all the celestials. All other *Gaṇas*, all gods together with the hermits–they who could assume forms they wished and could move in the sky followed Kumāra. All the Mother-goddesses flew into the sky along with the powerful Skanda, desirous of killing the great *Asuras*.

29-32. After traversing a long path, Skanda told the *Gaṇas*: "O mighty ones ! You descend on to the earth speedily." Hearing the words of Guha, the *Gaṇas* descended on the ground and going to the mountain nearby, made a terrific noise. The sound filling up the entire earth and the sky, entered *Pātāla*, the abode of *Dānavas*, through the passage of the sea. That was heard by Mahiṣa and the clever Tāraka as well as the *Asuras*—Virocana, Kumbha and Nikumbha.

33-34. Hearing the noise all of a sudden, which was intense like the fall of *Vajra* and wondering what it could be, they immediately went to Andhaka. O Nārada ! Those perturbed pre-eminent *Dānavas*, approaching Andhaka, discussed with him about that noise.

35-36. As the *Daityas* were discussing, the hog-faced leader of *Daityas*, Pātālaketu, came to *Rasātala* from *Pātāla*. He, being hit by an arrow, was aching and shivering again and again. Approaching Andhakāsura, he spoke in a feeble voice.

*Pātālaketu said:*

37-47. O *Daitya*-Lord ! I had been to the hermitage of Gālava. I forcibly began my attempt to destroy it. As I entered that hermitage in the form of a hog, O King ! I do not know, by which person, I was shot with an arrow. With my collar-bone broken by the arrow and afflicted with fear, I was made to run away hastily from that hermitage and he, too, came chasing me. O Asura ! The excellent sound of hoofs of the horse was heard; the warrior was shouting behind me, "Stop, stop". Due to fear, I came to the southern ocean. There I saw the people who were of various shapes and wearing various dresses. Some of them roared like cloud; others roared in echo; some others said: "We will indeed kill Mahiṣāsura." Yet other powerful ones said: "We will now kill Tārakāsura." O Lord of *Asuras* ! Having heard that, I was very much terrified. Leaving aside the ocean, I, mad with fear, jumped into a large hollow in the ground. That mighty one also followed me. Due to his fear, skipping my Hiraṇyapura, I have come to your refuge. You please favour me.

Having heard that, Andhaka said in a voice like that of a cloud: "You need not be afraid of him, O Dānava ! I shall certainly protect you."

Mahiṣa, Tāraka, the fierce Bāṇa, son of Bali, these valiant ones–Mahiṣa and others–went out with their followers to fight on earth without informing Andhaka.

48-49. O sage ! The *Daityas* with their weapons and army came to that place, where those *Gaṇas* of terrific forms made the loud noise. Then, the leaders of *Daityas*, seeing the *Gaṇas* of Kārttikeya, attacked at once, the fierce circle of Mother-goddesses.

50-63. The valiant Sthāṇu who was at their front holding *Parigha*, massacred the enemy army with rage, like Rudra (kills) the beings. Seeing Mahādeva striking, Kalaśodara, taking an axe in hand, killed all the great *Asuras*. The frightful Jyālāmukha, taking the *Asuras* by hand along with the chariots, elephants and horses, threw (them) into his wide mouth. Enraged Daṇḍaka too, lifting up the great *Asura* who was holding a *Prāsa*, threw him and his vehicle into the ocean. Śaṅkukarṇa, holding a pestle, was striking with a plough and pounding the *Dānavas*, like a minister (pounding) a king without manliness. The valiant leader of *Gaṇas*, Puṣpadanta, holding a sword and a shield, reduced the *Daityas* and *Dānavas* into two, three and several pieces. Wherever Piṅgala moved about with *Daṇḍa* and *Muṇḍa*, there, the *Dānavas* were seen in heaps. The *Gaṇa*-leader, the valorous Sahasranayana, whirling the spike, killed the *Asuras* with their horses, chariots and elephants. Bhīma killed the frontline Asuras, raining large boulders, as Indra does (fell) the high mountains with the raining of Vajra. The ferocious and mighty *Gaṇa*, Śakaṭacakra by name, who had five tufts, killed the enemies, forcibly whirling the Mudgara fast. In the battle, Giribhedī of swift movements, destroyed with his palm alone, the elephant with its rider and the chariot with the inmate. O sage ! The mighty Nāḍījaṅgha killed the *Asuras*, striking them with fists and knees and with bolts similar to *Vajra*. Kūrmagrīva and Hayagrīva killed the *Daityas* together with their vehicles by their head and feet and by plundering. Piṇḍākara and Kalipriya slew the *Dānavas* excited in the warfare, with snout and horn respectively.

64. Then, seeing their army being destroyed by the leaders of *Gaṇas*, Mahiṣa and the commander Tāraka rushed (to the battlefield).

65-69. The *Pramathas*, being struck by the excellent weapons of the *Dānavas* were enraged and fought covering them all round. Haṁsāsya hit Mahiṣāsura with Paṭṭiśa; Ṣoḍaśāsya with the trident; Śataśīrṣa with the fine sword; Śrutāyudha hit the *Daitya* on his head with the mace; Viśoka with the pestle and Bandhudatta with the pike. So also, he was poked by other *Gaṇas* with *Śūla, Śakti, Ṛṣti* and *Paṭṭiśa* in the battle. Still he did not even shiver like the Maināka mountain. Tāraka was tied and torn by Bhadrakālī; Ulūkhala, as well as Anekacūḍa, with excellent weapons in the battle.

70-72. Both the great *Asuras*, though struck by the *Pramathas* and the Mother goddesses, did not get perturbed. On the other hand, the two valiant ones went on harassing the *Gaṇas*. Mahiṣa, defeating the *Pramathas* by hitting speedily with his mace, raced with his weapon towards Kumāra. Seeing Mahiṣa, the son of Danu attack, enraged Cakrākṣa raised his discus and thwarted him.

73-75. The great warriors, *Gaṇas* and *Asuras*, holding discus and mace respectively, then fought, O Brāhmaṇa! It was fast, wonderful and splendid. Mahiṣa, whirling the mace, threw it on the *Gaṇas*. Cakrākṣa threw his discus towards the chariot. The discus with highly sharp teeth, severed the mace and attacked Mahiṣa. Then, the *Daityas* cried aloud, "Alas! Mahiṣa is killed."

76-77. Hearing this, Bāṇa speedily rushed there, whirling his *Prāsa* and hit the red-hubbed discus with five hundred (punches of) fist. Also, he tied down Cakrākṣa with five hundred arms. Though powerful, he (Cakrākṣa) was made motionless by Bāṇa.

78-80. Seeing Cakrākṣa and the discus bound by Bāṇāsura, Makarākṣa of immense strength, rushed with the mace in hand. The mighty one subdued (Bāṇa), by hitting him on the head with the mace. The proud *Asura* having had (defeat), felt ashamed and leaving the battle-ground, went away to Śālagrāma. Bāṇa, being hit by Makarākṣa, turned his back.

81-82. O celestial ascetic ! The entire army of *Daityas* was shattered. Having destroyed all the army of *Daityas*, the angered Lords of *Gaṇas*, stood chasing away the *Daityas* on the battlefield. Then, seeing his army destroyed, the mighty *Daitya*, Tāraka, holding aloft a sword, attacked the Lord of *Gaṇas*.

83-84. Then, the leaders of *Gaṇas*, Haṁsavaktra and others and also those Mother goddesses, vanquished in the battle by that unsurpassed (*Daitya*), holding the sword and (therefore) afflicted by fear, sought refuge in Skanda. Seeing Tāraka attacked with the sword and seeing the *Gaṇas* vanquished, the son of Maheśvara pierced his heart with the *Śakti.* He fell down on earth with his vital organ torn asunder.

85. O great sage ! When his brother was made one of subdued pride and was killed, Mahiṣa became terror-stricken and the wicked one left the battle-front and went over to Himālaya mountain.

86. Then, as the valiant Tāraka was killed and Mahiṣa being panicky went away to Himālaya, Bāṇa, due to fear entered the deep sea, even as his offending army was being hit by the *Gaṇas.*

87-88. Having killed Tāraka in the war-front, Kumāra, holding his *Śakti* and riding on the peacock decorated with a crest feather, went at great speed to kill Mahiṣāsura also. Seeing the Peacock-bannered, who with *Śakti* in hand was rushing behind him, he (Mahiṣa), leaving Kailāsa and Himālaya as well, reached Krauñca and entered a cave.

89. The venerable Guha, son of the Wielder of Pināka, painfully spared the life of the *Daitya* who entered (the cave therein). He stopped with this thought only: "How can I be a killer of my own kinsman ?"

90. There arrived then, the Lotus-born (Brahmā), Hara, Murāri (Viṣṇu) and the Lord of celestials (Indra). Having arrived, they said: "You fell Mahiṣa as well as the mountain (Krauñca) with your Śakti and carry out the task of the gods."

91-94. Hearing those words which were agreeable and true, Kārttikeya told the celestials with a smile: "How (shall I kill) the grandson of my grandfather (maternal) and therefore my brother (cousin) and son of my mother's brother? Very ancient indeed is this scripture, which the great sages versed in *Veda* sing, and believing in which, even the greatest sinner reaches heaven. (It says:) One shall not kill a cow, a Brāhmaṇa, an old man, a wealthy person, a young boy, one's relative, a lady—though wicked and guilty, as well as the principal preceptor and the teachers. So, knowing the foremost *Dharma,* O leading celestials ! I am not going to kill my brother, uncle's son. (However) I shall strike the enemy with the *Śakti* in such a way that the *Daitya* comes out of his hiding (of his own accord)."

95-98. O great sage ! Hearing the words of Kumāra, the venerable Indra having a design in his mind, told Guha: "Why do you say so ? You are not superior to me in intellect; listen to what Hari told you earlier. The firm opinion of the *Śāstras* is that one shall not kill many people for the sake of one individual; but one can kill a person for the sake of many; one does not become a sinner by that. Having heard this precept before, O son of Fire ! Namuci, though my brother, was killed along with his brother by me. Therefore, for the sake of many, you trample and kill Mahiṣāsura along with Krauñca with the *Śakti* given by Fire."

99-100. Hearing the words of Indra, Kumāra with red eyes due to anger and agitated, told Indra: "O you foolish Indra! What after all is the might of your arms or your body that you chide me as if you are the only wise one in the world?"

101. Indra replied to him; "O Guha ! I am strong on my own." Guha told him: "If you are mighty, come, come for a duel."

102. Indra said: "O son of Kṛttikā ! He who circumambulates this Krauñca faster shall become mighty."

103. Hearing his words, the swift Skanda left his peacock immediately and proceeded to go round (Krauñca) on foot.

104. Indra then getting down from the lordly elephant, stood after turning about on his feet. Guha, coming along, asked: "O fool ! Why are you standing here only ?"

105. Indra told him cunningly: "I went round it earlier than you." Kumāra asked Indra (again): "Did you go round first ?"

106. Both mutually contending, "I am first", "I am first", approached and asked Maheśa, Brahmā and Mādhava.

107. Then, Hari told Skanda; "You better ask the Mountain. He whom the Mountain speaks first, shall be the mighty one."

108. Hearing the words of Mādhava, the son of Fire went to Krauñca mountain and asked like this: "Who went round first ?"

109. So asked, the clever Krauñca said: "Indra did (it) first and you, Guha, did next."

110. His lips quivered due to anger (to hear Krauñca) speak thus. Then, he cleverly severed with the *Śakti*, Krauñca along with Mahiṣa.

111. As his son was killed, the mighty Sunābha as well as the King of Mountains came in haste. Seeing Mahiṣa killed by Guha, Brahmā, Indra, Rudra, Maruts, Aśvins and the prominent *Vasus* went to heaven.

112. The mighty Kumāra who seeing his uncle, desired to kill him with the *Śakti* raised, was dissuaded at once by the Discus-bearer (Viṣṇu) by embracing him with arms saying, "(He is) an elderly person."

113. Himālaya, going near Sunābha, held him by hand and led him away. Hari, having the vehicle of foe of snakes (Garuḍa), immediately took away Kumāra and his peacock to heaven.

114. Then, Guha said to Hari, the Chief of celestials: "O venerable one ! I lost my sense because of confusion; my brother (cousin), uncle's son, was killed; therefore, I shall desiccate my body."

115. Viṣṇu told him: "O Kumāra ! Go to Pṛthūdaka, the celebrated *Tīrtha* which destroys sins. Having a bath in (the river) Oghavatī and devotedly visiting Hara, you will become as resplendent as the Sun."

116. So told by Hari, Kumāra went over to the *Tīrtha* and visited Śambhu. Having taken bath and worshipping the gods, he, as lustrous as the Sun, proceeded to the mountain, the home of Hara.

117. Sucakranetra also performed austerities consuming only air in the great hermitage on the mountain and worshipped the bull-bannered Hara who was pleased and offered a boon.

118. That killer of Krauñca asked the boon from the Lord: "O venerable one ! You please bestow on me a weapon for severing the arms of the foe, so that I may cut off the hand of Bāṇa with my hand."

119. Śambhu told him: "Go, this boon has been given to your weapon, discus. You will cut down the madly grown forest of the arms of Bāṇa. There is nothing to worry."

120. After the wish was granted by the Killer of Tripura, the Lord of *Gaṇas* being pleased, approached Skanda. After prostrating himself to his feet and saluting him, he (Sukranetra) informed him of the grace of Hara.

121. Thus I have related to you, the (account of) killing of Mahiṣāsura and the death of Krauñca by the blow of the *Śakti* of the Son of the Three-eyed (Lord), (the account) which cleanses the sins of those who take refuge and enhances merit.

# CHAPTER FIFTY-NINE

## Episode of Pātālaketu; Andhaka Flees to Pātāla

*Nārada said:*

1. Please tell me by whom was that leader of the *Daityas* struck with arrows; he who of which wounds were infflicted by arrows arrived, when the *Daityas* were engaged in consultation.

*Pulastya said:*

2. O eminent sage ! There was in the lineage of Raghu, a king who vanquished the foes. His son was a noble person, the receptacle of a multitude of qualities, always happy, brave, mighty, a subduer of enemy's army and a remover of affliction of Brāhmaṇas, the blind, the poor and the wretched on the earth.

3. That illustrious king, Ṛtadhvaja by name, riding on a horse, struck fast Pātālaketu on the back with a crescent moon-like arrow, for the sake of Gālava.

*Nārada said:*

4. O exalted one ! Why did he accomplish this for Gālava? Why did the prince strike fast with an arrow ?

*Pulastya said:*

5-6. Earlier, sage Gālava had been performing austerity, while always staying in his own well-known hermitage. That Pātālaketu stupidly created impediments to his austerity and caused hindrance to his meditation. He was able to reduce him (the *Daitya*) to ashes but then, he did not like the loss of his austerity. He (once) looked up at the sky and heaved a very deep and hot sigh.

7. Then, a charming horse fell from the sky and there was heard an incorporeal voice too: "This is a mighty steed and trots a thousand *yojanas* in a day."

8. Then, taking hold of that charming steed and giving it to Ṛtadhvaja equipped with weapons, the eminent sage engaged himself in penance only. The king, then came and struck the *Daitya*.

*Nārada said:*

9. O you of best vows ! By whom was the horse sent down from the sky ? Whose was the incorporeal voice? Please tell me; I am very curious.

*Pulastya said:*

10. The mighty, well-known king of *Gandharvas* and songster of Indra, Viśvāvasu by name, immediately sent down the steed to the earth, only for the use of Ṛtadhvaja and for the sake of his (*Gandharva's*) daughter.

*Nārada said:*

11. What was the purpose of the *Gandharva* king for which he sent the (steed) of great speed ? What was the use of the king's Kuvalayāśva to the prince ?

*Pulastya said:*

12. Viśvāvasu had a daughter endowed with good manners and qualities and a very beautiful lady in all the three worlds. She, a mass of loveliness, as bright as the moon, was Madālasā by name, as if languid with passion.

13. The swift Pātālaketu, the enemy of gods, saw that beautiful girl playing in Nandana (garden) and kidnapped her. The excellent horse was given for her sake.

14. Having killed the enemy *Daitya,* the prince was unperturbed, though in possession of the handsome lady. The prince was regarded by that doe-eyed lady as Indra, just as the Lord of gods would be (regarded) by Śacī.

*Nārada said:*

15. When Mahiṣa and the great *Asura,* Tāraka, were thus destroyed, what did the clever son of Hiraṇyākṣa do again?

*Pulastya said:*

16-17. Having seen Tāraka and Mahiṣa killed on the battlefield, Andhaka, the killer of the army of gods, full of bad thoughts, was enraged at the *Daityas.* Then, taking only some retinue and holding *Parigha* in hand, he emerged out of *Pātāla* and roamed about on the earth.

18-19. Then, Gaurī, the auspicious Daughter of Mountain, being in the midst of companions on Mandara of charming caves, was seen by him roaming about. Having seen that daughter of the King of Mountains of lovely physique in the garden, Andhakāsura was at once afflicted with Cupid's arrow.

20-23. Then the *Asura*, being unable to think and blind due to eros, said: "Whose (daughter) is this beautiful damsel of charming limbs moving in the garden ? If she is not included in my Antaḥpura, then what is to be done with my useless life? If I do not have an embrace of this slim-waisted one, fie on my beauty ! What is the use of it being everlasting? He who unites me and that dark-haired and doe-eyed (damsel) is a kinsman, a counsellor, a brother in calamities."

24-29. When the Lord of *Daityas* was speaking thus, Prahlāda, the ocean of wisdom, closing his ears with his hands, said nodding his head: "Do not speak like this, O *Daitya*-chief ! For, she is the Mother of the universe, the wife of Śaṅkara, the wielder of trident and the protector of the worlds. Do not entertain the evil thought that instantly destroys your family; she is another's wife for you; do not sink down to *Rasātala*. Taking upon another's wife is despicable among virtuous ones and despicable among wicked people too; may your enemies resort to it. O *Daitya*-king ! Have you not heard the verse, true, salutary and beneficial to all people, sung by King Gādhi, when he saw his army return, after laying a seige of the enemy: "It is better to give up one's life than to desire inflicting injury on others; it is better to be silent than to speak lie; it is better to be impotent than to have intercourse with another's wife; it is better to beg one's food than to steal other's belongings."

30. Having heard the words of Prahlāda, he, blind with fury and afflicted by Cupid, ran after (her) saying, "Is she the mother of that foe ?"

31-34. Then, the sons of Diti followed him, like stones thrown by a machine. The imperishable Nandī, with discus in hand, forcibly dispersed them. The (*Daityas*) led by Maya and *Tāra* were stopped and made to retreat. Being beaten by *Vajra*, they, terrified, ran fast in ten directions. Seeing them tormented by Nandī in the battle, the *Dānava* Andhaka, struck Nandī with *Parigha* and felled him. Seeing Nandī fall down as well as Andhaka running (towards her), Gaurī, due to fear of the vile one, assumed hundred forms.

35-38. Then, in the midst of the group of goddesses, the great lord of *Asuras* moving about confused and with eyes tremulous due to passion, appeared like an elephant in rut moving about in the midst of female elephants in a forest. He was unable to recognise, who among them was the daughter of the Mountain. It is no wonder because these four are always unable to discern (things): A person born blind cannot see; one blind due to passion cannot discern; one mad with pride cannot discern; one overcome by greed cannot discern. Andhaka, even though looking on at her, did not recognise Girijā. Running about, he did not take hold (of the Devī) out of them, thinking them to be (mere) damsels. Then, the wicked one was subdued by Devī Śatāvarī.

39-41. Being struck by excellent weapons, he fell on earth. Seeing Andhaka fallen on the ground, the splendid one, Ambikā, who had assumed a hundred forms, left the place and disappeared.

Seeing Andhaka fallen, the leaders of groups of *Daityas* and *Dānavas* rushed, desirous of battle, making a loud noise. Gaṇeśvara stood up, hearing the noise of those attackers.

42-47. The enraged mighty one, Gaṇeśvara, taking *Vajra* and seeing the *Dānavas* with Maya, defeated them like Indra. Then, approaching and seeing Ambikā, he bowed down to her auspicious feet.

The Devī told those her own forms: "You go at your will. You move about on earth being worshipped by men there. Your residence will be in gardens and forests, in plants and trees. (Now) you go without any fear."

So told by the Daughter of Mountain, the forms (of the Devī), bowed down to Ambikā in order and went to all directions, being eulogised by the *Kinnaras.*

Andhaka, on the other hand, gained consciousness. Not seeing the Daughter of the Mountain but finding his army defeated, he fled to *Pātāla.* O sage ! That wicked Andhaka, reaching *Pātāla,* could neither eat during day time nor could sleep during night. He, being hit by the arrows of Cupid and overcome by lust, thought always of Gaurī.

# CHAPTER SIXTY

## Birth of Kedāra-tīrtha–Legend of Mura

*Nārada said:*

1. Where had Śaṅkara gone, for, Ambikā along with Nandī fought with Andhaka? You please tell me this.

*Pulastya said:*

2-4. Since Bhava indulged in sensual pleasures for one thousand years, he appeared to have lost vigour and stamina. Then, observing his own vigourless part, Maheśvara, the best of wise ones, made up his mind to undergo austerity. That omnipresent lord undertook the great vow, pacified Ambikā and placing Nandī as the guardian, roamed about on the earth.

5-7. He had put on an excellent medal round his neck, had ear-rings of great serpents and had a girdle of exquisite conchs round his loins. He held a skull in his right hand and a water-pot in his left. He stayed only for a day (in any place like) trees, slopes of mountains or hills and (banks of) rivers. He made the three worlds his place of stay. He subsisted (first) on only roots, (then on) water and (finally on) air for nine hundred years.

8-10. Then, on an even stone slab in the wide and beautiful slopes of Himālaya, he remained without breathing, putting *Vīṭa** in the mouth. Then, the resplendent *Vīṭa* breaking through the skull of Parameṣṭhī (Śiva) in the midst of the matted hairs, fell on the earth. By that falling *Vīṭa*, the hill was smashed and was made plain like level ground which is the well-known *Kedāra-tīrtha* par excellence and meritorious.

---

* A small piece of wood shaped like a barley corn and about a span long—MW *gilli* like piece of wood.

11-16. O Brāhmaṇa ! The bull-bannered Hara, then offered to Kedāra, a boon which enhances merit, destroys sin and brings about emancipation: "In the lotus-heart of those people keeping restraint, who drink water in your *Tīrtha,* observing the vow of *Brahmacarya,* abstaining from wine and meat and sustain themselves for six months without going in for food cooked by others, this (Kedāra) *Liṅga* will be established firmly. Never will they be inclined towards evil. *Śrāddha* (offered here) to the *Pitṛs* will become inexhaustible, undoubtedly. Bathing, gifts, austerities, *Homa, Japa* and such activities done here will have inexhaustible (results) and the people who die (here) will have no rebirth."

Obtaining this boon from Hara, the *Tīrtha* captivates the deities. Kedāra purifies people, like the words of the Three-eyed God.

17-19. Conferring the boon on Kedāra, Hara hurriedly went to Devī Kālindī, the daughter of Sun and the destroyer of sins, for taking bath. Then, stepping down for taking bath, Hara sank down in the great waters and repeated the Gāyatrī called Drupadā under the water. O Kalipriya ! As Śaṅkara got himself immersed in Devī Sarasvatī, a year and a half elapsed; Īśvara did not emerge.

20-21. In the meantime, Brahmā, the worlds and the oceans got agitated and the asterisms along with stars fell on the earth. Indra and other gods were stirred out of their seats. The great sages were muttering, "May there be welfare to the worlds."

22. The shaken *Devas* in the worlds came to ask Brahmā. Seeing him, they asked: "Why is it that the worlds are disturbed with (their life in) doubt ?"

23. The Lotus-born (Brahmā) told them: "I too do not know the cause. Come then; it is proper for you to ask the Wielder of Discus and Mace (Viṣṇu)."

24. So told by the Grandsire, the *Devas* led by Indra went to Murāri's abode, keeping the Grandsire in front.

*Nārada said:*

25. O divine sage ! Who is this Murāri—a Deva, a *Yakṣa,* a *Kinnara,* a *Daitya,* a *Rākṣasa* or a human being? Please tell me.

*Pulastya said:*

26. He who is endowed with the *Guṇas–Sattva, Rajas* and *Tamas*—and yet beyond *Guṇas,* the omnipresent one and the all-pervader is Murāri (Mura's foe), the killer of Madhu.

*Nārada said:*

27. Whose son is he spoken of, he who is known as Mura? How was he killed in a war by Viṣṇu? You please tell me that.

*Pulastya said:*

28. Listen, I will tell you about the killing of Murāsura. This anectode is wonderful, meritorious and it destroys sin.

29-30. Kaśyapa's own son was Mura by name, born of Danu. He saw the sons of Diti, vanquished in a battle by the foremost celestials. Then, being afraid of death, he performed austerities for quite a number of years and worshipped the omnipresent, unconquered Brahmā.

31-32. Then, pleased with him, (Brahmā,) the giver of boon, said: "O my boy ! Choose a boon."

The *Daitya* chose this as a boon from the Grandsire: "O unborn, omnipresent one ! Whomsoever I touch with my palm in a battle, those-be they immortal—shall die at the touch of my hand."

33-37. "Yes", said the venerable Brahmā, the Grandsire of the universe.

Then, the resplendent and mighty Mura came to the celestial mountain. Having come there, he challenged a *Deva,* a *Yakṣa* as well as a *Kinnara.* But, O Nārada ! No one fought a duel with that *Daitya.* Then, with rage, he, going to Amarāvatī, challenged Indra. Indra did not think of fighting with him. Then, he entered Amarāvatī with his hand raised. Nobody dared to stop him who was entering. Having gone to Indra's abode, Mura said to Indra: "O Indra (of thousand eyes) ! Give me a fight or else give up heaven."

38-41. O Brāhmaṇa ! So told by the *Daitya*, Indra (Harihara) then gave up the heavenly kingdom and became a dweller on earth. The excellent elephant and the *Vajra* of Indra were taken away by the foes. The resplendent Indra with his wife, son and *Devas* established a township on the southern (right) bank of Kālindī (river) and Mura staying in heaven, enjoyed great pleasures. The other ferocious *Dānava*–Maya, Tāra and others — waiting on Mura, enjoyed heaven like the pious ones.

42-44. The great *Asura* once arrived on the earth, (and went) alone riding on an elephant towards the river Sarayū. On the bank of Sarayū, he saw the valiant king by name Raghu, born in Solar dynasty and engaged in a sacrificial ceremony. Going near him, the *Daitya* said: "Give me a fight or else refrain from the sacrifice; the deities are not to be offered sacrifice by you."

45-47. O Brāhmaṇa ! Then the resplendent, wise and excellent ascetic Vasiṣṭha, son of Mitrāvaruṇa, came near him and said: "O *Daitya* ! Of what (use) to you are the vanquished ones? You bring under control those who are unconquered. If you want to strike, then restrain Antaka, the God of Death. He is the mighty one, O great Asura ! He does not carry out your orders. If you conquer him, all else on the earth is indeed subdued."

48. Hearing the words of Vasiṣṭha, the eminent *Dānava*, proceeded to vanquish Dharmarāja, the wielder of Daṇḍa.

49-50. Yama, hearing that he (Mura) is proceeding towards him, set out and considering his (Mura's) invincibility in warfare, went towards Keśava, riding on his buffalo. Having approached and bowing down, he informed him (Viṣṇu) of the activity of Mura. He (Viṣṇu) said: "You go and send the great *Asura* to me."

51. Having heard the words of Vāsudeva, Yama hurriedly (returned). In the meanwhile, Mura, the *Daitya,* arrived in (Yama's) city.

52. Yama told him who had come there: "O Mura ! What do you want to do? You tell me; I am going to do what you say, O leader of *Dānavas* !"

*Mura said:*

53. O Yama ! You better refrain from restraining the beings. If not, I will sever your head and fell it on the ground here.

***

54. To him, Dharmarāja said this: "If you restrain that great guardian of mine, I shall act as you say, O Mura !"

55. Mura told him: "Who is superior to you? Tell me about him: I shall vanquish him and stop him; there is no doubt."

56. Yama spoke to him: "Viṣṇu, the wielder of the discus and mace is my lord. That imperishable dweller in *Śvetadvīpa* controls me."

57. The foremost *Daitya* said to him: "Inform me as to where does he live? I will go there myself to restrain him."

58. Yama told him: "You go to the ocean *Kṣīroda* by name (*Kṣīra-sāgara*). There stays the venerable Viṣṇu, the protector of the world and the encompasser of the Universe."

59. Hearing those words, Mura said: "I will go to Keśava. But, O Dharma ! Till then, people should not be restrained by you."

60. He said: "You go; I will either strive for victory on your account or I shall take proper action whether to restrain or not."

61. Mura so told (by Dharma), went to the Milk-ocean, where Janārdana of four forms was lying on the bed of Śeṣa.

*Nārada said:*

62. How is Viṣṇu spoken of as having four forms, for, on account of his omnipresence and imperceptibility, Viṣṇu is spoken of as one only? Please tell me that.

*Pulastya said:*

63-64. O Brāhmaṇa ! O great sage ! Listen, how the Lord of the universe, the imperceptible one, the omnipresent one and the only one is having four forms. That unimaginable, indescribable, imperceptible, bright and peaceful supreme being called Vāsudeva is spoken of as *Dvādaśapatraka** (having twelve *Patrakas*).

*Nārada said:*

65. How bright ? How peaceful ? How unimaginable? How excellent ? Which are his twelve *Patrakas* (aspects) spoken about ? O great sage !

*Pulastya said:*

66. Listen to the guarded secret told by Brahmā, learnt by Sanatkumara who related it to me.

*Nārada said:*

67. Who was this Sanatkumāra (to whom) Brahmā himself spoke ? How did he impart it to you ? Tell me all this in order.

*Pulastya said:*

68-69. Dharma's wife was Himsā who begot four sons. They were serious students of *Yoga-śāstra*, O eminent sage ! The eldest was Sanatkumāra, the second Sanātana, the third Sanaka and the fourth Sanandana.

70-71. Having seen Kapila, another expert in *Sāṅkhya*, *Voḍhu*, *Āsuri* and the great *Pañcaśikha*, the foremost in *Yoga* and rich in austerities and giving seats (to them) who were young, although (he himself) was older, he spoke to Kapila

---

* Name of a *Yoga* or religious observance in which the twelve syllables viz. *Om namo bhagavate Vāsudevāya* are connected with the 12 signs of the Zodiac and with the 12 months–MW.

and others, the great mystic *Yoga* which cannot be expressed in words.

72. Having approached Brahmā, the lotus-born, Sanatkumāra asked him about *Yoga-vijñāna*. Prajāpati replied to him.

*Brahmā said:*

73. I will teach you if it is possible for you to listen to my words as a son and you, having *Sāṅkhya* knowledge, practise that wisdom.

*Sanatkumāra said:*

74. O Lord of *Devas* ! O all-pervader ! I am indeed your son, for, I am your disciple. O Grandsire ! There is no difference between a son and a disciple.

*Brahmā said:*

75-76. O Dharma's son ! There is a difference between a son and a disciple, depending on their respective *Dharma* and *Karma*. Still, listen to what I say (about the general difference). A son is called *Putra* because he protects (the father) from the hell called '*Put*'; a disciple removes all other types of sins—such is the statement of Veda.

*Sanatkumāra said:*

77. O divine Sir ! Which is this hell called 'Put' from which a '*Putra*' protects and which are the other sins removed by a disciple? Please tell.

*Brahmā said:*

78. O great sage ! These ancient episodes (*Purāṇa*) are sublime and associated with the stages of *Yoga*; it is meritorious, mighty and remover of fear. I will relate it to you by which sins are absolved.

# CHAPTER SIXTY-ONE

## Killing of Mura

*Brahmā said:*

1-17. Having sexual relation with another's wife, serving sinners and being cruel to all living beings are known to be the first hell. The great sin of stealing fruits, aimless roaming as well as cutting down the trees of importance are considered as the second hell. The evil (act) of accepting what is prohibited, killing or arresting a person who should not be killed, marriage with those who are not one's kins-are considered as third hell. Frightening all creatures, destroying the property of Bhava (Śiva), swerving away from one's *Dharma* are known to be the fourth hell. Murder, dishonesty towards friends, uttering falsehood, eating tasty food alone-are the fifth hell. Stealing away the fruits, etc. of pilgrimage, restraint which destroys *Yoga* and stealing of a pair of vehicles are said to lead to the sixth hell. Stealing the share of a king, secretly attending on the king's wife, doing things not congenial to the king are the seventh hell. Greed, excessive attachment, destroying *Dharma* and *Artha*, defiling with saliva-are known as the eighth hell. Stealing the property earmarked for a Brāhmaṇa, censuring Brāhmaṇas, enmity among kinsmen-are said to be the ninth hell. Violation of the rules of etiquette, hating the elite, infanticide, clandestine conduct against *Śāstra* and *Dharma* are described as the tenth hell. The destruction of the six auxiliaries and thwarting the employment of the six expedients are stated to form the eleventh hell, say the pious ones. Censuring the pious ones; always stealing, unclean action, forbidden conduct, not undergoing all the sacraments—all these are said to be the twelfth hell. The destruction of *Dharma*, *Artha* and *Kāma*, causing destruction of (means of) emancipation, trying to know (overhear) the conversation (of others) are said to be the thirteenth hell.

Destruction, action bereft of *Dharma*, activity which is to be shunned and arson are the despised fourteenth hell. Ignorance, jealousy, impurity, inauspiciousness as well as speaking untruth are indeed known to be the fifteenth (hell). Laziness, especially when it is associated with anger, being merciless towards everyone, setting fire to residential structures-are the sixteenth (hell). The desire for another's wife is spoken of as leading to hell. Feeling of intolerance and haughtiness are despised in the *Śāstras*.

18-20a. So a person who is undoubtedly free from these evils, '*Put*' and others, shall please the Lord of the universe by (begetting) progeny. He who waits on that Acyuta being pleased with the auspicious creation, shall completely destroy the horrible hell called '*Put*'. It is on account of this that (the son) is called *Putra*, O Sādhya !

20b-25a. Henceforth, I will relate to you the characteristics of the other sins: (Refraining from) donation towards deities, sages, beings, human beings and fathers; being greedy of other's wealth; making no distinction of *Varṇas* (are sins). He who abstains from even *Oṁkāra*, is considered a sinner. Speaking ill of *Guru* and also having (sexual) union with whom one should not have are major sins. Selling ghee and other things is a serious sin; so also accepting anything from a *Cāṇḍāla* and others, hiding one's own errors and disclosing other's errors are sins. Being envious, use of harsh language, unscrupulousness, and also the other two–making sound with the fingers and clapping the hands, speaking of anything outside *Dharma* by name or by utterance–(are sins). Cruelty, unrighteousness are spoken of as leading to hell.

25b-29. If a person having committed these sins, pleases Śaṅkara, then the person wins over completely the 'other sins' which are more on mental side. Whatever sin physical, oral, mental or greater, that which is committed by the father or the mother or by dependent persons or by brothers or by relatives in a birth, O son of Dharma ! All of them get absolved (in that birth only). This is the *Dharma* of a son and a disciple. If it is contrary, O Sādhya ! The order of things will be reversed. Therefore, a wise man shall have both a son and a disciple. A son shall be deemed superior to a disciple for the reason that a disciple absolves one from the 'other (sins)', while a son absolves from all.

*Pulastya said:*

30. Having heard the words of the Grandsire, the Sādhya, the one rich in penance, said: "I repeat thrice, 'truly I am you son'; please teach me *Yoga*, O Deva !"

31. To him replied the great *Yogī*: "If your parents give you over to me, then (I will teach) *Yoga*; you will be my heir, O my boy !"

32. Sanatkumāra said: "You please explain to me the idea of heirship that you spoke of."

33-35. O Nārada ! Having heard the words spoken by the superior Sādhya, the venerable Grandsire said with a smile: "Listen, O my boy ! There are six relatives (sons) who can be heirs: the son born of one's own wife, the one born of a wife (from another person), the adopted, the artificially (adopted), the one whose real father is not known and the abandoned. Obligation of debt, funeral rites and wealth, equivalence of Gotra, customs of the family as well as recognition (in the society)—these are perpetual in all these six sons.

36-37. A son of an unmarried woman, a son of a woman pregnant at wedding, a son purchased, a son of a woman married for the second time, a son who volunteers to be a son, a *Pāraśava* son (son of a Brāhmaṇa by a Śūdra woman–MW)–these six are also recognised as sons. But in the case of these (six), there is no question of repayment of debt, performance of obsequies, etc. by them; they bear only the name of the respective *Gotras* and their recognition in a family (is also superficial)."

38. Having heard those words of Brahmā, the elder brother of Sanaka asked him: "O Brāhmaṇa ! Please set forth the special characteristics (of these)."

39-46. Then, the Lord of celestials said: "Listen to the special characteristics, O my boy ! *Aurasa* is one who is born of one (from one's wife) as if one's own replica. When the husband is impotent, insane or addicted to vices, if the diseaseless wife with his permission begets a son (by another person), that son is called *Kṣetraja.* The son given over by his parents to another is called *Datta.* The son of a friend or a boy given over by a friend is *Kṛtrima,* say the elderly (people). *Gūḍha* (ka) son is one who is not known by whom in a house he was begot. A boy brought home from outside is called *Apaviddha.* The son of an unmarried woman is *Kānīna* and the son of a woman pregnant at the time of wedding is *Sahoḍhaja.* A boy purchased for a price is *Krīta. Punarbhava* is of two types: The girl once given in marriage to one, is given in marriage to another; (such a girl is called *Punarbhū*). The son of such (a woman) is known as *Paunarbhava* in this world. A boy who offers himself (to be the son) because of famine or addiction (of father) to some vice or for any other reason, is called *Svayaṁdatta.* O you of good vows ! *Pāraśava* is said to be the son of a Brāhmaṇa, born of a Śūdra woman, married or unmarried.

47. "O my son (boy)! It is for this reason that it is not proper for you to offer yourself. Go and bring your parents immediately."

48. Then, at the command of the Lord, he recalled his parents. O sage ! The couple came there to see the overlord.

49. Bowing down to Brahmā, they (said): Command us, O Lord ! After they sat comfortably, the Sādhya told them—

*Sanatkumāra said:*

50. O dear father ! Desirous of undergoing (training in) Yoga, I persuaded Brahmā. He asked me to be his son. Therefore, you will do well to give me over (to him).

51-52. So told by the son, the two said to the Grandsire, the preceptor of *Yoga*: "O Lord ! This is indeed our son.

From today onwards he shall become your son, O Brahmaṇa!" So saying, the two went to heaven as they came.

53-65. The Grandsire, on the other hand, taught *Yoga* of twelve *Patrakas* (petals) to his son Sanatkumāra, the Sādhya endowed with discipline: OṀ-kara is located in the *Śikhā* (back part of the head); *Meṣa* (Aries) stands at its head; the first petal is said to be in the month of *Vaiśākha*. NA-kāra is located in the face; *Vṛṣabha* (Taurus) as well as the month Jyeṣṭha are said to be there; it is spoken of as the second petal. MO-kāra is the two shoulders; *Mithuna* (Gemini) stands there and it is well-known as *Āṣāḍha* month; it is considered as the third petal. BHA-kāra is the two eyes; *Karkāṭaka* (Cancer) stands there; it is spoken of as *Śrāvaṇa* month and is considered as the fourth petal. GA-kāra is said to be the heart; *Siṁha* (Leo) resides there; it is spoken of as *Bhādrapada* month and is considered as the fifth. VA-kāra is to be known as the armour; *Kanyā* (Virgo) is established there; it is spoken of as *Āśvayuj* month and is considered as the sixth petal. TE-kāra is said to be (located) in the mind and *Tulā* (Libra) stands there; the month is *Kārttika* by name; (it is) considered as the seventh petal. VĀ-kāra is associated with the navel; there stands *Vṛścika* (Scorpio); this eighth petal is the month *Mārgaśīrsa* by name, O sage ! SU-kāra is said to be the buttocks and there stands *Dhanus* (Sagittarius); the month spoken of is *Pauṣa*; thus is the ninth (petal) explained. DE-kāra is in the two legs and *Makāra* (Timi-Capricorn) is said to be there; the month is well-known as *Māgha*; thus is considered the tenth petal. VĀ-kāra is the two knees; there stands *Kumbha* (Aquarius); this best petal; the eleventh is spoken of as *Phālguna*. YĀ-kāra is the two feet and *Mīna* (Pisces) exists there in *Caitra*, O sage ! This is spoken of as the twelfth petal of Keśava.

66-67. The wheel has twelve spokes, six navels with two each arrayed in threes but of unified single form–thus is described the supreme lord. The form of the supreme lord is set forth as being endowed with twelve aspects, by knowing which, O great sage ! One does not meet with death again.

68. The second (form of the Lord) is described: an imperishable form with the *Sattva-guṇa* being dominant, having four colours, four faces and four arms, having charming limbs and adorned with *Śrīvatsa.*

69. The third (form) called *Tāmasa,* is the excellent *Śeṣa*-form which is thousand-fold with a thousand faces and causing annihilation of the created beings.

70. The fourth (form) called *Rājasa* is of red colour and has four faces—the creator, the primordial man of two arms, wearing a garland.

71. These (latter) three are the manifest (forms) born out of the unmanifest, O great sage ! Thus are Marīci and other chiefs created; so also others in thousands.

72. O respectable sage ! Thus, I have described the form of the primordial Viṣṇu. (This knowledge) promotes wisdom and prosperity.

The wicked Mura approached the Four-armed Lord again at the suggestion of Yama.

73-74. O sage ! The killer of Madhu asked him who had come: "O Asura ! For what purpose have you come here?" He replied: "To have a duel with you." The (Lord), the killer of groups of *Asuras,* said again: "If you have come here for a duel with me, then, why is your heart trembling time and again, as if of a person afflicted with fever. Therefore, I am not going to fight with a coward."

75. So told by the Killer of Madhu, Mura with his mind agitated, put his hand on his heart saying, "How? Where? Whom?" and felled (himself).

76. Hari, on the other hand, hurled the discus softly and dexterously and severed that lotus-heart of the enemy. The *Devas* became free from grief and were eulogizing the Lord, Padmanābha.

77. Thus I have told you the killing of the *Daitya,* Mura, tactfully accomplished by the Bearer-of-the-sharp-discus. On account of this, the supreme lord, Nṛsiṁha became famous as Murāri.

# CHAPTER SIXTY-TWO

## The Legend of Maṅkaṇa

*Pulastya said:*

1. Then, going to the abode of Murāri and after prostrating themselves before the Lord, the celestials asked the cause of the turbulence in the universe.

2. Having heard that, the venerable one said: "Let us go to the abode of Hara. He, the most wise, knows (why) the mobile and immobile universe is perturbed."

3-6a. So told by Vāsudeva, the *Devas* led by Śakra (Indra), went to mount Mandara, keeping Janārdana in front. There, they could not see either the Lord or the Bull or the Devī or even Nandī. They being covered by the darkness of ignorance, found the mountain vacant.

Seeing them blinded of their sight, the great resplendent Lord Viṣṇu said: "Don't you see Maheśa standing in front of you?" They said to him: "We are not at all seeing the Lord, the spouse of Girijā. We do not know the cause which has blinded us."

6b-14. The Lord of universal form told them: "You have offended the Lord (Śiva); you are the worst sinners; you being engrossed in your own interests, have killed the foetus of Mṛḍānī. Therefore, your intelligence and discrimination have been swept away by the Trident-bearing Lord. Hence, you have not been able to see, though he is in front of you, and though you are seeing him. So, to purify your bodies and to visualise the Lord, you set your mind on *Īśvara* with devotion, after being purified by *Tapta-kṛcchra* (vow).

Perform ablution (to the *Liṅga*) first with more than hundred pots of milk; ablution with curds in sixty four pots; ablution with *Havis* (ghee) in thirty-two pots; sixteen pots are spoken of for clean *Pañcagavya*; ablution with eight pots of honey; for water, twice the number of these pots, O celestials ! Then (uttering) one hundred and eight names, the Lord is to be smeared devotedly with *Gorocanā, Kumkuma* and sandal (paste). One should worship with *Bilva* leaves, with flowers (like) Lotuses, *Mandāras, Pārijātas* and *Atimuktas* along with camphor, *Agaru* and sandal. Then, fumes of *Agaru, Kāleya* and sandal are to be offered. Śatarudrīya text is to be recited in *Pada* and *Krama* modes as specified in *Ṛgveda* (tradition). If you do in this way, you will visualise the Lord of *Devas* and not through any other way."

15. So told by Vāsudeva, the *Devas* asked Keśava: "O Madhusūdana ! Please relate the mode of *Tapta-kṛcchra,* by performing which one attains physical purification for all times."

*Vāsudeva said:*

16-17. For three days one should drink hot water; for three days, hot milk; for three days, hot ghee and for three days (only) air is to be consumed (i.e., no liquid or solid food). The quantity of water to be consumed everyday (for three days) is twelve *Palas;* that of milk is eight *Palas;* that of ghee is six *Palas,* O celestial !

*Pulastya said:*

18-20. When told thus, the celestials led by Indra, performed the vow of mysterious *Tapta-kṛcchra,* for the purification of the body. After observance of the vow, the celestials were absolved of the sin. Then they, free from sin, spoke to Vāsudeva, the Lord of *Devas:* "O Lord of the universe! O Keśava ! Where is that Śambhu whom we can bathe with milk and other things according to the procedure?"

21. Then, Viṣṇu told the celestials: "Śaṅkara lies here in my body. Don't you see him established (here), engrossed in *Yoga* ?"

22. They told him: "We are unable to see the destroyer of Tripura, ourselves. O Lord of celestials ! Please tell us the truth as to where is Maheśāna found."

23. Then, Hari, the imperishable self, Murāri, showed the *Devas, Īśvara's Liṅga* which was established in the lotus of his heart.

24-26. Then, the immortals performed ablutions with excellent milk and other things, in order, to the eternal, to the unchangeable and to the imperishable *Liṅga*. Smearing with *Gorocana* and sweet-smelling sandal, they properly worshipped the Lord with *Bilva* leaves and lotuses. After providing (scented) fumes to the supreme Lord and devotedly offering excellent herbs and having repeated one hundred eight names, they prostrated themselves.

*Nārada said:*

27. Even as they (celestials) were meditating thus, how did the two Lords of *Devas*, Hara and Acyuta, being endowed with *Sattva* and *Tamas*, assume that *Yoga* ?

*Pulastya said:*

28. Knowing the thought of the celestials, the omnipresent Lord became one of imperishable *Visvamūrti* (all-form), having auspicious marks and bearing all weapons.

29-30. The *Devas* saw that Śaṅkara with Mādhava having two eyes and a half, ear-rings of both gold and snakes, matted hair and hair as a tuft, banners of *Garuḍa* and *Vṛṣabha*, adornments of necklace and serpents, loins covered with both yellow (garment) and skin, having discus, sword, plough and *Śārṅga* (bow) in hand as well as *Pināka* (bow), trident, *Ajagava* (bow), *cowrie* (shell), *Khaṭvāṅga*, skull, bell and conch with a twanging sound, O great sage !

31. Brahmā and other *Devas*, immediately after seeing that Hari-Śaṅkara, making their minds fixed, made obeisance, saying, "salutation to you, the imperishable and the omnipresent one."

32-33. Having observed the gods being of concentrated mind, Hari, the Lord of *Devas* took them all and rushed at once to his own hermitage in Kurukṣetra. Then they saw the supreme *Deva* being in the form of Sthāṇu in the midst of water. Having seen Sthāṇu, they all sat down after uttering, "salutation to Sthāṇu."

34. Then the Lord of the celestials (Indra) said: "Please come and bestow a boon on us; O Lord of the universe ! the universe is agitated; please rise out of water, O one fond of guests !"

35-36. *Vṛṣabha-dhvaja* (Śiva) heard those pleasing words and having heard it, the all-pervading, blemishless lord stood up immediately. Hara came out and being saluted by the celestials including Indra, spoke courteously with a smile: "Salutation to the God of gods."

37. All the *Devas* told him: "O Śaṅkara ! Please terminate the great vow. The three worlds are agitated, being tormented by your effulgence."

38-41. Then, Mahādeva said: "I have terminated the great vow." Afterwards, the celestials with pure mind went to heaven, satisfied.

O great sage ! Later the earth together with oceans and islands shook. Then, Rudra thought, "Why is the earth perturbed?" and the Trident-bearer went all round Kurukṣetra. He saw *Uśanas* (*Śukra*), rich in penance, on the bank of Oghavatī (river). Then said the Lord of celestials: "O Vipra ! Why are you performing penance agitating the universe? Please tell me quickly."

*Uśanas said:*

42. This severe penance is being performed with a desire to propitiate you. O Three-eyed Lord ! By that, I desire to learn *Sañjīvinī-vidyā*, the science of resuscitation.

*Hara said:*

43. O one rich in penance ! I am pleased by this severe austerity being performed. Hence, you will learn fully the science of resuscitation.

44. Having obtained the boon, Śukra refrained from penance. Still the earth covered by oceans, hills and trees was not stable.

45-47. Mahādeva went to the holy *Sapta-sārasvata* (region). There he saw the sage by name Maṅkaṇa, dancing. Engrossed in emotion, he danced impetuously, stretching his arms like a child. Because of his heavy steps only, the earth together with hills shook. Approaching and holding him by hand, Śaṅkara said these words with a smile: "O great sage ! What have you thought of ? For what reason are you dancing? What joy is there? Please tell me now."

48-49. That Brāhmaṇa said: "O best of the twice-born ! Listen to the cause of my joy. Many years went by, as I performed penance for purification of my body. Then I found vegetable juice (instead of blood) oozing out from a wound in my hand. O foremost of *Dvijas* ! I am very much delighted by that and hence, being so pure, I am dancing."

50. Śambhu told him: "O *Dvija* ! See, by mere clapping, extra white ash comes out of my hand, but I do not have any thrill; really, you are mad."

51. Then, listening to those words, Sage Maṅkaṇaka (Maṅkaṇa) bowed down to that Śiva (*Vṛṣabha-dhvaja*) and giving up dancing, wonder-struck as he was, prostrated to the feet of Śiva, bent with modesty, O great sage !

52-56. Śambhu told him: "O *Dvija* ! You attain that abode of Brahmā which is indeed difficult to reach. This pool Pṛthūdaka shall become prominent on the earth, giving very great benefits. The celestials, *Asuras*, *Gandharvas*, *Vidyādharas* and *Kinnaras* will be present here. May the Sārasvata (region) be the prime resort of Dharma and the remover of dirt of sin. *Suprabhā*, *Kāñcanākṣī*, *Suveṇu*, *Vimalodakā*, *Mahodarā*, *Oghavatī* and *Viśālā Sarasvatī*—these seven Sarasvatī streams will reside (perpetually flow) (here) always and all will endow the meritorious benefit of having a sip of *Soma*. You too, having established a prominent icon (*Liṅga*) in Kurukṣetra will reach the most meritorious abode of Brahmā, hard to attain."

57-58. O sage ! Being told so by Lord Śaṅkara, the restrained one, after having established a *Liṅga* in Kurukṣetra, went to *Brahmaloka*. As Maṅkaṇaka left, the earth became stable. Then, Śambhu went to his holy and empty (quiet) abode Mandara.

59. O *Dvija* ! Thus have I related to you, why Śaṅkara had gone then for austerities and returned to the empty (quiet) mountain, desirous of seeing Pārvātī and was united with her.

## CHAPTER SIXTY-THREE

### The Story of Daṇḍa

*Nārada said:*

1. What did the *Dānava*, Andhaka, do in the nether world, on going there ? And also what did Śaṅkara do, while in Mandara? Please tell me.

*Pulastya said:*

2-3. O Brāhmaṇa ! Andhaka residing in the nether world was tormented by the fire of love. Having bodily torment, he told this to all the *Dānavas*: "He who brings that Daughter of Mountain to me immediately is my friend; he is my kinsman; he is my brother; he is my father."

4-6. When Andhaka, the foremost *Daitya*, afflicted by eros, said thus, Prahlāda spoke this in a voice as deep as that of a cloud: "O brave one ! She who is the Daughter of Mountain, is, in truth, your mother; the Lord with three eyes is the father, listen to the reason for this. O *Dānava* ! Years ago, your father, always pious, having no sons, propitiated Lord Hara for the sake of a son.

7-11. "O Dānava King ! The Three-eyed Lord gave a son, though blind, to him desirous of a son, saying thus: "O Hiraṇyākṣa ! My three eyes were covered by Girijā for sport, when I was engaged in *Yoga.* Then arose dense darkness. From that darkness was born this being, having a voice like that of a dark cloud. O *Daitya* ! Take this one, your son, obtained by efforts. When this person does any act not approved by society or when this wicked one desires even the mother of the three worlds or when he kills a Brāhmaṇa, then I will myself dry up his body, O *Asura* !"

12-18. "So saying, Śambhu returned to his place, Mandāra mountain. Your father also came to *Rasātala* taking you with him. Because of this, O Dānava ! The Daughter of Mountain is your mother and Śambhu, the master of all this universe, is indeed your father. You are also one of proper conduct with amazing qualities and one versed in *Śāstras.* A person of your type should not entertain thoughts of such evil design. Bhava (Śiva), the Lord of the three worlds, the unmanifest one, the unconquerable one is prostrated by everyone. She is his wife. You are not worthy of her, O vanquisher of immortals ! It is not possible to obtain the virtuous Daughter of Mountain-*King* without conquering Rudra together with his *Gaṇas,* and this desire is hard to gain. He, who can cross (swim) the ocean with one's arms, or fell the sun onto the earth or even uproot Mount Meru, shall conquer the Wielder of Trident. There may be a mighty person who is able to do all the feats described but even by him it is not possible to know Hara. This is the absolute truth, I assert."

19-22. "O *Daitya* ! Have you not heard, how King Daṇḍa, foolishly desiring another's wife, was destroyed together with his kingdom? There was a King Daṇḍa by name, who had a large contingent of army and retinue. That mighty one, chose Bhārgava (Śukra) as his priest. The king performed many sacrifices under the supervision of Śukra. Now, Śukra had a daughter by name Arajā. Once, Śukra went to the

*Asura,* Vṛṣaparvan. Being honoured by him, the foremost Bhārgava stayed there for a long time."

23-24. "O great *Asura* ! Arajā of a charming physique, was attending on the fires in her house. Then, there came the king (Daṇḍa). He asked: 'Where is Śukra ?'

The attendants said: The venerable Śukra has gone to assist in the performance (of sacrifice) of the son of Danu."

25. "The king asked: Which lady stays in the hermitage of Bhārgava ? They told him: O King ! Arajā, the daughter of the Guru, stays there.

26-28. "The son of Ikṣvāku went inside the hermitage to see Śukra's daughter. Then, the valiant one saw Arajā. O Andhaka ! Having seen her, the king Daṇḍa, under the strong influence of death was at once afflicted by Cupid. Then, the mighty one sent away the servants, brothers, friends and even the disciples of Śukra and went behind (Arajā) alone.

29-30. "O Dānava ! The glorious daughter of Śukra got up (in reverence) and with a brotherly feeling, gladly honoured him who had come to her. Then, the king told her: O young lady ! Oblige me now who am being tormented by Cupid, with the waters of your embrace.

31-32. "O Asura ! She with all modesty, told that great King: My father is very wrathful; he can burn down even the celestials; O foolish one ! you have come on your own; in fact, you are my brother and I am your sister; you are a disciple of my father.

33. "He said: O frail one ! Śukra burns me down in course of time; O one of slender waist ! the fire of love is burning me even now.

34. "She said to king Daṇḍa: Wait for a while; you ask your Guru only; he will give me over to you without doubt.

35. "Daṇḍa said: "O charming damsel ! I cannot bear the lapse of time. If the duration of sacrifice is to be awaited, impediments come in, O pretty lady !

36-37. "Then said Virajā (Arajā): 'O prince ! I am unable to give myself to you that way. Women are not indeed independent. What use is there in speaking to you at length? O King ! You together with the servants, relatives and friends will before long, get lost by the curse of Śukra.'

38. "Then, the King said: O pretty one ! Listen to the action of Citrāṅgadā, to what happened long ago in the prosperous divine era.

39-45a. "The virtuous daughter of Viśvakarmā was one Citrāṅgadā by name. She, endowed with beauty and youth was like a lotus pond without a lotus. Once, that lotus-eyed one, surrounded by her companions, went to the dense forest called Naimiṣa for bathing. As she stepped down for bathing, there came the wise King Suratha by name, the son of Sudeva. She told aside to her companions these significant words: This prince will be tormented by Cupid. Hence, it is proper for me to offer myself to his handsome one.

"The companions told her: O pretty one ! You are young and you are not bold. O sinless one ! There is no freedom for you here to offer yourself. There is your father, who is most pious and a master of all *Śāstras*. It is not proper for you now to offer yourself on your own to the king.

45b-50a. "In the meanwhile, the pure and truthful King Suratha, tormented by the arrows of Cupid, came closer and said to her: O lovely one ! O lady with bewitching eyes ! You entice me by mere sight. Cupid had smitten me with the arrows of your side-glance. Therefore, you please make me lie down on the bed of your breasts. Otherwise, Cupid will scorch me down because of seeing you again and again.' Then, that lady of fair limbs and lotus-like eyes offered herself on her own, in spite of being dissuaded by her companions. Thus, in the days gone by, that king was saved by that pretty maiden. Therefore you will also, O one of broad hips ! do well to save me.

50b-55. "Arajā told Daṇḍa: Do you not know what happened to her later? I will tell you. Then, the pretty one gave herself on her own to the King Suratha.' Thereafter her father cursed her: Since you gave yourself by flouting

*Dharma* because of feminine nature to this dull-witted person, there cannot be any marriage (between you two). Without marriage, you will neither get happiness from your husband nor will you have the benefit of a son nor will you be united with your husband. The moment the curse was uttered, Sarasvatī carried away upto thirteen *yojanas*, the King who had not yet fulfilled his desire. As the King was carried away, she too swooned.

56-57. "Then all those companions sprinkled waters of Sarasvatī (over her). Being sprinkled completely with cold water, she, the daughter of Viśvakarmā became almost dead, losing all activity. Considering her dead, the afflicted companions went in haste, some to bring firewood and some to bring fire. When all of them had gone into the dense forest, the pretty lady regained consciousness and looked on all the sides. She did not see either the King or the deeply attached companions.

58-63. " 'She jumped into (the waters of) Sarasvatī. O King! the lady of tremulous eyes (was speedily carried away) by the waters of Kāñcanākṣī and was thrown into the waters of the mighty river Gomatī, turbulent with waves. O lord of the realms ! Then, she (Gomatī) too, having known her (Citrāṅgadā's) fate, threw her in a thick forest thronged by lions and tigers. Thus, have I heard the condition of the lady who acted on her own. Therefore, guarding my pure character, I will not give myself to you.'

"Listening to her words, Daṇḍa of prowess equal to that of Śakra (Indra), said with a laugh to Arajā, in regard to his own interest but causing destruction to himself."

*Daṇḍa said:*

64. O lady of slim waist ! Give your attention to hear what happened afterwards to her, her father and to the king Suratha.

65-67. When the king was washed away and she fell in the thick forest, a Yakṣa named Añjana (Guhyaka) moving in the air saw (her). Then, he came near the damsel and talked to her with difficulty. He said: "Come on, O fortunate one ! I will take you to Suratha. O lady of black eyes ! You will surely be united with him. Therefore, proceed immediately to visit the Lord, Śrīkaṇṭha (Śiva)."

68-69. So told by that Yakṣa, the lady of beautiful eyes, came immediately to *Śrīkaṇṭha*, to the south and north of Yamunā river. Visiting Maheśa, Śrīkaṇṭha, and bathing in Yamunā river, she stood with her head bent, till the sun came to the middle (of the sky).

70-73. Then, there came Ṛtudhvaja, a *Sāmavedin*, the holy preceptor of *Pāśupata* and rich in penance, for performing ablution to the Lord. Having seen her standing as if weeping and without grace, the hermit went into meditation to know as to who she was. She, then, having prostrated herself before the sage, stood with folded hands. He asked her: "O my girl! Whose daughter are you who are like a heavenly lady? When have you come here into the forest, bereft of men and animals?" At that, the lady of slender waist, related to the sage all that had happened.

74-81. Having heard that, the sage got angry and cursed the best of the Artisans (*Viśvakarmā*): "Because this his daughter, though to be given to another (in marriage) was not at all united with her husband by the wretched one, may he become a monkey." After saying thus, he, the illustrious one, again took bath as per precepts and having attended on the evening twilight, worshipped Śaṅkara.

After worshipping Hara, the supreme lord of *Devas*, according to precepts laid down, he came and told the lady with beautiful eyebrows, weeping and longing for her husband: "O fortunate one ! Go to the holy place of *Saptagodāvara*. O lady with beautiful thighs ! as you will be there attending on Mahādeva, the great Hāṭakeśvara, Devavatī, the excellent and well-known daughter of the *Daitya* Kandaramālin will come. Another one, poor daughter of Añjana, a Yakṣa, known as Damayantī, will also arrive there. So also, one more lady, Vedavatī, the excellent daughter of

Parjanya (will join there). When the three ladies come together in the *Sapta-godāvara-tīrtha*, the place of Mahādeva called Hāṭaka, then will you be united (with your husband)."

82-83. The young lady Citrāṅgadā, so told by the hermit, proceeded in haste to *Sapta-godāvara-tīrtha*. Having arrived in that *Tīrtha*, she stayed there, always remaining pure, worshipping the Lord of *Devas*, Śiva, and partaking of fruits and roots.

84-86. That sage endowed with wisdom, then, wrote a significant verse (addressed) to Śrīkaṇṭha, desirous of doing good to her: "Is there not a single celestial, *Asura*, *Yakṣa*, *man* or a *Rākṣasa* (moving about at night), who by one's valour, would erase this grief of the doe-eyed (damsel)?" So saying (i.e., writing), the hermit, thinking about the wide-eyed only, went to visit the venerable lord Puṣkaranātha and the river Payoṣṇī, honoured by the group of sages.

## CHAPTER SIXTY-FOUR

## The Story of Suratha and Citrāṅgadā

*Daṇḍa said:*

1. O Arajā ! Many years passed by as Citrāṅgadā was there (*Sapta-godāvara*) comfortably and remembering the hero Suratha.

2-4. Viśvakarmā too, being cursed by the hermit, got the form of a monkey and fell down on to earth from the top of Meru, prompted by fate. O lovely lady ! He lived on Śālveya, a great mountain in a thick forest, full of bushes on the banks of the river Śālūkinī. O lady of excellent features ! Many many years rolled on as he lived there, eating fruits and roots in the forest.

5-11. Once, the tiger among *Daityas*, Kandara by name, was moving in the heaven, taking with him his beloved daughter, the famous Devavatī. The monkey-chief saw that lady of excellent face, who had come to that forest along with her father and held her hand forcibly. Then, having seen his worthy daughter held by the monkey, that *Daitya* Kandara got enraged and went after him holding a sword. Having observed the best of *Daityas* attacking, the mighty monkey went away to Himālaya along with that charming lady. The monkey visited Śrīkaṇṭha, Mahādeva on the bank of *Yamunā.* Not far from that place was a hermitage hidden and abandoned by a hermit. Leaving Devavatī in that holy and great hermitage, the monkey dived into Yamunā (*Kālindī*), even as Kandara was seeing. He took his daughter as dead together with the monkey and the effulgent one went to his own home, the nether world (*Pātāla*).

12-18. The monkey also, carried away by the swift current of *Kālindī* was brought to a land *Śivi* by name, which was full of virtuous people. Then, having speedily crossed (the river), the mighty (monkey), desirous of going towards Kapilavaṇa where the lady of beautiful eyes had been kept, however, saw Añjana, the best of Guhyakas coming with his daughter Damayantī. The monkey, who wanted to go (to Devavatī) indeed mistook that she herself was Devavatī. Even as he was thinking that the trouble of diving into the waters was not in vain, that beautiful lady ran away afraid of him and fell into the river *Hiraṇvatī.* Seeing his daughter falling into the waters of the river, the grief-stricken Guhyaka went to mount Añjana. There, the noble one, being pure and taking upon the vow of silence, spent several years engaged in austerities.

19-22. Damayantī too, was carried away fast by the river Hiraṇvatī and was taken to a very holy place Kosala, inhabited by pious people. As she was moving about weeping, she saw a banyan tree which was covered by the aerial roots and (looked) like Īśvara with matted hair. Seeing the wide shade, the lady of excellent face rested there. Sitting on a stone slab, she heard a human voice: "Is there not a person who could tell that hermit, rich in penance, that his son has been tied down to the banyan tree ?"

23-25. Having heard that voice with significant words, she saw obliquely up and down and on all sides.

O virtuous lady ! At the highest point of the tree, she saw a child of five years, tied carefully with tawny matted hair. Seeing him speak, the sorrowful Damayantī said: "O my child! Tell me by which sinner were you tied up ?"

26-33. He told her: "O honourable lady ! I have been tied with matted hair on this banyan tree by the most wicked monkey and I am alive due to the power of my austerities. Long ago Lord Maheśvara was there in Maṇipura. There resided my father Ṛtadhvaja, a store-house of austerity. To that noble person practising austerities was I, an adept in all *Śāstras*, born due to great *Yoga*, together with a ṣwarm of bees. O lady with pleasing face ! My father recognising me as Jābāli, bowed down to me and said (the following); you listen to it — 'For five thousand years you will be a child and your boyhood will be for ten thousand years. You will be a youth for twenty thousand years and twice that (i.e. forty thousand years) will be your old age. You will undergo tight bondage for five hundred years in your childhood. You will suffer bodily torture for ten hundred years in your boyhood. Similarly, you will enjoy the best pleasures for two thousand years in your youth. In your old age, you will undergo for forty hundred years, severe hardship of lying on the ground and eating rotten food.'

34-40. So told by my father, I, as a child of about five years was moving about on the earth. (Once while) going to Hiraṇvatī for bathing, I saw a big monkey. He said to me: "O you fool ! Where are you taking this Devavatī whom I had kept in the holy hermitage." Then, carrying me, a radiant child, tied me with matted hair on top of this banyan tree, O beautiful lady ! O timid lady ! So also my bondage was made secure, being inside a complex contrivance with twisted ropes of creepers, by the wicked monkey. The contrivances of creepers made above, below and at all cardinal points cannot be broken without using force. Restraining me here, the monkey-chief went away to *Amara-parvata* of his own accord. I was myself observing all this and I have told you, O excellent one ! O lady of charming limbs! Who are you ? For what purpose have you come into this dense forest without your husband? Please tell me."

41-44. She said: "My father is the Lord of Guhyakas, Añjana by name; I am Damayantī by name, born of the womb of Pramlocā. In my horoscope, it was said by sage Mudgala: This lady shall no doubt become the queen of a great king. Simultaneously with this utterance, drum sounded in the heaven and she-jackals cried inauspiciously. The sage said again: 'There is no doubt, she will become the principal queen of a king. But as a maiden, she will be subject to a very perilous predicament.'

45-46. "So saying, the sage hurriedly went away. Then, my father wanted to go to a holy spot taking me with him, when a monkey sprang up from the bank of Hiraṇvatī. Being afraid of (the monkey) I threw myself into the river water and I have been brought to this place, devoid of human beings."

*Daṇḍa said:*

47-48. Having heard the words uttered by her, Jābāli told her: "O beautiful lady ! Please go to Śrīkaṇṭha on the bank of Yamunā. My father goes there during midday to worship Śiva; please inform him (of this); by that you will get prosperity.

49-53. "Then, Damayantī proceeded in haste to the river Yamunā in the Himālayas, in order to rescue the hermit, rich in penance. Subsisting on roots, bulbs and fruits, she without taking long time, arrived in that place of Śaṅkara which the hermit frequented. After prostrating the overlord of *Devas*, Śrīkaṇṭha, saluted by the world, she saw the inscription, O great sage ! Grasping the meaning thereof, the lady of sweet smile, inscribed the verse uttered by

Jāpamāli (i.e. Jābāli) and another one about herself: "I have been told by Mudgala : You will become a queen. But I am put in this (wretched) state. Is any one capable of rescuing me ?"

54-59. After inscribing thus on the stone slab, she went to bathe in Yamunā. She saw there a fine hermitage, full of sweet notes of intoxicated cuckoos. 'That most pious sage does indeed stay within this (hermitage)', thinking thus, she entered that great hermitage. Then, she saw the virtuous Devavatī sitting (before) the deities, with a dry face and tremulous eyes, appearing like a withered lotus creeper. That daughter of *Daitya* too, saw the daughter of Yakṣa coming towards her. Thinking who she might be, she, getting up, became still. Then, both embracing tightly out of friendship questioned each other and each related her story to the other. The two excellent women knowing the truth about each other, through a variety of eager conversations, stayed there.

60-65. In the meanwhile, Ṛtadhvaja, the most honourable hermit, arrived there to worship Śrīkaṇṭha and then saw the inscription. Having seen it, he read it and grasped its meaning. The hermit, rich in penance, meditated for a while and came to know everything. Then, hurriedly worshipping the Lord of *Devas*, Ṛtadhvaja went in haste to Ayodhyā to meet the Ikṣvāku king ! After meeting the great king, the hermit said thus: "O king. O Tiger among men ! Please listen to my plea. My son endowed with all excellence and well-versed in all *Śāstras*, is tied down by a monkey-chief on the outskirts of your kingdom. No one, other than your son is capable of rescuing him. O foremost among kings ! Your son by name Śakuni is an adept in the technique in this regard."

66-71. O lady of slender waist ! Having heard the words of the hermit, my father ordered his dear son Śakuni by name, to rescue Jābāli. Then, being sent by the father, my valiant brother arrived in the part of the forest with the great sage.

Observing the banyan tree which was very tall and white all round due to aerial roots, he saw the son of the sage bound on the top of the tree. Having examined the noose of creepers all round and having observed the son of the sage bound on the banyan tree with his own matted hair, he, the mighty prince, took the bow and tied the string. He easily cut (the noose) of the ascetic's son simultaneously with arrows. Then, the noose of creepers tied on all the four quarters by the monkey long ago was severed by arrows after five hundred years.

72-75. The sage (Ṛtadhvaja) immediately climbed the banyan tree covered by creepers. Having seen his father approach him, Jābāli though bound, saluted with his head with utmost respect as per custom. The sage hugged him and smelt his head. He began to free him, but was not successful because of the strong knots.

Immediately, the mighty Śakuni, bending his bow and (taking) arrows, climbed the banyan to free the matted hair. He (too) was not able to (untie) the bonds made tight by the monkey-chief.

76-79. When he (prince) (along with the hermit) was not able to untie the matted hair, Śakuni got down with the great sage. He took hold of his bow and arrows and created a shelter of arrows. He easily cut the branch into three pieces with two crescent-headed arrows. When the branch was severed, the ascetic, rich in penance, carrying the burden, got down from the tree through the path of the steps of arrows. As his son was brought down, Ṛtadhvaja proceeded to river Yamunā along with the archer prince and Jābāli, bearing the burden.

## CHAPTER SIXTY-FIVE

### The Story of Suratha and Citrāṅgadā (continued)

*Daṇḍa said:*

1-3. In the meanwhile, the two maidens, the pretty daughters of *Yakṣa* and *Asura*, came to see Hara and that hermit, the best of *Yogīs*. They found the Lord with dried and faded flowers and full of remains of offerings of flowers, as Ṛtadhvaja had gone away. Then, seeing the Lord of *Devas* (in that state), those two excellent maidens bathed and worshipped (the Lord) day and night according to the precepts.

4-10. As the two were staying there, a sage, Gālava by name, came to that forest to see Śrīkaṇṭha, the unmanifest one. Having seen the pair of maidens, the sage entered thinking who they could be, after taking ablution in the clear waters of Yamunā. Then, sage Gālava worshipped Śrīkaṇṭha. The daughters of the *Yakṣa* and *Asura* were singing a song melodiously. Then, hearing the music, Gālava took them for *Gandharva* maidens. There was no doubt there. After worshipping the god *Īśāna* according to the precepts and after completing *Japa*, Gālava relaxed and was bowed down to by the maidens. Then, the sage questioned: "Please tell me whose daughters are you who are devotedly decorating the abode of Bhava?" The two beautiful maidens spoke to the best of sages, about all that had happened. Gālava, the best of ascetics, became appraised of their precedents.

11-12. Staying there that night, the sage, treated respectfully by them, got up in the morning and after worshipping Gaurīśa (Śiva) according to the precepts, went to the maidens and said: "I shall go to the superior *Puṣkarāráṇya*; I take leave of you; you do well to permit me."

13. Then, they too, said: "O Brāhmaṇa ! It is difficult to meet you (again)" and also asked politely why he was going to Puṣkara grove ?

14. The effulgent hermit told them with pride: "The ensuing (full-moon) day in *Kṛttikā* asterism in the month of *Kārttika* is meritorious in Puṣkara only."

15. The two said: "We will go wherever you go. O Brāhmaṇa ! We are not interested in being here without you."

16-19. "Yes", said the best sage. Afterwards, the maidens prostrated to Maheśvara and eagerly went to Puṣkara grove along with the sage. Other sages also had assembled there in thousands; kings and people from the countryside (were also there), except the one Ṛtadhvaja. Eminent kings including Nābhāga and Ikṣvāku and the sages (had come) to take bath in Puṣkara on the *Kārttika* full-moon day. Gālava too, with the two maidens descended for bath in the bow-shaped middle enclosure of the waters of Puṣkara.

20-21. Going under water, he saw many female fish advancing again and again with love towards a big (male) fish lying in water. He (the male fish) said to them: "You (move) freely and you do not know this Dharma; public scandal, strong and severe, is difficult to bear."

22-23. They (females) said to the big fish: "Why? Do we not see the hermit Gālava moving about as he wishes, along with the two maidens? If that spiritual-minded person, rich in penance, himself is not afraid of public scandal, why are you, living under water, afraid of ?"

24. That Timi (big fish) then said: "This person, rich in penance, does neither know it (*Dharma*) as he is blind with passion nor does he know fear, he being very foolish."

25-26. Hearing these words of the fish, the shameful Gālava who had dipped himself in water did not come up but stayed there with his senses controlled. The two maidens of lovely thighs, went up the bank after ablution and stood expecting eagerly to see that eminent sage.

27. The festival at Puṣkara was over. The people–sages, kings and those from the countryside–all went back as they came.

28-29. There stood *Citrāṅgadā*, daughter of Viśvakarmā, of glittering teeth, of lovely limbs and of slender waist, looking here and there. Those two maidens were also standing there, looking for the eminent sage Gālava in that holy spot, bereft of people and Gālava under water.

30-32. There came a *Gandharva* maiden of upright character, Vedavatī by name, the daughter of Parjanya and born of the womb of Ghṛtācī. Approaching the holy bank, she took bath in the middle part of Puṣkara and saw the three maidens standing on the opposite bank. Approaching Citrāṅgadā, she asked softly: "Who are you ? Why are you staying in this desolate place ?"

33-39. She replied her: "O lady with lovely hips ! Know me to be Citrāṅgadā, the famous daughter of Viśvakarmā, the divine architect. O good lady ! I went (once) to take bath in the famous *Kāñcanākṣī*-virtuous Sarasvatī, the mother of *Dharma*, in Naimiṣa (forest). I, who was worthy of being married to a celestial and who had gone there was requested by Suratha of Vidarbha afflicted with love and he surrendered to me. I gave myself to him though dissuaded by my friends. Then, I was cursed by my father and got separated from the king. O good lady ! I had made up my mind to die but was dissuaded by a Guhyaka. I went to see Śrīkaṇṭha and then to see the Godāvarī waters. From there, I came to this exalted holy spot. I could not see Suratha, my lord, the gladdener of my heart. O young lady ! Who are you ? You have come now, after the festival is over. You tell me the truth, O lovely one !"

40-52. She said: "Listen, who am I, of slender waist and unfortunate and why I have come to Puṣkara, after the festival is over. O friend ! I, by name Vedavatī, was born of Parjanya and Ghṛtācī. While enjoying myself in a part of a forest, I was noticed by a monkey. Approaching me, he (monkey) said: "O Devavatī ! Where are you going ? By whom were you brought to mount Meru from the hermitage on earth?" Then I said: "O monkey ! I am not Devavatī; I am Vedavatī by name and I am residing in Meru only." Then, being chased by that wicked monkey, I immediately climbed the tall *Bandhujīva* tree. That tree broke down, being forcibly hit by the foot of the monkey. Then, I hugged on to its big branch. The monkey threw the tree into the waters of the ocean and I, terrified, fell along with the tree. Then, all beings– the movable and the immovable– saw the tree falling freely from the sky. Seeing me falling down, the people cried, 'alas!', 'alas!'. Siddha Gandharvas said: 'Alas, this lady is the queen of the venerable Indradyumna, the valiant son of Manu and the performer of a thousand sacrifices, as told by Brahmā himself.' Hearing those sweet words, I became unconscious and I did not know by whom the tree was shattered to a thousand pieces. Then, I was carried away at once by the strong wind (friend of fire) and am brought here and you were seen, O lovely one ! Get up then; let us go. Let us see, who those two maidens on the north bank of Puṣkara are.

53-56. So saying, that lady of exquisite physique along with the lady of slender form, went to see the two maidens and ask them their purpose out of curiosity. Having gone there, she asked them. Both of them said everything as it occurred and the other two also introduced themselves. Then, all the four of them reaching the *Sapta-godāvara-waters*, stayed there worshipping Hāṭakeśvara on the bank. For the sake of these, the three persons—Śakuni, Jābāli and Ṛtadhvaja roamed about for many-many years.

57-61. As ten hundred years elapsed, the sage (Jābāli), carrying the burden on his head was tired and being despondent entered Śākala country with his father. In that country, the prosperous king Indradyumna, son of Manu, was ruling. He, having learnt (of their arrival), went out to receive them with honour (Arghya and Pādya). Jābāli and Ṛtadhvaja were very well honoured by him. That son of Ikṣvāku, the wise Śakuni, his own brother's son was also received well. Then the sage Ṛtadhvaja said these words to Indradyumna: "O King ! Our daughter (maiden) known as Damayantī is lost. O King ! For her sake, we have roamed all over the earth. Please get up to provide transportation facility."

62-64. The King then said: "O Brāhmaṇa ! My excellent wife is also lost. (I could not find her) though I tried my best. To whom shall I say this? A big mountain-like tree falling from the sky was shattered to thousand pieces with arrows, hearing the words of Siddhas. At the same time, the one of slender waist was rashly pushed aside by me. I do not know where she (fell). Therefore, I will go to search her."

65-67. So saying, the king getting up hastily, provided chariots to the two *Dvijas* and to the son of his brother. Riding the chariots, they immediately set about searching on the earth from one end. Arriving in *Badarikāśrama*, they saw a young man with matted hair, the very storehouse of penance, emaciated due to austerities, wearing soiled cloth, tired and pensive and heaving heavily.

68-71. The valorous king Indradyumna approached him and asked: "O hermit ! Why have you taken up this severe penance in the prime of your youth? Please speak to me about your aim."

He said: "Who are you ? Please tell me. You are enquiring with friendliness about me, who am afflicted with grief, am wretched and engaged in penance."

He replied: "O hermit ! I, the son of Manu and dear brother of Ikṣvāku, am the mighty king in Śākalapura. I have told you about (myself)." That king (hermit) also related to him all the past events.

72-73. Having heard this, the royal sage (Indradyumna) said: "No, do not give up your body. I will come (with you) to search the slender-bodied lady; you are my cousin." So saying, he hugged the king (hermit), who was a strict follower of righteousness. Taking him on to the chariot, he (Indradyumna) immediately introduced him to the two sages.

74-76. Having seen the king (hermit), Ṛtadhvaja with his son, said: "O King ! Come, come. I will do a good turn to you. That maiden Citrāṅgadā whom you saw in Naimiṣa, has been sent to *Sapta-godāvara-tīrtha* by me only. (So) come on, let us go for the same purpose. Three other maidens as well will meet us there."

77-78. So saying and pacifying the son of Sudeva, the sage along with his son and Indradyumna and keeping Śakuni in the forefront, started the journey in the chariot drawn by horses towards *Sapta-godāvara-tīrtha* where the damsels had gone.

79-80. Just at this juncture, the lady Ghṛtācī, stricken with grief, roamed about Udayagiri, searching for her daughter. That Apsarā came across that monkey and asked him: "O monkey ! Did you not see (my) daughter? Please speak the truth."

81-84. Having heard her words, that monkey replied: "I met a damsel called Devavatī and I have confined her in a big penance grove, abounding in animals and birds on the holy banks of *Kālindī* river, in front of the temple of *Śrīkaṇṭha*. I have told you the truth." She told the good monkey: "She was known by name Vedavatī and not Devavatī. (Anyway) come, let us go (there)." Having heard the words of Ghṛtācī, the monkey followed her swiftly towards the river *Kauśikī*.

85-88. Those three eminent royal sages as well as the two hermits, arrived at the river *Kauśikī* in chariots moving fast with horses. Alighting from the chariots, they reached the river for ablution. Ghṛtācī too, came to that holy river for a bath. That monkey following her was seen by Jābāli. Immediately after espying (the monkey), he informed his father and the valiant king: "O father ! Here indeed that monkey is coming in haste, by whom I was tied fast on the tree with matted hair in the past."

89-90. Listening to the words of Jābāli, Śakuni with rage, bending down his bow with the arrow, said thus: "O Brāhmaṇa ! Please give me orders. O father ! Please tell me, so that I shall kill this monkey with a single arrow today."

91-92. So told by him, the great sage intent on the well-being of all beings, spoke to Śakuni these appropriate words:

"O my dear prince ! No one is killed or arrested by anyone else. Killing or arresting is a sequel to one's past deeds."

93. Śakuni, so told, asked the sage: "O Brāhmaṇa ! Please order me; please direct me as to what I should do."

94-99a. That sage, so told (by Śakuni), spoke to that monkey-leader: "My son had been tied up with the matted hair on the banyan tree by you. Even with great efforts, it was not possible to disentangle him from the tree. Then, the tree was cut into three pieces by this noble king. My son is carrying that branch (piece) on his head; please untie it. Ten hundred years have elapsed since he bore the branch. There is no person who is capable of untying him." Having heard the words of the sage, the monkey untied slowly the matted hair of Jābāli and in a short while the matted hair was disentangled. Then, the noble sage, Ṛtadhvaja was happy and was ready to offer a boon. He said to the monkey: "You ask for a boon you long for."

99b-109. Hearing the words of Ṛtadhvaja, he begged for this wish (to be granted): "I am the eminent Viśvakarmā, reduced to the state of a monkey. O Brāhmaṇa ! If you want to grant me my wish, then this harsh curse on me may please be withdrawn. O ascetic ! Know me to be Tvaṣṭā, the father of Citrāṅgadā, turned into a monkey by your curse. All those many sins committed by me due to the evil fickleness of a monkey, be absolved."

Then Ṛtadhvaja said: "There will be the end of the curse when you beget a mighty son in Ghṛtācī." O lady of slender waist ! Having been spoken thus, that noble monkey being very glad, immediately descended into the great river for ablution. Afterwards all of them took bath and (offered worship to) the fathers in order. They, being happy, went away in chariots.

Ghṛtācī soared into the heavens. That fast-moving monkey, the best of the apes too, went after her. That noble monkey ogled the beautiful Ghṛtācī. That passionate lady too, eyeing that eminent monkey, the best of the mighty and recognising him as Viśvakarmā, longed for him.

Then, on the pretty mountain in Kolāhala, the monkey made love to her and the lady too, responded to the best of the monkeys. Thus, after sporting for a long time (they) arrived at the Vindhya mountain.

110-117. Those noble men, tired, arrived at that holy spot *Sapta-godāvara-tīrtha* at midday in chariots. Having arrived, they being thirsty, got down (from the chariots) for resting. Their charioteers and horses too bathed and drank water to their full. The divine steeds were let out for grazing for a while in the pretty grassy forest lands. All of them being contented, ran towards the exquisite temple.

Hearing the trot of the horse's hoofs, those best of the ladies saying, "What is this ?" Went inside the temple of Hāṭakeśvara and going up the top floor, looked all round. They saw the best of men taking ablution in the waters of the *Tīrtha.* Then, having spotted Suratha, sporting matted hair, the horripilated Citrāṅgadā told her friends with a smile: "That youth, who has the lustre of a dark cloud, has an attractive physique, has stout arms, is indeed the prince, who was chosen by me formerly as my husband. This one, who is of golden hue and wears white matted hair, is indeed Ṛtadhvaja, the foremost of the ascetics. There is no doubt about this."

118-119. Then, the delighted Damayantī, told her companions: "This one here is his (Ṛtadhvaja's) son Jābāli; there is no doubt." So saying, she (along with others) got down from the top floor and sitting before the Lord, Śambhu, sang songs of welfare.

"Salutation to you, O Śarva ! O Śambhu ! O three-eyed one ! O one of charming body ! O lord of the three worlds ! O spouse of Umā ! O destroyer of Dakṣa's sacrifice ! O one causing destruction to Cupid's body ! O remover of grave sins ! O high-souled one ! O one of highly terrific form ! O one causing annihilation of all beings ! O bringer of prosperity! O Maheśvara ! O wielder of the trident ! O foe of Cupid ! O resident of cave ! O one having space as garment! O great one with the head ornament of moon ! O bearer of matted hair ! O one whose body is adorned with a garland of skulls ! O one who agitated the lord of celestials by his left eye ! O remover of eyes of Bhaga ! O Bhīmasena ! O protector ! O lord of beings ! O burner of Cupid's body ! O one living in open space ! O Śiva ! O Mahādeva ! O Īśāna! O Śaṅkara ! O ferocious one ! O existent one ! O bull-bannered one ! O Kaṭabha ! O master of great sophisticated dance ! O one desiring ash ! O one never dissociated (from Pārvatī) ! O Rudra ! O Rudreśvara ! O Sthāṇu ! O Ekaliṅga! O beloved of Kālindī ! O Śrīkaṇṭha ! O blue-necked one ! O unconquered one ! O one dreadful to the foe ! O lord of happiness ! O Vāmadeva ! O Aghora ! O Tatpuruṣa ! O Mahāghora ! O one of non-dreadful form ! O one of peaceful form ! O beloved of Sarasvatī ! O one of thousand forms ! O one of unique origin ! O omnipresent one ! O fire of delusion! O Rudra ! O terrific one ! O Hara ! O supporter of the earth ! O pleasing one ! O one residing in all holy spots ! O swan ! O overlord of desires ! O ruler of Kedāra ! O perfect one ! O Mucukunda ! O receptacle of honey ! O wielder of sword ! O dreadful one ! O master of learning ! O master of Soma ! O master of love ! O one residing in the lotus-heart of the Daughter of Mountain ! O one lying on the sea ! O Gayāmukha ! O Gokarṇa ! O source of Brahmā ! O one of thousand faces, eyes and feet ! O Hāṭakeśvara ! Salutation to you".

120-126. In the meanwhile, all those sages and kings arrived to visit the triple-eyed Hāṭakeśvara, the creator of the three worlds. They, coming up after a good bath, saw the noble damsels standing before him (the Lord) and singing an exquisite song. Then, the son of Sudeva looking at his beloved, the daughter of Viśvakarmā, was glad at heart and shone with horripilation. Ṛtadhvaja, a meditative soul too, seeing the young lady Citrāṅgadā standing, recognised the lady and was happy. Then, others too, approaching the Lord of *Devas,* Hāṭakeśvara, worshipped the triple-eyed Lord and adored him in order. Citrāṅgadā too, seeing Ṛtadhvaja and others, got up along with the slender-bodied damsels and prostrated. That happy hermit along with his son greeting them, went inside with ease together with the kings.

127-129. O pretty lady ! The noble monkey arrived along with Ghṛtācī, desirous of visiting Hāṭakeśvara, after taking ablution in the *Godāvarī-tīrtha.* Then, Ghṛtācī noticed that slender lady (Vedavatī) of pretty looks. That young lady of beautiful complexion too, seeing her mother became very happy. Then, Ghṛtācī embraced her daughter tightly with affection and smelled (her head) again and again with eyes wet.

130-131. The honourable Ṛtadhvaja, then told the monkey: "You go to Mahājana (city) in Añjanādri to bring the *Guhyaka.* You also bring immediately the valorous Lord of the *Daityas,* Kandaramāli from *Pātāla* and the *Gandharva* King Parjanya from Heaven."

132. As the sage was saying thus, Devavatī spoke to the monkey; "O monkey-chief ! You would also please bring Gālava here."

133-136. After being told so, the monkey-chief of extraordinary prowess, went to Añjana (mountain), invited (*Guhyaka*) and proceeded to Amara mountain. Inviting Parjanya there and sending him to the majestic *Āśrama* in the *Sapta-godāvara-tīrtha,* the monkey went down to *Pātāla.* Inviting Kandaramālin there, the most powerful monkey emerged out of *Pātāla* and moved on the earth fast. Finding Gālava, the source of austerity, near Māhiṣmatī, (the monkey) flew in and brought him immediately to *Sapta-godāvara-tīrtha.*

137-142a. Taking ablution there as per prescription, (Gālava) came in (to visit) Hāṭakeśvara and saw Damayantī and Devavatī who were there. (Devavatī too), seeing that Gālava, got up and prostrated. Those noble kings also, worshipping that sage, rich in penance, felt extremely happy and sat with ease.

At that juncture, as they sat down, those high-souled ones, the *Yakṣa, Gandharva* and *Dānava* invited by the monkey arrived. Immediately after seeing them arrive, those daughters with wide eyes, hugged their fathers with their eyes wet, due to affection. Seeing Damayantī and others united with their fathers, the pretty daughter of Viśvakarmā had tears in her eyes.

142b-146a. Then, that sage Satyadhvaja told her the truth: "Do not feel sad. O daughter ! This monkey is your father."

Hearing these words, she overcome with shame thought: "How did this Viśvakarmā assume now the form of a monkey? (What is the use of) my being born, an evil daughter ? Hence I will give up my body." Thinking thus in her mind, she spoke to Ṛtadhvaja: "O Brāhmaṇa ! Please save me weighed down by sin; I, having committed patricide, desire to die; please permit me."

146b-150a. At that, the sage said to the slender lady: "Do not feel miserable now. There will be termination (of this curse) by (an event) that is going to happen. So do not give up your body. Your father will once again become the divine carpenter, when a child is born of Ghṛtācī. No doubt, need be entertained in this."

When the sage endowed with *Yogic* power said thus, Ghṛtācī came near that Citrāṅgadā and said this: "Give up grief. In ten month's time, a son equal to your father is going to be born of me without doubt."

150b-155a. Citrāṅgadā so told, then became bright with happiness. The lady of charming limbs, postponed her marriage till she saw her father. All other damsels too postponed their marriage till that time, desirous of fulfilling her wish.

After ten months elapsed, the *Apsarā* gave birth to a son, Nala, there on the banks of *Godāvarī*. As the child was born, Viśvakarmā was relieved of his monkey-form. The divine carpenter came near his dear daughter and hugged her affectionately. Glad at heart, he recalled Śakra, the ruler of the celestials along with the celestials and *Kinnaras.*

155b-159. Śakra, being recalled by Tvaṣṭā, arrived there, surrounded by groups of immortals. Mahendra, together with the celestials, reached that Tīrtha called Hāṭaka. As the *Devas*, *Gandharvas* and *Apsarās* assembled there, Indradyumna spoke to Ṛtadhvaja, the best of the sages: "O Brāhmaṇa ! May the daughter of Kandaramālin be given (in marriage) to Jābāli; may your (son) accept the hand of *Daitya*'s daughter in marriage; may the beautiful Śakuni marry Damayantī; may this Vedavatī be mine after offering *Havis* as per custom." "Very well", replied that sage to the king, the son of Manu.

160-163. Then, Gālava and other Ṛtviks happily conducted the holy marriage rite by offering oblations to fire as per custom. Then the *Gandharvas* sang and the *Apsarās* danced. First, Jābāli's hand was held by the *Daitya*'s daughter. Following it, Vedavatī's hand was held ceremoniously by Indradyumna. Then, Yakṣa's daughter held the hand of Śakuni. O auspicious one ! Suratha held the hand of Citrāṅgadā. O lady of slender waist ! Thus marriages were completed in order.

164-168. As the marriages were over, the ascetic told Śakra and the other gods: "You all must stay always in this *Sapta-godāvara-tīrtha*, especially in this excellent month of *Vaiśākha* (Mādhava)." Saying "very well", all the celestials being happy, went to Heaven in order. The sages taking with them the sage (Ṛtadhvaja) and his son went away eagerly. The kings with their spouses reached their cities. They enjoyed sensual pleasures with gay abandon.

O auspicious one ! This is the story of Citrāṅgadā as it happened in former days. Therefore, O excellent lady with lotus-petal like eyes ! You accept me. So saying, the prince cajoled with soft words, the doe-eyed daughter of the Brāhmaṇa (Śukra) with charming thighs. She, however, told the king thus.

## CHAPTER SIXTY-SIX

### Setting out of Andhaka's army

*Arajā said:*

1. O King ! I am not going to give myself to you for the sake of guarding you and me from the curse. What is the use of speaking so much ?

*Prahlāda said:*

2-3. The foolish prince whose heart and soul were overpowered by lust, forcibly raped the daughter of glorious Bhārgava who was arguing thus. After making to lose her character, the king blind with haughtiness, went out of the *Āśrama* and reached his own city.

4-5. That young lady Arajā, sullied because of being sprinkled with semen, went out of the *Āśrama* and stood outside with her head bent down, thinking of her father and crying again and again like Rohiṇī, the beloved of Moon, attacked by a Mahāgraha.

6-9. After a long time and after the *Yajña* ceremony closed, sage Śukra came back to his *Āśrama* from *Pātāla.* Having come, he saw in the outskirts of the *Āśrama,* his daughter having marks of menses, appearing like a line of cloud in the sky tinged with the twilight colour. Observing her, he enquired: "O daughter ! By whom have you been seduced ? Who is it that plays with the enraged serpent having venom ? Where ? I will proceed today only. Where did that sinful person of too bad a conduct go ? Who is that sinful one who has ruined you of pure conduct ?"

10-11. Then, she, looking at her father again and again and trembling and crying, spoke very slowly due to shyness: "By your pupil Daṇḍa, though dissuaded several times, have I, crying without a protector, been reduced forcibly to the state of being censured."

12-15. After listening to these words of his daughter, he, with his eyes red due to rage, purifying himself by washing his hands, said thus: "That misbehaved one has made Arajā swerve from her righteous conduct, flouting the fear of my orders and my dignity. Because of having seen (my daughter) bare-bodied, he along with his country, army, servants and vehicles, shall be reduced to ashes within seven days." So cursing that Daṇḍa, the eminent sage told his daughter: "O auspicious daughter ! You stay here doing austerities for absolving yourself of sin."

16-18. Having cursed Daṇḍa, the son of Ikṣvāku in this way, the venerable Śukra went down to *Pātāla,* the excellent abode of *Dānavas.* Then, on the other side, Daṇḍa proud of his strength, together with his country, army and vehicles was reduced to ashes within seven days. Thus the gods avoid *Daṇḍakāraṇya.* Lord Śambhu, however, made it the abode of *Rākṣasas.*

19-21. Thus, wives of others lead (a person who goes after them) to great disgrace and reduce to ashes not only his merit but also his physical pleasures. Therefore, O Andhaka! you should not entertain this evil thought. Even an ordinary woman will burn down, what to say of the Daughter of the Mountain ? O King of *Daityas* ! Śaṅkara cannot be conquered by either the celestials or *Asuras.* It is not possible even to meet him, let alone fighting him on the battlefield.

*Pulastya said:*

22-24. When told so, the effulgent, enraged Andhakāsura with his eyes red and heaving, spoke thus to Prahlāda: "O *Asura* ! Is that lone three-eyed one with his body smeared with ashes and bereft of righteousness, able to fight with me a duel in the battlefield? Andhaka is not afraid of Indra or of human beings in any way. How would such a person be afraid of the Bull-bannered One (Śiva) because of his seeing the Pura ?"

25-40. O Nārada ! Having heard his harsh words, Prahlāda said: "This course which contradicts both *Dharma* and *Artha* (standards) and therefore should be censured, should not be taken up by you. What disparity they say is there between fire and moth, between a lion and a jackal, between an elephant and a mosquito, between gold and stone, that much of disparity is there between Hara and you, O Andhaka ! O valiant one ! You have been warned by me; you will be warned again and again.

Listen to the words of the noble, divine sage Asita: 'He who is of a righteous conduct, who has controlled his pride and rage, who is cultured with learning, who does not inflict pain on others, who is contented in his own wife and avoids other's wives, has no fear of any sort in this world. He who is bereft of righteousness, who is always fond of quarrels, who inflicts pain on others, who is not endowed with (the knowledge of) *Veda* or *Śāstra*, who is covetous of other's wives and wealth, who associates himself with persons of unequal *Varṇa*, does not find happiness either here or in the other world. The venerable Prabhākara was endowed with righteousness; the son of Varuṇa (Vasiṣṭha) had given up anger; Manu, the son of Arka, was endowed with learning; sage Agastya was contented in his own wife. These meritorious actions without any association of sin, were attended to by these in their family tradition (and hence) they became effulgent, able to curse and bless and were honoured by the celestials and *Siddhas*. Udgamita was unrighteousness; Vibhu was always interested in quarrels; the evil-minded Namuci was inflicting pain on others; King Sanaka was too haughty; Hiraṇyākṣa, the son of Diti, was desirous of grabbing other's wealth; his younger brother (Hiraṇyakaśipu) was also foolish and one of deep evil intentions; Yadu (though) of excellent grace was stealing gold; these in the past ages were ruined because of their bad conduct. Therefore *Dharma* should not be renounced; *Dharma* is the excellent resort; those without *Dharma* go to the fearful hell of *Raurava*. *Dharma* is spoken of by (great) men as the ferry here as well as in heaven and *Adharma* (leads) to downfall in this as well as the other world. Those who follow *Dharma* should always shun resorting to other's wives. Other's wives only lead to twenty-one hells. For the people of all *Varṇas,* this is the (principal) *Dharma* enjoined in this world. He who cherishes liking for other's wives and other's wealth, goes to the horrible *Raurava* hell for many years.' O *Asura*-king ! Thus did the imperishable divine sage Asita, speak of the procedure of *Dharma* to Aruṇa, the lord of birds, in the past. Therefore, an intelligent person should avoid other's wives from a distance. The other's wives lead short-sighted persons to disgrace."

*Pulastya said:*

41-45. When told so, Andhaka said to Prahlāda: "You alone be devoted to *Dharma*; I do not observe *Dharma*." So saying to Prahlāda, Andhaka told Śambara: "O Śambara ! Go to the great mountain Mandara and tell Śaṅkara: O beggar ! Why and with what (authority) are you looking after this heaven-like great mountain Mandara having (many) caves ? You tell me who gave you this ? The gods led by Indra are standing at my bidding. Then, why are you residing in Mandara ignoring me ? If this excellent mountain is liked by you, then carry out my words. This lady who is your wife, be immediately handed over to me."

46-49. On being told thus, Śambara proceeded fast to Mandara. There he went to that place where the Wielder of Pināka was with Devī. The son of Danu, the messenger of Andhaka, went and said exactly in the same way (as instructed).

Hara spoke to him in reply, even as the Daughter of the Mountain was hearing: "This Mandara has been given to me by the honourable Thousand-eyed One (Indra). Hence I cannot vacate it without the orders of Vṛtra's foe. With regard to what the *Dānava* has said 'let Pārvatī be handed over to me', well, she may go if she likes; I am unable to hold her back."

50-51. O eminent sage ! Then Pārvatī told Śambara: "O valiant one ! Go and tell the wise Andhaka:(Let us have) a duel between us in which I will be a pedestrian and you, a king. Having put on stake our very life, the one who wins will have claim (over the other)."

52-54. The clever Śambara being told so, returned to Andhaka. Having gone back, he related all that was spoken by Gaurī. Having heard it, the *Dānava* king with his eyes burning with fury and sighing, called Duryodhana and said this to him: "O valiant one ! Go immediately and beat the war-drum without hesitation, like a woman of bad character."

55-64. Then, Duryodhana ordered by Andhaka, struck hard the war-drum vehemently as if with all his strength. That war-drum struck by the strong Duryodhana made a terrific loud noise, like a (female) donkey. Hearing such a noise, all the great *Asuras* immediately came to the meeting saying, "What is this?" The valorous commander told them all as was the case. They, too, the best of the mighty, got ready, eager for a war. They along with Andhaka set out on elephants, camels, horses and chariots. Andhaka, riding on a chariot measuring five *Nalvas* (furlongs), set out, determined to defeat the Lord Śiva.

Jambha, Kujambha, Huṇḍa, Tuhuṇḍa, Śambara, Bali, Bāṇa, Kārtasvara, Hastī, Sūryaśatru, Mahodara, Ayaṣ, Śaṅku, Śibi, Śālva, Vṛṣaparva, Virocana, Hayagrīva, Kālanemi, Saṁhrāda, Kālanāśana, Sarabha, Sabala, Vala, heroic Vṛtra, Duryodhana, Pāka, Vipāka, Kāla and Śambara—these and may other heroic warriors set out enthusiastically, holding varieties of weapons to fight on the battlefield. Thus, that evil-minded and foolish king of *Daityas*, Andhaka, thinking of fighting with Hara, reached the high mountain Mandara, dragged by the noose of Death.

# CHAPTER SIXTY-SEVEN

## Vision of Sadāśiva

*Pulastya said:*

1. Hara too, preparing for the battle called *Nandī* and told him: "Inform Śailādi and others who are under your control."

2-4. Then, as per the orders of Maheśa, *Nandī* acted faster. The blessed one, having touched water recalled the leaders of *Gaṇas.* Being recalled by Nandī, all the leaders of *Gaṇas* in thousands, ran in haste and bowed down to the Lord of Celestials. *Nandī,* the imperishable one, with folded hands, introduced all those *Gaṇas* who had arrived to the magnanimous Śaṅkara.

*Nandī said:*

5-18. O Śambhu ! These bright ones with three eyes and matted hair whom you see are well-known as *Rudras,* eleven crore (in number). These monkey-faced ones and valorous like tigers whom you see are the doorkeepers of these (*Rudras*), well-armed and rich in glory. The six-faced ones whom you see, those holding spears and peacock-bannered are *Kumārakas* called *Skandas,* sixty-six crore (in number). O Śaṅkara ! These are sixty-six crore (*Gaṇas*) called *Śākhas* having six faces and these are *Viśālas, Naigamas* in similar numbers. O Śambhu ! These are seven hundred crore best *Pramathas.* O Lord of Celestials ! To each one of these there are as many Mother-goddesses. These leaders of *Gaṇas* are all three-eyed, holding tridents with their body smeared with ashes and are called *Śaivas.* So also, O omnipresent Lord ! These other *Gaṇas,* the *Pāśupatas* innumerable in number and having ash as weapon, have arrived for (your) assistance. Other *Gaṇas,* the Kālamukhas who are ferocious, holding the *Pināka* (bow), having long matted hairs and devoted to you have come here now. These foremost brave *Gaṇas* decorated with red sandal, fighting with *Khaṭvāṅga* and of noble vow have joined (us) for the battle. O omnipresent Lord ! These other *Gaṇas* called *Nirāśrayas*, who have space as their clothing, who have matted hair and who have bell as their weapon, too, have arrived here. So also, these imperishable *Gaṇas* called Mahāpāśupatas, the bull-bannered ones, have come riding birds. They have two eyes and a half, appearing like lotuses and their chest is marked with *Śrīvatsa*. They are wielding discus and trident and worship Bhairava with Viṣṇu without difference. These lion-faced *Gaṇas*, carrying tridents, bows and arrows are Vīrabhadra's and others who were born of your hair. These and many others have arrived in hundreds and thousands for your assistance; order them as you please.

19-20. Then, all the *Gaṇas* went near the Bull-bannered One and prostrated. He bade the *Gaṇas* sit, after comforting them with hospitable treatment. The Mahāpāśupatas bowed down to Maheśvara. He, seeing them, made them rise up and embraced those leaders.

21-24. Then, observing this most wonderful sight, all those leaders of *Gaṇas* were surprised and thought: "What is this?" The foremost of the *Yogins*, Śailādi, seeing the *Gaṇas* with their eyes wide open with wonder, told the Lord of celestials, the wielder of trident and the master of *Gaṇas*, with a smile: "O Lord Maheśvara ! All the *Gaṇas* are indeed surprised, for the embrace you gave to the Mahāpāśupatas. O omnipresent Mahādeva ! Please tell us at your will, how their obvious form, knowledge and wisdom became nourishers of the three worlds."

25. Listening to the words of the leader of *Pramathas*, the promoter of the beings said to all the *Gaṇas* who were able to think about the existing and the non-existing.

*Rudra said:*

26-30a. Hara was worshipped with concentration by you endowed with devotion but obsessed by egoism and so decrying the position of Viṣṇu. By your ignorance, the identity that I am Lord Viṣṇu and that imperishable one is myself was obscured. There is no difference between us; a single body appearing as two. You did not comprehend me or Hari, as these, the tigers among men, endowed with devotion, O *Gaṇas* ! Because you with erroneous perception have despised Hari, your wisdom was obscured and so you were not embraced by me.

30b-32a. As he said these words, the *Gaṇas* told Maheśvara: "How is that you have identity (with him) ? You are of blemishless consciousness; you are shining like the pure quartz crystal, peaceful, bright and without any stigma; he, on the other hand, is shining like collyrium; how is (the identity) proper ?"

32b-43a. Hearing their meaningful words, the Cloud-bannered Lord, laughed and said to the *Gaṇas* in a voice as deep as that of a cloud: "Listen, I will relate to you those things which enhance my own glory. You are in no way fit for the highest knowledge. The secret is being revealed to you, lest there should be a scandal. Always have the same devotion in mind to him (as you are having) unto me. Consider that which you have resorted to as having one form and one body. I am not pleased with being anointed with milk, ghee and so on, howsoever carefully (carried out) or with the best sandal paste and so forth. You may wilfully sever my body with a saw. Even then, the eternal Viṣṇu will be found in my body. Both, he who takes food once a day and he who is devoted to Viṣṇu are similar in this world. There is no need to doubt. The people do not speak of the difference sometimes. That is why I do not put you in some strange hell. That lotus-eyed Jagannātha permeated by me, who was despised by you, is the lord of everything, the all-pervading one and the Lord of *Gaṇas*. There is no match to him in the world of the movable and the immovable. That venerable Lord of the universe is of white form, yellow and red. Therefore there is no truth greater than him in the universe. That venerable Sadāśiva, worshipped by all, alone sustains the *Sāttvika*, the *Rājasa*, the *Tāmasa* and the mixed."

43b-52a. Having heard the words of Śaṅkara, Śailādi and other *Pramatha*-chiefs said: "O worshipful one ! Please tell us the attributes of Sadāśiva."

Having listened to those words of the *Pramathas*, the Lord of Celestials exhibited that unsullied, ungazeable (most radiant) grand form of Śiva having a thousand faces, thousand feet and thousand arms, holding the staff and occupied by beings everywhere; divine weapons were seen abiding in the staff. Then again, the *Gaṇas* saw Śaṅkara having one face bearing the marks of Rudra and Viṣṇu in thousands. One half of the body was of Viṣṇu and the other half of Hara. He was riding on the bull with the banner of the bird and was riding the bird with the banner of the bull. Even as the Three-eyed Lord, supreme with qualities assumed (different) forms, the *Gaṇas*, the Mahāpāśupatas came into being. Then, Śaṅkara of multiforms became one of single form. In a moment he was white, in another moment red, in yet another moment yellow and black as well as variegated, colourless and also Mahāpāśupata. In a moment he appeared as Rudra and Indra, in another moment as Śambhu and Sun. In half a moment, he appeared as Śaṅkara, as Viṣṇu and in another moment, he appeared as Śarva, as the Grandsire.

52b-56. Then, seeing that most astounding (event), the *Gaṇas* of Śiva realised Brahmā, Viṣṇu, Indra and Bhāskara as identical. When they cognised the eternal god of gods as one and the same, then those attendants (of Śiva) became purged of their sins. When they were purged of their sins and did not differentiate Hari-Īśvara, Śambhu shone, delighted at heart and said these words with joy: "O you of excellent vows ! I am pleased by this wisdom of you all. Choose an unlimited boon cherished by your minds; I will grant it."

They said: "O worshipful sovereign ! You please bestow this boon on us. May the great sin accrued to us for seeing difference, get absolved."

*Pulastya said:*

57-59. "Well", said Śarva and made them purged of the stain (sin). The Unmanifest One embraced all those chiefs of *Gaṇa* troops. Thus the *Gaṇa*-chiefs came to (Mandara) mountain together with the omnipresent Lord, the one who drives away the miseries of the devout, the one riding the bull and the cloud and the one who could be known through the statements of *Veda* and stayed there. The lofty, white-bodied mountain covered by the *Pramathas* of cloud colour and associated with the feet of Īśvara shone, like Hara's mighty bull of the hue of autumnal cloud shines with his body covered by blue hide.

## CHAPTER SIXTY-EIGHT

### The Defeat of *Daityas*

*Pulastya said:*

1. In the meanwhile, Andhaka together with the *Daityas* arrived at the excellent Mandara mountain whose caves had been occupied by the *Pramathas.*

2-5. The *Pramathas* seeing the *Dānavas* gave out shrill cries. The enraged *Pramathas* blew the trumpets also many times. That tremendous noise like that of annihilation, filled the two worlds. Vināyaka, the lord of obstacles, who was in the aerial route heard (it). Much enraged, he came down to the excellent mountain Mandara and surrounded by the *Pramathas*, saw his father as well. Bowing down with devotion, he said to Maheśvara: "O Lord of the Universe ! O one eager for war ! Why are you sitting still? Rise up."

6. Then, at the words of Vighneśvara, the Lord of the Universe told Ambikā: "We will go to kill Andhaka. (You should stay) yourself being alert."

7-8. The Daughter of the Mountain embracing Lord Hara again and again and looking at his face, said with affection: " Go to (kill) Andhaka." Then, the most pleased Gaurī, offered attractive yellow sandalpaste to the master of celestials and bowed down to his feet.

9-10. Then, Hara said to the companions—Mālinī, Jayā, Vijayā, Jayantī and Aparājitā: "You should stay alert in the house, well-guarded. The Daughter of the Mountain should be carefully guarded from dangers."

11-16. Thus ordering them all, the happy master, riding the bull, went out of the house. Those Gaṇas went after him. The leaders of the *Gaṇas*, going out of Īśvara's abode, gathered round and shouted 'Hail !' O great sage ! As Maheśvara, the wielder of trident, the protector of the world, was proceeding for battle, pleasing, lucky and auspicious omens wished him victory. A female jackal on his left side was proceeding forward shouting in a pleasing voice. The teams of carrion-eating creatures were joyfully moving, desirous of flesh and feeling thirsty for blood. Śiva's right arm up to the nails (finger tips) shook. The Hārīta bird flew past silently, turning its face away. Observing such an omen, Lord Śasiśekhara (Śiva), transcending the past, future and present, told Śailādi with a smile—

*Lord Śiva said:*

17. O Nandī ! O Gaṇeśvara ! Today victory is awaiting us and not defeat. The omens occurring (to the effect) are found.

18. Listening to those words of Śambhu, Śailādi told Śaṅkara: "O Mahādeva ! What doubt is there? You will conquer the multitude of foes."

19-21. So saying, Nandī commanded the *Rudra-Gaṇas* along with the Mahāpāśupatas to fight. Those warriors carrying varieties of weapons attacked with force and felled the *Dānava* army, like lightning (fells) trees. Being hit by the mighty *Pramathas,* those *Daityas* and *Dānavas* with *Kūṭa* and *Mudgara* in hand, began to kill the *Pramathas.*

22-24. Then in the sky, the gods led by the Sun came along with Indra, Viṣṇu and Brahmā to witness (the war). O Nārada ! Then in the sky, the sound of the drums mixed with the (sound of) singing and of instruments etc. was produced. As the gods were witnessing, the enraged Mahāpāśupatas and other *Gaṇas* were killing that *Dānava* army.

25-36 ab. Having seen the army with four divisions being killed by the *Gaṇa*-chiefs, the enraged Daṇḍa quickly went forward, taking a dreadful *Parigha* made of iron and tied with silk garment. The *Parigha* in his hand was shining like the Indradhvaja held up. That mighty one, whirling it, killed the *Gaṇas, Rudras* and others upto Skanda in the war and they fell down stricken with fear. Seeing the army being destroyed, Vināyaka, a *Gaṇa*-chief, ran speedily after Daṇḍa, the chief *Dānava.* Seeing Gaṇapati attacking, the wicked and valiant *Daitya* hurled the *Parigha* on the head (of Gaṇapati). O Brāhmaṇa ! The *Parigha* hitting (the head) of Vināyaka decorated with *Vajra,* was reduced to hundred pieces, like lightning (striking) the crest of Meru. Seeing the *Parigha* becoming useless and seeing the attacking *Gaṇa*-chief, the *Dānava* forcibly pulled him and held him fast in his arms. Then, he struck Mahodara on his head with the *Mudgara.* Gaṇeśa, Mahodara (struck) the *Daitya*-chief with the axe. The *Dānava* fell on the earth split into two, like a log of wood. Still the *Dānava*-chief did not loosen his arm.

Mahodara tried to get himself released but could not. Then, seeing Vināyaka tied by the arm, Kuṇḍodara, another valiant *Gaṇa*-chief, holding a pestle, immediately hit his (Daṇḍa's) arm all round. Then, the *Gaṇa*-chief Kalaśadhvaja severed the heart of Rāhu with the *Prāsa*. As Daṇḍa was killed and Rāhu turned back, the five *Gaṇa*-chiefs pouring venom of wrath and blazing like the fire of deluge entered into the army of valiant *Dānavas*.

36cd-43. Observing his army being killed, the mighty Bali, equal to wind in speed, forcefully threw his mace and struck Vināyaka on the head, temples and hands, injured Kuṇḍodara's hand and made Mahodara's head, shorn of the skull. (He made) Kumbhadhvaja shaken in his joints and Ghaṭodara broken at thigh joint. Finding the *Gaṇa*-chiefs hapless, the mighty *Asura*-chief with doubled valour ran fast to kill the eminent *Gaṇa*-leaders like Skanda and Viśākha. The venerable Maheśvara who saw him advancing, then called Śailādi, the foremost of the *Gaṇas* and said: "O valiant one ! You go and kill the *Daitya* in the battle."

So told by the Bull-bannered Lord, the son of Śilāda, taking hold of a discus, confronted Bali and struck him on his head. Bali lost his consciousness and fell on the ground. The mighty Kujambha, learning his nephew (brother's son) swoon, took hold of a pestle and whirling it fast, threw it on Nandī with rage. Honourable Nandī, quickly held the oncoming pestle in his hand and struck Kujambha with the same. He fell down on earth, dead, in the warfare. Killing Kujambha with the pestle, Nandī killed in hundreds with *Vajra*.

44-51. They, being killed by the *Gaṇa*-leader, took refuge in Duryodhana. Duryodhana, seeing the *Daityas* subdued by the master of the *Gaṇas* with strokes of *Vajra*, whirling with full force the noose, as lustrous as lightning, threw it on Nandī saying, "You are dead." Nandī snapped the oncoming noose with *Vajra*, as a back-biting person (snaps) a secret. Observing the noose being severed, he advanced towards the *Gaṇa*, clinching his fist. Then (Nandī), wielder of *Vajra*, immediately severed off his head, appearing like a palm fruit, with his *Vajra*. (Duryodhana) being killed, fell at once. The *Daityas* ran helter-skelter in panic.

Then, Hastī, seeing his son killed, attacked Nandī. Taking hold of a bow of tremendous speed, (Hastī), with arrows appearing like Yama's club, pierced those bull-bannered *Gaṇas* together with Nandī. Being covered by the arrows of the *Dānavas*, like a hill by the showers of clouds, Vināyaka and others, though valiant, fled in all directions in panic, like bulls chased by a lion. Then, Kumāra seeing the *Gaṇas* turning their back, armed himself with a sharp *Śakti* (spear) and confronted the foe at once and pierced the heart (of the foe) with the spear (*Śakti*). The *Dānava*-warrior, Hastī, fell on the ground with his heart pierced by the spear, during the warfare.

52-56. Beholding that army of enemies shattered, the wrathful *Gaṇa*-chiefs with Nandī as their head (went on) killing the *Dānavas*. Being struck by the *Pramathas*, the *Daityas* fled back but returned stronger again to face the *Gaṇas* in the battle. Seeing them return, the tiger-faced Nandiṣeṇa too returned speedily, sighing and with his eyes burning with anger. O Nārada ! When the *Gaṇa*-leader, with a sharp *Paṭṭiśa* in hand returned, Kārtasvara too returned holding a mace. Seeing that great *Asura*, Kārtasvara blazing like fire, advancing, (Nandiṣeṇa) whirled that *Paṭṭiśa* and struck on the head (of the *Asura*) who cried aloud in a discordant voice.

57-65. When his brother, son of maternal uncle, was killed, Turaṅgakadhvaja, forcefully throwing the noose, tied the valiant *Gaṇa*-chief Nandiṣeṇa together with his *Paṭṭiśa*. Seeing Nandiṣeṇa tied like that, the best of the mighty, Viśākha, enraged, came with a spear in hand and took position. Seeing the foremost of the valiants, Ayaḥśiras with noose in hand, engaged the strong Viśākha, the cock-bannered, in fight. Seeing Viśākha cornered in war, the best of the *Gaṇas*, Śākha and Naigameya at once rushed towards the foe. Ayaḥśiras was struck by Naigameya with the spear on one side and by Śākha on the other, with a view to help Viśākha. He (Ayaḥśiras), being attacked by the three sons of Śaṅkara, fled the battlefield and approaching Śambara (begged him): "Protect me from Gaṇeśvara immediately." Being cut with the spear (*Śakti*) by the four sons of Śaṅkara, the noose got destroyed at once and fell on earth from the sky. As the noose was severed, Śambara with pitiful looks fled helter-skelter. O divine sage ! Kumāra (then) pounded the (*Asura*) army. O great sage ! The fear-stricken and desolate army together with the *Dānavas*, being killed by the sons of Śiva and (his) *Gaṇas* and their limbs becoming listless due to panic, sought refuge in Śukra.

## CHAPTER SIXTY-NINE

### Jambha and Kujambha killed

*Pulastya said:*

1-5. Then, as Kujambha died and the army was routed by the *Pramathas*, the great warrior, the terrified Andhaka, approached his preceptor, Śukra and entreatingly said: "O venerable Brāhmaṇa-sage ! Under your aegis we are attacking the gods and *Gandharvas*, the celestials and *kinnaras* as well. But, O venerable Sir ! See this, my well protected army, which is being pushed away by the *Pramathas*, as a woman none to care for (would be pushed). O Bhārgava ! My brothers Kujambha and others are killed. The *Pramathas* are innumerable, like the merits of Kurukṣetra. Therefore, do (something) in such a way that it will not be known by the enemies. You better do that, by which we can win over the foes in the battle."

*Pulastya said:*

6-8. O divine sage ! Having listened to the words of Andhaka, the most superior teacher, Śukra, spoke these words, consoling and gladdening the king of *Dānavas*: "Then I will try for your benefit and do good to you." So saying, Śukra (Kavi), a follower of pure vows, then went on repeating the *Sañjīvinī-Vidyā* in accordance with the precepts. As the Vidyā (sacred incantation) was being repeated, all the leaders of *Asuras* who had been killed by the *Pramathas* in the warfare, got up.

9-11. As the resurrected *Daityas*, Kujambha and others, came again for waging war, Nandī told Śaṅkara: " Those *Daityas* who had been killed on the battlefield by the *Pramathas* with their best efforts, have been brought to life once again by Bhārgava with (his) incantation. O Mahādeva! has not thus, that tremendous action (of the *Pramathas*) on the battlefield been nullified by utilising the power of incantation of Śukra, O Īśa ?"

12-13. When Nandī, the joy of his family said thus, the Lord affectionately replied, (stating) the best means of accomplishing his object: "O leader of *Gaṇas* ! Go and bring Śukra near me. I will restrain him according to the circumstances after meeting him."

14-18. When Nandī, the *Gaṇa*-leader was told so by Rudra, he then came to the army of *Daityas*, with a desire to seize Śukra. But the powerful Bhayaṅkara, the foremost of the *Asuras* saw him and obstructed his way, like an animal (obstructing) a lion in forest. Nandī, falling on him, struck him with the discus as powerful as the thunderbolt. He then fell down unconscious and Nandī moved fast. Then, the *Rākṣasas*, the tigers in battles, Kujambha, Jambha, Bala and Vṛtra, chased Nandī. So also, other eminent *Dānavas*, Maya, Hrāda and others followed the *Gaṇa*-leader in the battle, carrying various weapons.

19-23. Then, Brahmā and other gods saw the *Gaṇa*-leader being beaten by the powerful (*Daityas*). Seeing him, the venerable one said to Indra and other gods: "Go to the help of Śambhu. This is the best opportunity." Hearing the words uttered by Brahmā, the gods including Indra, quickly joined the army of Śiva from the sky. Their stream joining the army of the *Pramathas,* shone like the big streams of rivers joining the ocean. Then, there was a terrific tumult of noise in the two armies of celestials and *Pramathas.*

24-27. Taking the chance, Nandī hastened and took hold of Bhārgava, like a lion (takes hold of) a forest animal. Putting down all the guards, the leader of the *Gaṇas* took Śukra away and presented him before Śiva. Lord Śarva put Kavi (Śukra), who was brought to him, into his mouth. Those foes of celestials saw Bhārgava covered in the mouth (of Śarva). That foremost Kavi was devoured and placed in the stomach by Śambhu. Bhārgava ardently praised that venerable one with these words—

*Śukra said:*

28-30. Salutation to you, to the giver of boons, to Hara endowed with all qualities; salutation, salutation to Śaṅkara, to the great master, to the lord of the universe; salutation to you, O life ! O guardian of the world ! O Vṛkṣāpi ! O fire for Cupid ! O foe of time ! Salutation to you, to Vāmadeva; Salutation to Savitṛ, to the multiform one, to dwarf, to one moving always; salutation to Mahādeva, to Śarva, to Īśvara. (Prose) O three-eyed one ! O Hara ! O Bhava ! O Śaṅkara ! O spouse of Umā ! O cloud-bannered one ! O one attached to caves and cremation grounds ! O one smeared with ash ! O wielder of trident ! O lord of beings ! O lord of cows ! O most excellent Puruṣa ! Salutation, salutation to you.

31-38. Pleased at being devotedly lauded thus by the best Kavi, Hara said: "O Bhārgava, choose a boon." He asked: " O venerable one ! Give me now this boon, so that I may get out of your stomach." Then, Hara closing his eyes, said: "O best of the twice-born ! Please come out."

Immediately after he was told so by the Lord, the best Bhārgava began to move in the Lord's stomach. Moving about, he (Śukra) saw the earth, ocean and the nether world along with the movable and the immovable objects in the cavity of the stomach of Śaṅkara. (He saw there) *Ādityas, Vasus* and *Rudras* as well as the groups of *Viśvedevas, Yakṣas, Kimpuruṣas* and groups of *Gandharvas* and *Apsaras.* (He saw there) the sages, human beings, sādhyas, animals, worms, insects, reptiles, trees, bushes, fruits, roots and plants. (He saw there) the acquatic and terrestrial beings, those that do not wink and those that wink, the unmanifest and the manifest, the bipeds and the quadrupeds. Having seen (all these), Bhārgava roamed about overcome by curiosity. As Bhārgava was roaming there, one divine year elapsed. Still, he did not find the end of it. Kavi became exhausted. Finding himself tired and unable to get out, he resorted to Mahādeva, bent down with devotion.

*Śukra said:*

39-43. O one of multiforms ! O one of mighty form ! O one assuming a form having innumerable eyes ! O thousand-eyed one ! O Mahādeva ! I have come to your refuge. Salutation to you, O Śaṅkara ! O Śarva ! O Śambhu ! O one of thousand eyes and feet ! O one with ornaments of serpents! Having seen the entire universe in your stomach, I am confounded. I surrender myself to your refuge.

When he (Śukra) said these words, the noble Śambhu, then said this with a smile: "O moon of the family of Bhārgavas! You come out through the penis; now you are my son. All the movable and immovable beings laud you by the name 'Śukra'. Let there not be any doubt about this." So saying, the venerable one ejected him through his penis and that Śukra emerged. Having come out, that moon of the Bhārgava family, the high-souled one of superior strength, attaining the nature of being Śukra, bowed down to Śambhu and went back immediately to the army of great *Asuras*.

44-46. When Bhārgava came back, the *Dānavas* were pleased and made up their mind again for a fight with the leaders of *Gaṇas*. Then, the leaders of *Gaṇas* along with the group of celestials, fought a violent battle with those *Asuras*; everyone was desirous of victory. O ascetic ! Then, as the *Asura* troops (and the celestials) were fighting, the battle took a violent form.

47-58. In the battle, Andhaka (fought) with Nandī, Ayaḥśiras with Śaṅkukarṇa, wise Bali with Kumbhadhvaja, Virocana with Nandiṣeṇa. Aśvagrīva fought with Viśākha and Śākha with Vṛtra; so also Naigameya (fought) with Bāṇa and the best of the *Rākṣasas* with Bala. Tuhuṇḍa, the best of the *Dānavas*, fought in the battle with that Vināyaka of superior prowess, wielding an axe. Hastī (fought) with Kuṇḍajaṭhara and Hrāda with the powerful Ghaṭodara. These *Dānavas*–six hundred *Daityas*–the best of the powerful fought with the *Pramathas*, O divine sage ! The powerful *Asura*-chief Jambha by name, obstructed the oncoming Gaṇotkaṭa who was like Śatakratu (Indra), the wielder of *Vajra*. The *Asura*-lord, Śambhu fought with Brahmā; the *Daitya*-chief, deceitful Kujambha fought with Viṣṇu; Solka (fought) with Vaivasvata (*Yama*); similarly, Triśiras with Varuṇa; Dvimūrdha (fought) with Pavana (*Vāyu*); Virūpadhṛk with Soma along with Mitra; that ferocious great *Asura* having a single eye, Kālanemi (was also fighting). The effulgent great *Asura* Vidyunmālī, violent on the battlefield, though single, gave fight to eleven *Rudras*. Naraka (engaged) the two *Aśvins*; Śambara (fought) with the Bhāskaras; Nivātakavacas and others with the *Sādhyas* and the groups of *Maruts*.

59-67. As thousands of such duels of the *Pramathas* with the *Dānavas* were fought, there elapsed six hundred divine years, O great sage ! When those celestials and others were not competent to fight with the *Dānavas*, (the *Dānavas*) opening their mouth, went on gradually swallowing the celestials forcibly. Then, that army became devoid of the *Pramathas* and gods. (The Giriprastha once) occupied by the *Pramathas* and also the celestials became devoid of them. Seeing the Giriprastha empty and the *Pramathas* and celestials being swallowed, the self-restrained Rudra in fury, created Jṛmbhāmbikā (goddess Yawn). Under its influence, the sons of Danu, being lazy and speaking slowly and giving up arms, yawned with distorted faces. As the *Dānavas* yawned, the perplexed *Gaṇa*-lords and the celestials, hastily emerged out of the bodies of *Daityas*. The supreme celestials with lotus-like eyes, emerging out of the bodies with the lustre of clouds, appeared like lightning issuing out of clouds. Then, O one rich in penance ! All the high-souled groups of celestials, having come out, fought again with rage. Then, all the *Dānavas* were being defeated in the war again and again, day and night by the best of gods, protected by Śarva.

68-74. There, the imperishable one of eighteen arms and of three eyes, meditated after the lapse of seven hundred years. Having touched (i.e. sipped) the waters of Sarasvatī and having taken bath as prescribed, the contented and devoted Hara, threw a handful of flowers on the head. Then, he made obeisance with his head, performed circumambulation, waited on Āditya with Hiraṇyagarbha etc. and performed Japa. The powerful wielder of trident, having uttered clearly, "salutation, salutation to you, the witness", danced with deep emotion, waving round his staff-like arms. When the Lord of gods was dancing, the *Gaṇas* as well as the celestials, danced with emotion, following Hara. Having attended on twilight and having danced to his satisfaction, the Lord of gods made up his mind again for a combat with the *Dānavas*. Then, all the *Dānavas* were defeated by all the troops of powerful celestials who had no fear and were protected by the arms of Śiva.

75-79. Having seen his army vanquished and considering Śaṅkara unassailable, Andhaka called Sunda and said this: "O Sunda ! You are my brother and are my confident in all matters. Therefore, having listened to the words that I speak to you, you do what is appropriate. This high-souled one is an adept in warfare and unconquerable for various reasons. However, the Daughter of the Mountain, having lotus-like eyes is in my heart. Therefore, get up, let us go there, where that lady of charming smile is. O Dānava ! There, I shall entice her in Śambhu's form. You become Nandī Gaṇeśvara, Śiva's attendant. After going there and enjoying her, I shall conquer the *Pramathas* and the celestials."

80-82. When (Andhaka) said so, Sunda said, "Very well", (and) became Śailādi and Andhaka became Śaṅkara. The powerful chiefs of the *Asura* army, having assumed the forms of Nandī and Rudra, arrived at Mandara mountain with their bodies wounded by weapons. Holding the hand of Nandī (i.e. Sunda), Andhaka (as Śiva), the foremost of *Asuras*, entered Hara's residence with a fearless mind.

83-90a. Then, the Daughter of the Mountain, having seen Andhaka coming at a distance in the guise of Maheśvara, with (bodily) splendour made dull by the (wounds) inflicted by weapons and leaning on Sunda in the guise of Śailādi, entered (her house).

Having seen him, (Pārvatī) told Mālinī, Yaṣasyā, Vijayā and Jayā: "O Jayā ! See, (how) the body of the Lord is made by the unscrupulous enemies, for my sake; so get up quickly. Bring old ghee, (piece of) cloth, salt and curds. I will myself treat the wounds of the Wielder of Pināka. You immediately do (to) cure the wounds of this my lord."

So saying, she got up from her excellent seat and welcomed with respect, taking him to be the Bull-bannered One. Having removed them (wounds) with the leaves of reeds, she keenly searched further for marks (scars). Then, she saw those two standing at the sides. O sage ! Having come to know him as the terrible *Dānava*, fraudulently concealing his person, Pārvatī then went away (from that place).

90b-96a. Andhakāsura, grasping the intent of Devī, left Sunda and ran swiftly after the beautiful spouse of Hara.

The *Daitya* ran in the same way as she went. Having utter disregard (to the *Daitya*) and stepping without hesitation, Pārvatī saw him attacking and took to heels in panic. Leaving the house, she then went into the garden with her companions. O bull among sages ! He, mad with passion, pursued her there too. Still, she did not curse him in order to preserve her penance. Because of fear from him, Gaurī entered the radiant white *Arka* flower. O sage ! Vijayā and others went incognito in the thick bushes. Then, as Pārvatī vanished, the son of Hiraṇyākṣa, holding Sunda by hand, again came back to his army.

96b-108. O best of sages ! When Andhaka came back to his army, the fierce fight between the *Pramathas* and the *Asuras* began again.

There in the battle, the best of celestials, Viṣṇu, the wielder of discus and mace, killed the army of *Asuras*, desirous of doing good to Śaṅkara. The best of *Dānavas* were pierced (in groups of) five, six, seven or eight by the arrows discharged from the *Śārṅga* (bow), as the clouds (are pierced) by the rays of the sun. Janārdana killed some with the mace and some with the discus. He severed some with the sword and reduced others to ashes by (mere) sight. Dragging (some) others with the plough, he pounded them with the pestle. *Garuḍa* struck with the flapping of his wings, with beak and with chest.

That primordial person, the creator and the Grand-old-sire (Brahmā), whirling his large lotus, sprinkled (every one) with water. Having come into contact with Brahmā's water which contained (the waters of) all holy spots, the *Gaṇas* and the groups of celestials indeed became increased by hundred-fold. Those *Dānavas*, at the contact of that sin-destroying water, became extinct together with their vehicles, as mountains (became extinct) by (the touch of) *Vajra*.

Seeing Brahmā and Hari killing the powerful *Asuras* in the battle, Indra also arrived, making up his mind to fight.

O Nārada ! Seeing him attack, the powerful *Dānava*-chief, unconquerable by the gods and the *Dānavas*, Bala, bowing down to the wielder of the mace and Brahmā (lotus-born) sitting in the aerial car, in order, hastened to fight lifting his fist. Observing him attack, the leader of celestials, whirling the *Vajra* in his arms with force, as if with a thousand arms, threw it on the head of Bala. O sage ! Though that *Vajra* was really the foremost of the weapons, became (reduced to) thousand pieces at once. Bala advanced and the master of gods, the king of celestials, became panicky and retreated, O great sage !

109. Seeing that he was retreating, Jambha surrounded by the *Bhūtas*, said this: "Stop, you are the king of the mobile and the immobile (beings) and running away (from the battlefield) is not commended in the code of conduct of a king."

110-111. O eminent sage ! Hearing the words of Jambha, Indra (of thousand eyes) was frightened and immediately approached Viṣṇu. Coming closer, he said: "O Lord Viṣṇu ! Listen to the words (of Jambha). You are the master of the past and the future. Jambha is mocking at me very much, calling as weaponless. O esteemed one ! Please give me a weapon; I am taking refuge in you."

112. Hari told that Indra: "Now, you go leaving aside the *Vajra* (and) approach Agni for a weapon. He will undoubtedly give you (one)."

113. O Nārada ! Listening to the words of Janārdana, Indra (Śakra) of inestimable prowess, took refuge in Agni and said these words—

*Śakra (Indra) said:*

114. O Agni ! My *Vajra* was broken into hundred (pieces) while striking at Bala. Jambha is challenging me; therefore, please give me a weapon.

*Pulastya said:*

115-116. The venerable Agni told him: "O Indra (Vāsava)! I am pleased with you, that you have taken refuge in me only, giving up pride." So saying, Agni caused a weapon *Śakti*, to emerge out of his *Śakti* (capacity), gave it to Indra and (then) the venerable shining one went to heaven.

117-121. Then, holding that terrific *Śakti* having hundred bells, the destroyer of enemies, attacked Jambha, desirous of killing him. Śakra along with that (*Śakti*) and the army ran after (Jambha). Then Jambha became angry and struck the best of the elephants (the vehicle of Indra). Being struck by the fist of Jambha, the elephant with its temples and forehead split, fell down, like a mountain struck by the *Vajra* of Indra in the days of yore. Indra quickly jumping from the collapsing kingly elephant, landed on the earth, skipping away the Mandara mountain. Seeing that Indra (Hari) falling (on the earth), *Siddhas* and *Cāraṇas* then said: "O Indra ! stop, do not, do not fall on earth today."

122. Listening to their words, he of controlled mind, halted for a while and told them: "How can I fight with the foes, when I am falling ?"

123-125. The *Devas* and *Gandharvas* said to him: "O king! Do not feel miserable. You fight ascending the chariot that we send to you." So saying, Viśvāvasu and others sent to Indra a large chariot made of pure gold, adorned with series of tinklers, bearing auspicious marks, having the banner of monkey and yoked with restrained horses.

126-127. Seeing the chariot arrive but without a charioteer, Indra then said. "How shall I fight and how shall I steer the horses in the battle. If someone shall become my charioteer now, then I will kill the enemies; otherwise not, on any account."

128. Then those *Gandharvas* said: "O Lord ! A charioteer is not found amongst us; you better steer the horses yourself."

129-130. Being said so, the venerable one, the Lord of celestials, leaving the excellent chariot, fell on the earth dishevelled. His head was unsteady, hair was loose and the grip on the weapon was lost. Seeing the thousand-eyed Indra fall, the earth trembled.

131. As the earth shook, the wife of sage Śamīka, engaged in austerities, said: "O lord ! Leave the boy outside happily."

132-133. Hearing the words of his wife, he asked, "What for ?" She said: "O lord ! Listen to what the astrologers have said. O best of sages ! When this earth trembles, whatever that is thrown outside, becomes doubled."

134-135. Hearing those words, the twice-born one, then took the boy, his son, and at once left him on the earth outside without hesitation. The twice-born one who went inside again for (bringing) the pair of cows was stopped by his wife: "(The time) is over and it will harm you."

136-138. Being told so, the divine sage quickly went outside and saw there two boys of identical form standing. Seeing the pair of boys, honourable by the celestials and his wife of wonderful insight, he said: "I am not getting to the truth; you please tell me what I ask; what indeed will be the traits of this second boy ? Tell me now the actions that were related by Gālava."

139. She replied: "I will not tell you today; O Lord ! I will tell you later." He said: "You tell me today only; if not I will not eat my food today."

140. She said: "O Brāhmaṇa ! Listen; I will tell you what is beneficial; because you asked me today with anxiety, he will have to be named Kāru."

141-143. When she said so, the innocent boy knowing everything about chariot, went to render assistance to Indra. The *Gandharvas* led by Viśvāvasu blessed the boy with splendour, knowing him to be going for the assistance of Indra only. The boy endowed with the splendour of *Gandharvas*, approached Indra and said: "Come on, O Lord of gods ! I will be your favourite charioteer."

144. Hearing that, Indra said: "O my boy ! Whose son are you? How can you steer the horses ? There appears a doubt in me."

145. He roared: "O Indra ! Know me to be the son of Śamīka and born of the earth. (I am) endowed with the splendour of *Gandharvas* (and) I know all about horse-carriages."

146-147. Hearing that, the venerable Indra, the best of *Yogīs* appeared in the sky; so also, the son of the twice-born one, well-known as Mātali. Then, Indra, the foremost among the celestials mounted the grand chariot and Mātali, the son of Śamīka held the reins.

148-154. Then, coming to Mandāra mountain, he entered the army of the enemies. While going in, the glorious one saw a large bow fallen there along with the arrows, having five colours–white, red, black, crimson and yellow. The best of celestials took hold of that (bow) with the arrows. Then, making obeisance mentally to the *Devas,* endowed with *Rajas, Sattva* and *Tamas,* he (Indra) fixed the arrow onto the bow, pulling the bow-string. Then, the terrible arrows with feathers of peacock and named Brahmā, Viṣṇu and Śiva, moved about in the battle, killing the *Asuras.* O Nārada! That Indra covered the sky, the corners, the earth, the quarters as well as the enemy-side with a multitude of arrows. The elephant was hit; the horse was split; the charioteer fell on to the earth; the elephant-driver came (fell) down on the earth; Jambha too was hurt by the arrow. The foot-soldiers, hit by the arrows of Indra, fell on the earth. Most of the leaders of the army were killed in the battle.

155-156. Observing then, that invincible army destroyed by Indra's arrows, Kujambha as well as Jambhāsura, holding terrific maces, attacked the imperishable lord of celestials (Viṣṇu). The venerable one, Viṣṇu, seeing them attack, quickly struck Kujambha with the enemy-destroying *Sudarśana* (discus) and he, losing life, fell on the earth from the chariot.

157-161. When he, the brother was killed by Mādhava, Jambha was overcome by anger. In a fit of rage, he, mentally afflicted, attacked Indra in the battle, like a deer (attacking) a lion. Seeing him advancing, the high-souled Indra, leaving aside the bow with the arrow, took hold of the *Śakti* which was like the *Daṇḍa* of Yama and released it to kill Jambha. Seeing the *Śakti*, resounding with the sound of bells, Jambha hit it with the mace. (*Śakti* however) reducing the mace to ashes at once, pierced Jambha at heart. The enemy of celestials being pierced at heart by the *Śakti*, fell on earth with life departed. Seeing him fallen senseless on earth, the frightened *Daityas* turned back. As Jambha was killed and the army of *Daitya* was destroyed, the delighted *Gaṇas*, while worshipping Viṣṇu were praising the heroism of Indra as well. That Indra (*Gotrabhit*–splitter of mountains) approached Śiva and stood there.

## CHAPTER SEVENTY

### Andhaka is granted Boon

*Pulastya said:*

1. When that *Daitya* army was destroyed, Śukra said to Andhaka, the Lord of *Asuras*: "O brave one! Come on, come on, today. The great *Asuras* are dead; we shall once again go to the mountain and fight with Śiva."

2-3. Andhaka told him: "O Brāhmaṇa ! What you said is not right. I do not go away from the battlefield, bringing discredit to my family. O tiger among the twice-born ones ! you see my invincible prowess. I shall conquer the *Devas*, *Dānavas* and *Gandharvas* together with Indra and Maheśvara."

4-5. Saying these words, enraged Andhaka, son of Hiraṇyākṣa pacified and said these pleasing words to the charioteer: "O powerful driver ! Take the chariot to the vicinity of Śiva, so that I shall kill the *Pramathas* and the army with a shower of arrows."

6-9. O sage ! Hearing these words of Andhaka, the charioteer, then drove the big-bodied steeds of black colour towards the place. Though impelled with all efforts, the steeds, sinking in their thighs, carried the chariot towards Hara with great difficulty. The steeds carrying the *Daitya*, though equal to wind in speed, reached thhe *Pramatha* army after more than a year. Then bending the crescent moon-like strong bow, he (*Daitya*) struck Indra, Upendra and Maheśvara with arrows (*Nārācas*).

10. Seeing the army covered by the arrows, the venerable Janārdana, the bearer of discus, the protector of the three worlds told the celestials.

*Viṣṇu said:*

11-13. O excellent celestials ! Why are you standing ? You will have prosperity by killing him. Therefore, be fast striving today, desirous of victory. May his steeds be subdued along with the charioteer; let his chariot be broken; let the enemy be made devoid of chariot. Śaṅkara will later burn him down who is made devoid of the chariot. The rising enemy should not be ignored by the intelligent preceptor of gods.

14-20. So told by Vāsudeva, the *Pramathas* along with the immortals (gods), made haste with Indra and with the Discus-bearer (Viṣṇu). In a mere twinkling of the eye, Janārdana with his mace, struck down the thousand horses, having the lustre of cloud. That Skanda pulling away the charioteer from the big chariot, rent his heart with the *Śakti* and threw him who had lost his life on earth. O sage ! Immediately Vināyaka and the other *Pramathas* along with Indra and other gods, broke the chariot together with its banner and axle. That one of great valour, devoid of chariot and giving up the bow, at once attacked the gods taking hold of the mace. Then, that foremost *Daitya*, going (forward) eight steps, told Mahādeva these reasonable words in a voice as deep as that of a cloud: "O beggar ! You are with your army and I am without companions at the moment; still I will conquer you; see my valour today."

21-22. Hearing those words, Śaṅkara put all the *Gaṇas* together with the groups of celestials along with Brahmā into his own body. Making those *Pramathas* and the gods stay in his body, Śaṅkara said: "O evil-souled one ! Come on, come on, I am also remaining alone."

23-25. Seeing that great wonder of the disappearance of the entire celestials and *Gaṇas*, the *Daitya*, holding the mace, advanced towards Śaṅkara with force. Seeing him advance, the venerable one, wielding the trident, let the excellent bull and stood on the Giriprastha as a foot-soldier. After a violent and tense fight with the attacking *Daitya*, Bhairava, who frightens the three worlds, pierced his chest.

26-30. The venerable Śiva, the Eternal One, the giver of prosperity and the promoter of beings assuming a destructive form having terrific tusks, being as resplendent as a million suns, being clad in lion's skin, having matted hair, having necklace of serpents, having a smear of filthy mud (or wearing soiled cloth), having tiger's arms, having fiery eyes-severed the enemies with the lance. O great sage ! Though the *Dānava* (Andhaka) was cleft at the chest, he took hold of Bhairava along with the lance and ran away fast for about a *Krośa*. Then the venerable one, somehow supporting himself by himself, tore quickly the mace-wielding enemy with the lance. That *Daitya*-lord, however jumped, holding the lance in his hands and threw the mace on the head of Hara.

31-36. The great *Yogī*, the lord of creatures and the power of sustenance of beings stayed there only. Then blood flowed profusely from the wound on his head, caused by the fall of the mace. From the eastern stream was born a *Bhairava*, well-known as Vidyārāja with the lustre equal to that of fire and adorned by a garland of lotuses. From another blood (stream) was born a *Bhairava* known by the name Rudra, decorated with lance and honoured by the entire world. From another (third) blood (stream) were born four *Bhairavas*, from Caṇḍa to Ekakapāli, well-known by the scholars on earth. From the blood on the earth was born a

*Bhairava* adorned with a lance and well-known as Lalitarāja, shining like Śobhāñjana. O sage ! Thus, This *Bhairava* is spoken of as having seven forms. Vighnarāja is considered as the eighth. These are the eight *Bhairavas*.

37-41. O Brāhmaṇa ! Thus, The great *Asura* of the lustre of rainbow, was fixed to the trident and held like an umbrella by the high-souled one. O Brāhmaṇa ! From the wound of the trident, his blood dropped copiously by which Mahādeva of seven forms was submerged upto his neck. Then there was a lot of sweating (on the forehead) of Śaṅkara due to fatigue. From such a forehead was born a girl smeared with blood. O Vipra (Brāhmaṇa) ! From the drop of the perspiration that fell on earth from the face of Śiva, was born a boy, as lustrous as a heap of burning embers. He, being very thirsty, drank Andhaka's blood. The girl born of the wound, licked quickly the blood (of the wound of Andhaka).

42-44. Then Lord Mahādeva, Śaṅkara, lustrous like young sun and the giver of boons in the world, told these noble words for prosperity: "O doer of welfare ! The celestials, great sages, *Pitṛs, Yakṣas, Vidyādharas* as well as human beings worship you. They please you along with oblations and with multitude of flowers in their hands; there is no doubt. (You will have) the auspicious name Carcikā, because you are smeared with blood."

45. So told by the benevolent Lord, Carcikā again went back to Girivindhyavāsinī. The beautiful lady roamed all over the earth and went to the excellent place, Hiṅgulakā mountain.

46. After she went away, the benevolent Lord bestowed on Kuja (one born of earth), a boon that was the best: "You will have lordship as a planet. Auspiciousness or inauspiciousness of the world will be (because of you) and you will have eclipse from other planets."

47-49. Hara, the venerable *Bhairava,* made Andhaka dried of his strength and reduced him to skin and skeleton only without blood, by the sun and fire of his eyes for a thousand divine years. The King of *Asuras* became absolved of sins, by the fire emerging from Śambhu. Then, cognising Īśa as the lord of beings, as of multiforms, as the protector of all the movables and immovables, as the overlord of everything, as the imperishable one, as the protector of the three worlds, as the benevolent one, as the most distinguished one, as the one prostrated to and worshipped by all the Celestials and others, as the primordial one, Andhaka, thereafter made this eulogy.

*Andhaka said:*

50-55. Salutation to you, O terrific one ! O one of frightening form! O guardian of the three worlds ! O wielder of the sharp trident ! O skull-bearer ! O one having garland of serpents ! O triple-eyed one ! Please protect me, one of evil intentions. Victory to you, O Lord of everything ! O one of all-form ! O one whose feet are bowed down to by the celestials as well as *Asuras* ! O husband of the mother of three worlds ! O Bull-Bannered One ! I, who am afraid, have come to your refuge, O Protector ! O master ! Gods call you Śiva; *Siddhas* as Hara and the great sages as Sthāṇu; *Yakṣas* speak of you as Bhīma; human beings as Maheśvara; *Bhūtas* as the lord of *Bhūtas*; nocturnal beings worship (you) as *Ugra*; holy Pitṛs (worship you) as Bhava; salutation to you; I am a servant of you; O Hara ! Protect me; O protector of the world ! Destroy my sins; you are the three gods; you are the three *Yugas*; you are the three *Dharmas*; you are the one (adorned) with three lotuses; O omnipresent one ! O triple-eyed one ! You are Trayyāruṇi; you are the *Veda*; you are the imperishable one; purify me; I have come to your refuge; you are *Triṇāciketa*; you are established in three states; you are learned in the six *Aṅgas*; you have no attachment to women and related objects; you are the master of the three worlds; purify me, O Śambhu ! I am your servant; with fear, I have taken refuge in you.

56-64. O Śaṅkara ! O Great Lord of *Bhūtas* ! O Girīśa ! Grave sin has been committed by me, whose mind was overpowered by the enemy *Kāma*. I entreat you; I bow down to you with my head; I am sin; I am a sinner; I am an evil-souled one; I am born of sin; save me, O God of Gods ! Please be a destroyer of all my sins. There is no offence on my part, for I, such an evil-doer, have been touched by you. O Īśvara! Be pleased with me; you are the doer; you are the sustainer; you are victory and you are great victory; you are the auspicious one; you are Oṁkāra; you are Īśāna; you are the imperishable one; you are the immovable one; you are Brahmā, the creator; you are Viṣṇu, the protector; you are Maheśvara; you are Indra; you are the syllable, *Vaṣaṭ*; you are virtue; you are the foremost of the *Tuṣitas*; you are the subtle one; you are the manifest form; you are the unmanifest form; you are *Dhīvara*; all this universe–the immovable and the movable–is pervaded by you; you are the beginning, the end and the middle; you are also the thousand-footed one; you are the victory; you are the thousand-eyed one; you are the one called *Cittapa*; you are the stout-armed one; you are the infinite, all-pervading, omnipresent, Haṁsa; you are the one rich in virtue and the imperishable one; you are the lord of speech, the unperturbed one, Rudra, Paśupati and Śiva; you are the three *Vedas*; you are the one of restrained anger, of restrained enemies, of restrained senses; you are victory, the wielder of trident; protect me; I have taken refuge in you.

*Pulastya said:*

65-66. O Brāhmaṇa ! Being prayed to thus by the Lord of *Daityas*, the pleased Maheśvara of reddish-brown eyes, told the son of Hiraṇyākṣa: "O Leader of *Dānavas* ! I am pleased; I am satisfied, O Andhaka ! May you fare well; you choose the boon you desire; I will grant you that."

*Andhaka said:*

67-69. Ambikā is mother to me; you, Tryambaka, are my father; I bow down to the feet of the mother; they are to be greatly respected by me. Now that Īśāna is benevolent, may my vast misdeeds–physical and mental–and the evil thoughts be absolved. So also, O Maheśvara ! May my *Dānava* characteristics leave me; may my devotion to you be firm; please grant me this boon.

-eyed Lord. Inviting the *Gaṇas* along with Nandī and placing Bhṛṅgī in front, Śiva showed him (to them) saying, "This is indeed Andhaka." Seeing the enemy, the *Dānava*-lord, whose muscles were utterly dried and who had acquired *Gaṇa*-headship, they praised the Bull-bannered Lord.

75-77. Then, the venerable one embracing the gods told them: "You go to your places and enjoy the three types of happiness. May Indra too go to the excellent Malaya mountain and after attending to his job there, may he go to heaven." So saying, making obeisance to the Grandsire and embracing Janārdana, Śiva sent away the celestials, after bidding them farewell.

78-89. Mahendra went to Malaya and after doing his work there, departed to Heaven. After Indra and other leaders departed, the venerable Śiva, Hara, let the *Gaṇas* out of the middle of his body. The *Gaṇas* too, after meeting Śaṅkara, seated on their respective vehicles, departed to the excellent places in their respective regions, where there are cows yielding one's wish, trees yielding fruits of one's wish, (where) rivers are flowing with nectar and ponds have *Pāyasa* as mud, O Nārada !

When the *Pramathas* went back to their respective places, Maheśvara taking Andhaka by hand and with Nandī came to the Mountain (Mandara). Hara returned home, after the lapse of two thousand years. He saw the Daughter of the Mountain staying in the white *Arka* flower. Soon after seeing him endowed with all characteristics return, she abandoned the *Arka* flower and immediately called out her companions.

Being called by Devī, Jayā and others quickly arrived. Surrounded by them, she stood looking forward to meet Hara. Then the Three-eyed Lord seeing Girijā, Andhaka, the *Dānava* and also Nandī, embraced Girijā with joy. Then he said: "O Devī ! This Andhaka has been made your servant by me. O lady of charming smile ! See your son come back." So saying, he told Andhaka: "O my son ! Come on, come on quick. Take refuge in the mother; she brings welfare to you."

So told by the all-pervading Lord, Nandī and Andhaka, the *Gaṇa*-leader, approached Ambikā and both of them, bowed down to her feet. O great sage ! Andhaka, then bending down with devotion, recited a prayer to Gaurī, which is of great merit. It destroys sins and is in consonance with *Veda*.

*Andhaka said:*

OM. Obeisance to you. I prostrate myself before Bhavānī, who is dear to the past and future beings, the sustainer, the creator, the mother of Skanda, the beloved of Mahādeva, the giver of milk, the consciousness, the mother of three worlds, the supporter, the mother of gods, the *Veda*, the *Smṛti*, compassion, bashfulness, love, the mother of *Kāma*, to the one always purifying, the destroyer of *Daitya* army, Mahāmāyā, Sumāyā, Vaijayantī, the auspicious one, Kālarātri, the mother of Govinda, the daughter of the King of Mountains, the one worshipped by all gods, the one worshipped by all *Bhūtas*, *Vidyā*, Sarasvatī, to the queen of the Three-eyed Lord. I take refuge in *Mṛḍānī*, the refuge; obeisance, obeisance to you.

90. Being prayed to by Andhaka, the splendid one was satisfied and said: "O my son ! I am pleased; ask for the best boon."

*Bhṛṅgī said:*

91. O Pārvatī ! May my sins of three types become extinct; O Ambikā ! May my devotion be always in Īśvara.

*Pulastya said:*

92. Gaurī, then told the son of Hiraṇyākṣa: "Be it so; worshipping Śarva in my vicinity, you be the master of the *Gaṇas.*"

93. Thus, Maheśvara assuming a terrifying body through his power and having an odd number of eyes, made him who had such (a large body) into having the frightening form of *Bhṛṅgī.*

94. O great sage ! This holy anecdote enhancing the fame of Śiva, purifying and giving prosperity, is related to you. This should be recounted to the most pious Dvijas, by one seeking virtue, longevity and health.

## CHAPTER SEVENTY-ONE

### Birth of Maruts

*Nārada said:*

1. O best of the twice-born ! It behoves you to recount to me what was done by Mahendra in Malaya, and what was the job successfully accomplished by him ?

*Pulastya said:*

2. O sage ! Listen to what Mahendra did in Malaya for the welfare of the world as well as for his own welfare.

3-8. After being defeated by the troops of celestials, the *Asuras* led by Maya and Tāra were engaged in going to the nether world at the words of Aghāsura. O Vipra (Brāhmaṇa)! (on their way), they saw the big mountain Malaya whose caves were resorted to by *Siddhas,* which was thickly covered by creepers and was full of intoxicated beasts, which was over-grown with very cool sandal trees infested by serpents and over which had spread the fragrance of *Mādhavī* flowers. Seeing that cool shade, those (*Asuras*) led by Maya and Tāra who were tired and emaciated by exercise, desired to camp there. As they camped there, the sweet-scented cool southern breeze wafted slowly, gratifying the sense of smell. All the great *Asuras* took delight in that place, making enemity with those living there who were worshipped by one and all.

9-11. Coming to know about them, Śaṅkara then sent Indra to Malaya. That Indra, while going, saw the Mother-Cow (Surabhi) on the way. Circumambulating her, Indra saw the shining mountain and (further) saw all the *Dānavas* who were rejoicing and indulging in enjoyments. The Killer of Bala (Indra), then challenged all those great *Asuras*. They too, unperturbed, came strewing a multitude of arrows.

12-17. O Brāhmaṇa-sage ! Seeing them come, (Indra) seated in a chariot and appearing wonderful, (completely) covered them with showers of arrows, as cloud would do on seeing a mountain. After covering Maya and other *Dānavas* with arrows, Indra killed Pāka with sharp-tipped arrows having heron feathers. Then the omnipresent lord of all immortals got the name Pākaśāsana because of subduing (*Pāka*) forcefully with the arrows. He severed another *Asura*, Pura by name, the son of Bāṇāsura, with arrows having feathers; therefore, he became Purandara. O Brāhmaṇa ! Killing like this, *Gotrabhit* (Indra) conquered the *Dānava* army in the battle. That defeated (army) went to *Rasātala*. It was for this purpose that Indra was sent to Malaya mountain by Tryambaka. O best of sages ! What else would you like to hear ?

*Nārada said:*

18. O Brāhmaṇa ! Why is Indra, the lord of gods called *Gotrabhit* ? This doubt lurks in my mind.

*Pulastya said:*

19. Hear from me why Indra is spoken of as *Gotrabhit* and also what the destroyer of foes did after Hiraṇyakaśipu was killed.

20. O Nārada ! Losing his son, Diti asked Kaśyapa: "O Lord! You are my benefactor; give me a son who kills Indra."

21-22. Kaśyapa then told her: "O lady of dark eyes ! If you would remain pure and (engage in prescribed) activities for a thousand divine years, then would you bear that son who would be the leader of the three worlds and the killer of foes; not otherwise, O my dear !"

23. So told by her husband, that Diti took up the vow. The sage (Kaśyapa) impregnating her, went over to *Udayaparvata.*

24-25. After he departed, the Thousand-eyed (Indra), the foremost of the celestials immediately came to the hermitage and said these words to Diti: "I will do your service if you permit." " Very well", said she, impelled by destiny.

26. Purandara attended to activities like collecting fuel and so on obediently to achieve his purpose and was looking out for a fault (on the part of Diti), like a serpent searching for a hole.

27-28. Once, at the end of ten hundred years, she, engaged in penance and endowed with great purity had a wash for her head. Keeping her head on the knees and spreading out her hair, she fell asleep. The ends of her hair were touching her feet.

29-37. O Nārada ! That god of thousand-eyes knowing it to be the chance, entered the womb of the mother through the nasal passage. Entering the womb of the mother of *Daityas,* Purandara grew up and saw a big boy with his face turned upwards and keeping the hand on the waist. So also Indra saw on his face, a piece of flesh sparkling like pure crystal and he took it in his hand. Then Indra, full of rage, pressed the piece of flesh in his hands. Because of it the piece became hard. Half of it grew upwards and another half grew downwards. That piece of flesh grew to become a hundred-knotted *Vajra*. O Brāhmaṇa ! With that hundred-knotted *Vajra*, he cut the foetus borne by Diti seven-fold and that (foetus) cried long. Then Diti awoke and she came to know about the doing of Indra. She heard the voice of her baby-boy crying. Indra, however, said: "O you ! Silly one! Do not cry in such a rattling voice." Having said so, he severed each of them (seven) seven-fold again. They became Indra's divine servants, Maruts by name. Being placed in front, they move with various pleasing activities.

38-39. Then, Indra along with the *Vajra*, emerging out of the womb, told Diti with folded hands, afraid of being cursed: "It is not my fault; he was my enemy; therefore, he was killed by me; O madam ! You should not be angry with me."

*Diti said:*

40. There is no fault of yours in this. I think it had been destined earlier, for he got killed even as the period was complete.

*Pulastya said:*

41. So saying and pacifying those children, the passionate Diti, immediately sent them with the Lord of gods.

42. O great sage ! Thus in the days of yore, the venerable Mahendra afflicted by fear, aborted and severed with *Vajra*, his own brothers in the womb; hence, he became well-known as *Gotrabhit*.

## CHAPTER SEVENTY-TWO

### The Birth of Maruts (continued)

*Nārada said:*

1-2. Who were these Maruts, the best of the sons of Diti, of whom you spoke about, who were in the atmospheric region earlier ? Please tell me. O best of men ! You also tell me about those who were in the aerial path in the bygone *Manvantaras.*

*Pulastya said:*

3. Listen, I will relate to you the birth of earlier Maruts from *Svāyambhuva-Manvantara* to the present *Manvantara.*

4-6. Svāyambhuva's son was known by the name Manu Priyavrata. His son was Savana, known all over the world. O divine sage ! That king died childless. His wife Suvedā wept, overcome by grief. She did not allow (the body) to be burnt. She, as a forlorn one, remained embracing (the body of) her husband, wailing repeatedly," O my lord; Oh ! My lord."

7. Then from the sky an incorporeal voice spoke—

"O queen ! Do not wail any more. If you have virtue of the best order, then enter the fire with (the body of) your husband."

8. The distressed queen Suvedā, hearing that voice from the sky said: "I am bewailing for this unfortunate king who is childless and not for myself, O aerial being !"

9. He then said: "O young woman ! Do not bewail; seven sons will be there to this king; quickly enter the fire; I have spoken the truth; you trust me now."

10-14. So told by the Sky-farer, that lady, loyal to her husband, having laid (the body of) the worthy husband on the pyre and lighting it with fire, entered the fire thinking (of him only). After a while, that king endowed with splendour, arose together with his wife. Then, he, able to move at will, soared into the sky along with his queen, the daughter of Sunābha. To that bull among kings was born excellent sons endowed with vigour and prowess, who became great and famous kings on earth. The queen had her monthly course as she went. Because of his divine association, he remained in the sky with his wife for five days. Then, on the sixth day, thinking that her period should not go in vain, the king moving at will had sexual intercourse with the beautiful lady. Then his semen fell from the sky. At the end of the ejection of semen, the king with his queen proceeded to *Brahmaloka* through the divine path, O one rich in penance. His sons were valiant, adept in *Astras* and truthful.

15-20. The cloud-coloured semen that fell from the sky was seen eagerly by the wives of (seven) sages–Samādā, Nalinī, Puṣyatī, Citrā, Viśālā, Haritā and Alinīlā. Having seen that fallen on a lotus and thinking it to be ambrosia they did not speak to the sages (their husbands), rich in penance, with a desire to get youthfulness for ever. Then, having taken bath and worshipping their respective husbands as per precept, the ladies, with the permission of their husbands, drank that semen of the king contained in the lotus, taking it to be nectar. The moment they drank the semen ejected by the foremost king, those wives of ascetics became devoid of *Brāhmaṇical* splendour and all the sages divorced their defiled wives. O sage ! The ladies gave birth to seven sons who wailed ferociously. The whole world was filled with the sound of their wailing.

21-23. There came the venerable Brahmā, the Grandsire of the world. Having approached the children, he said: "O valiant ones ! Do not cry. Maruts will be the name of you who stay in the sky." So saying, Brahmā, the lord of gods and the Grandsire of the world moving in the sky, took them and ordained them to be Maruts. They were the Maruts in the first *Svāyambhuva-Manvantara.*

24-26. O Nārada ! I will tell you about the Maruts in the *Svārociṣa-Manvantara;* listen. The lustrous son of Svārociṣa was Ṛtadhvaja by name. His seven sons were as powerful as

*Ādityas.* Those kings went away to Mahāmeru mountain for performing austerities and for worshipping Brahmā with a view to attain the position of Indra. Then the wise Thousand-eyed One (Indra) was indeed afflicted with fear.

27-30a. O Nārada ! He, an adept speaker, spoke to Pūtanā, the chief of *Apsarās*: "O Pūtanā ! O sportive one ! Go to the Mahāmeru mountain. There the sons of Ṛtadhvaja are performing severe penance. O lovely one ! Act in such a way that their penance is hindered. O charming one ! Let them not accomplish (their desire)."

So told by Indra, Pūtanā, endowed with beauty, speedily came to the place where penance was being performed by them.

30b-38a. Not far from their hermitage was the river Mandodavāhinī. All those brothers came to that river for ablution. She of charming features too, got into the river for a bath. O sage ! Those kings saw her taking bath and were perturbed; so their semen was ejaculated. A female aquatic being swallowed it. It was Śaṅkhinī, the spouse of Mahāśaṅkha, the foremost of sharks.

The brothers whose austerity was ruined, went back to their paternal kingdom. That *Apsarā* going back to Indra, made a truthful report.

Then, after a long time, that shark in the form of a *conch* was lifted up with large nets by a fisherman. Having seen that huge *conch* lying on the ground, the fisherman reported it to the sons of Ṛtadhvaja. Those noble ones, the followers of *Yoga* among *Yogins*, came there. They carried (the conch) to their residence and left it in the pond of the city. In course of time, that Śaṅkhinī gave birth to seven babies. Even as they were born, she attained salvation.

38b-41. The Children not having either the mother or the father and moving in water, cried for their mother's milk. Then there arrived the Grandsire and said: "O my sons! do not cry; be quiet. You will become gods, moving in the aerial region." So saying and taking them with him, Brahmā appointed them as gods in the atmospheric region and went to his abode. So were the Maruts pacified in the *Svārociṣa-Manvantara.*

42-46. O one having penance as wealth ! Listen about the Maruts at the time of Uttama (Manu). The king of Niṣadha, born in the family of Uttama was famous as Vapuṣmān (one with a worthy physique), who had a body comparable to the sun. His son, Jyotiṣmān had excellent qualities and was pious. He performed austerities on the banks of Mandākinī, desiring a son. His wife of lovely hips, the daughter of the preceptor of gods was attending on him who had undertaken such an austerity. She brought (to him) fruits, flowers, fuel, *Darbha* grass, water and such things. The lady of lotus-petal-like eyes very well attended to the service of guests too. Attending on her husband, she became emaciated and was (reduced) to only veins.

47-48. (Once) that lady of charming body, endowed with splendour, was seen in the forest by the seven sages. Then seeing that lady of charming body, emaciated through austerity, they enquired the purpose of her austerity as well as that of her husband. She said: "Our austerity is for a son."

49-50. O Brāhmaṇa ! Those seven great sages became benevolent and said: "You go back. By the grace of the great sages, you will have seven sons endowed with the excellences of both of you; there is no doubt." So saying, all those great sages went away.

51-55. That saintly king with his wife went back to his city. Then, after a long time, that slim, dear queen of the king got impregnated by that excellent king. When the wife was pregnant, the king died. That devoted wife, who too wanted to follow her husband, was dissuaded by the ministers but she did not refrain (from it). Placing (the body of her) husband on the pyre, she too climbed on it. Then from the middle of the fire, a piece of unburnt (flesh) fell into the water, O sage ! That, being soaked in cold water, got divided into seven. They grew into Maruts in the *Uttama-Manvantara.*

56. O lover of singing ! Instruments and of quarrel ! I will speak about the Maruts who were in the *Tāmasa-Manvantara.*

57-62a. The son of Tāmasamanu was one Citraka, famous as Dantadhvaja. Desiring a son, he offered in fire his flesh, blood, bones, hair of the body and of head, the thick sinew, marrow, liver and the semen. King Citraka (offered these) for getting a son; so we have heard. Soon after the semen was dropped on the seven flames, there was a voice: "Do not throw in" and the king, however, died. Then from the fire emerged (seven) babies having seven types of splendour and they cried ferociously, O sage ! Hearing their noise, the venerable Lotus-born came there and after consideration, made them the celestial Maruts. O Brāhmaṇa ! These were the Maruts, the group of gods, in the *Tāmasa(-Manvantara)*.

62b-75. O one rich in penance ! Hear about those who were the Maruts in the *Raivata(-Manvantara)*. In the family of Raivata, there was a wealthy person known by the name Ripujit who conquered all enemies. He had no son. Having worshipped the Sun, the repository of brilliance, through austerities, he obtained a girl, Surati. Taking her (with him), he went home. O Brāhmaṇa ! As she was residing in her father's house, her father died. She, engulfed by grief, prepared herself to give up her life. O Nārada ! Then the Seven Sages dissuaded her (from committing suicide). All those hermits had set their mind on her. Unable to get over the grief, she lighted the fire and entered it. The sages saw it and with their mind fixed on her, became pensive. Seeing her dead, the sages went away saying, "Alas! Alas!" From the fire, then emerged seven boys. They being separated from their mother, wailed. The Grandsire, the protector of the world, pacified them and made them the group of Maruts. O one having penance as wealth ! These were the Maruts who were born in the *Raivata-Manvantara.*

Hear me; I will relate (to you) about the Maruts in the *Cākṣuṣa-Manvantara.* There was a truthful, pure hermit, well-known as Maṅki (Maṅkaṇaka) in the *Sapta-sārasvata-tīrtha.* He performed a severe penance. O sage ! The gods sent Tuṣitā to create impediments to him. The lovely woman, having come to the bank of the river, disturbed him. Then his semen got ejaculated in the waters of *Sapta-sārasvata*. Sage Maṅkaṇaka cursed that perplexed enemy: "Get away, O silly one ! You will get ample retribution for this sin. Your destruction is going to happen during a sacrificial performance." Cursing thus, the celebrated sage went back to his hermitage and from the seven (streams of) Sarasvatī, seven Maruts were born.

76. O great sage ! Thus you are told about the *Maruts* spreading in the world who were born in earlier ages, by listening to whose birth, one evades rebirth and will have abundance of virtue.

## CHAPTER SEVENTY-THREE

### Killing of Kālanemi

*Pulastya said:*

1-3. O lover of quarrel ! It was for this purpose that *Daitya* Bali was made the king. Prahlāda was his minister and Śukra, his priest. Learning that Bali, the *Daitya*, the son of Virocana was coronated, all the *Asuras* came to meet him. Seeing all the members of his clan arrive and receiving them rankwise, he asked thus: "What is propitious to me ?"

4-9. At that they told him: "O handsome *Asura* ! Listen to what is propitious to you and also what is beneficial to us. Your grandfather Hiraṇyakaśipu was powerful and was the heroic protector of *Dānavas*; he was Indra in the three worlds. The excellent celestial Viṣṇu who assumed the body of a lion came and tore him asunder with nails before the very eyes of the *Dānava*-chiefs. O mighty one ! The kingdom of the high-souled Andhaka was taken away for their (gods) sake by Lord Śaṅkara, the wielder of the trident. Again, your another father Jambha too was killed by Indra. Kujambha was also killed like an animal by Viṣṇu, before everybody.

Śaṅkha, Pāka and your brother Sudarśana were killed by Mahendra. Your father Virocana was also killed, I tell you."

10-14. O Brāhmaṇa ! Having heard the destruction of his clan by Indra, the *Dānava* together with all those powerful *Asuras* got prepared (for a war). Some *Asuras* proceeded for war with the gods on chariots, some on elephants, some on horses and others on foot. The strong Maya, the ferocious commander, went in front; in the middle of the army was Bali and Kālanemi at the back. Śālva whose prowess was well-known, went restraining the left flank and the terrible one, by name Tāraka, the dreadful right flank. O lover of quarrel! Thousands, millions and billions of *Dānavas* advanced for a war with the celestials.

15. Having learnt the endeavour of *Asuras*, Indra, the Lord of celestials told the celestials: "(Let us proceed) with our army to fight with the assembly of *Daityas.*"

16-21. Saying these words, the powerful Lord of celestials ascended the chariot, whose horses were controlled by the venerable Mātali. When Indra ascended the chariot, the celestials moved out riding their respective vehicles, looking forward for a battle. *Ādityaṣ, Vasus, Rudras, Sādhyas, Viśvedevas, Aśvins, Vidyādharas, Guhyakas, Yakṣas, Rākṣasas, Pannagas,* saintly kings, *Siddhas* as well as various *Bhūtaṣ* in groups advanced hastily (to the place) where the army of the *Daityas* was standing; some riding elephants, some riding chariots, some on horses and some riding shining aerial cars carried by birds, O Nārada ! At that juncture, the wise Vainateya arrived and riding on him arrived Viṣṇu, the excellent one among celestials.

22. Indra along with all the leading celestials, bowed down with his head to the imperishable Lord of the three worlds who had arrived.

23-25. Then, at the head of the army of gods went Kārttikeya, the wielder of mace. Viṣṇu, went guarding the rear and in the middle was Indra. O sage ! Jayanta was the guard on the left side and the powerful Varuṇa, went as the guard on the right side. Then the immortals' glorious army guarded by Skanda, Indra, Viṣṇu, Varuṇa and Sūrya, having an assemblage of arms, wielding various missiles and weapons, encountered the enemy army near the mountain.

26-34. The battle between the *Devas* and the *Asuras* took place on the pleasing and auspicious slopes of the eastern mountain which had with flat rocks and which was treeless and birdless. O sage ! There was violence in both those armies because of their coming close, as between an ape and an elephant on that excellent mountain in the days of yore. O celestial hermit ! The tawny battle dust raised by the chariots on the battle-front was like a cloud tinged with twilight red in the sky. Then, there was tumultuous fighting; nothing could be visualised; only the sounds of those uttering 'cut', 'pierce' were incessantly heard. Then, (there was) terrible slaughter of the *Dānavas* together with that of the *Devas*. There arose a stream of blood bringing down the dust. As the dust subsided, the multitude of *Devas* along with wise Skanda, immediately attacked that large *Dānava* force. The *Devas* protected by the arms of Kumāra, killed the *Dānavas* and the striking *Dānavas* guarded by Maya, killed the *Devas*.

35-36. O Nārada ! Then, the best of the celestials being without a relish of the portion of nectar, along with their army were defeated by the *Daityas* in the war. Having seen the celestials defeated, the enemy-killing Lord, having the banner of Vainateya, lifted his *Śārṅga* bow and there afterwards killed (the *Dānavas*) with streams of arrows.

37-40. Those *Dānavas*, the sons of Diti, being struck by Viṣṇu and by *Garuḍa*, resorted to the powerful *Asura*, Kālanemi. O Brāhmaṇa ! Assuring them security, he went there, where Mādhava was and grew (in size), like a disease neglected. The mighty one (*Asura*) threw into his wide mouth taking hold of whomsoever–*Deva, Yakṣa, Kinnara*–he would touch by his hand. With impetuosity, accompanied by the sons of Diti, the foremost of the *Dānavas*, though weaponless, crushed swiftly with hands, feets and nails, the army of *Devas* including Indra, the Sun and the Moon in the war. Performing (actions) similar to fire, he had the form of fire of deluge encompassing horizontally and vertically the earth and the heaven and desired to burn down all this world.

41. Seeing the very powerful enemy growing, all the leading *Devas*, *Gandharvas*, *Siddhas* and *Sādhyas* and other chieftains fled in various directions with tremulous eyes due to fear. Those leaping *Daityas* puffed up with pride, made Viṣṇu adored by the hosts of immortals and having a charming crown, lose his glory, by hurling (on him) various weapons and missiles.

42. Seeing the *Daityas*, Maya, Bali and others with Kālanemi as chief (acting) thus, Viṣṇu pulling incessantly (the string of) *Śārṅga*, covered them along with their chariots, elephants and horses who were of reduced prowess, by eying them with the eyes reddish due to rage, with chest-piercing, well-feathered thunderbolt-like arrows called *Nārāca*, like a cloud (covering) a mountain.

43. Being covered by such arrows as *Nārācas* and crescent-moons, shining like the *Daṇḍa* of Yama and discharged by the hands of Hari, those (*Daityas*) led by Bali and Maya, exceedingly panicky, pushed in haste the hundred-faced *Dānava*-chief, Kālanemi to the forefront. He faced the Lord of the army of *Devas*, Keśava of unmatched prowess and the protector of the world.

44-46. Seeing him of hundred-heads, holding the mace and appearing like the peak of a big mountain, Viṣṇu kept aside the *Śārṅga* and immediately took hold of the discus in hand.

Encountering the Lord himself, the *Dānava*, laughing for a long time at the Lord, the feller of *Daitya*-tree and the wearer of garland, spoke in a voice resembling that of a cloud: "This is the conqueror of the son of Danu, the agitator of the army of the sons of Danu, the most wrathful foe, the one who killed Madhu with weapon, the one who brought an end to Hiraṇyākṣa, the one delighted in being worshipped with varieties of flowers. Where does this matchless, mischievous one go, when he had fallen within my sight? If he enters into a fight with me, really the lotus-eyed one does not go home. The celestials with terror-afflicted eyes will see him taking to dust, with his limbs loosened by the blow of my fist."

47. So saying to Madhusūdana, Kālanemi with his lips quivering in a fit of rage, threw his mace on the Lord of birds, as Indra (hurls) his *Vajra* on the mountain.

48-54. Observing the falling frightful mace thrown by the *Dānava*, Viṣṇu cut it with the discus, like the past action (disrupting) the wishes of one who is very unfortunate. Smashing the terrible mace of the *Dānava*, Viṣṇu then went near him and swiftly severed his stout arms. With the arms severed by the formidable Viṣṇu, Kālanemi appeared like a hill burnt down. Then, Mādhava with rage, cut his head with the discus and felled it on the ground, like a ripened *Tāla* fruit. The armless and headless torso (of Kālanemi) which was like a topless *Tāla* tree in a forest, stood motionless like the excellent mountain Meru. O sage ! Vainateya, the lord of birds, felled it on the earth with his chest. (It fell) like the head of Rāhu, destroyed (cut) by the *Vajra* of Mahendra, falling from the sky on to the earth. When the commander of the *Dānava* army was killed, the *Daityas* and *Asura*-chiefs, except Bāṇa, subdued by the celestials, fled away, abandoning their weapons, with their hair, armour and clothing loosened.

## CHAPTER SEVENTY-FOUR

### Prahlāda's advice to Bali

*Pulastya said:*

1. As Bāṇa's army returned (to the battle field), the *Dānavas*, with their weapons, desirous of fighting again, proceeded quickly towards the army of *Devas*.

2. Viṣṇu of unlimited prowess, knowing the son of Bali to be invincible, called all the celestials and said—

" You fight without any worry."

3. Then, as directed by Viṣṇu, the Devas led by Indra waged war against the *Dānavas*. Viṣṇu, however, disappeared.

4. Learning about Mādhava's departure, Śukra told Bali: "O Bali ! Govinda has left the celestials; now you conquer."

5-11. He, the lustrous one, pleased by the words of the Purohita at the departure of Janārdana, taking hold of a mace, attacked the army of *Devas*. Then, Bāṇa, carrying weapons in his thousand arms, attacked the army of *Devas* and killed the *Devas* in thousands. O sage ! The mighty *Maya* also assuming various forms through magical power (*Māyā*), gave fight to the army of immortals. Vidyujjihva, Para, Bhadra, Vṛsaparva, Sitekṣaṇa, Vipāka, Vikṣara–all these too chased the army and the *Devas*. Being beaten by the sons of Diti, the *Devas* led by Indra, almost turned their back after Lord Janārdana departed. All the (*Dānavas*) led by Bali and Bāṇa, keen on conquering the three worlds, chased from the back, the frustrated troops of celestials. Being destroyed by the sons of Diti, the *Devas* with Indra were afflicted with fear and leaving Heaven, they went over to Brahmaloka.

12-14. As the celestials with Indra went over to Brahmā's abode, Bali along with his sons, relatives and followers, became the enjoyer of Heaven. O Brāhmaṇa ! The powerful Bali became Indra; Bāṇa became Yama; Maya was Varuṇa; Rāhu was Soma and Hrāda, Agni; Svarbhānu was Sūrya and Śukra was Bṛhaspati. Whoever other *Devas* were there, in place of all of them, the foes of celestials were appointed.

15. At the end of *Dvāpara* and the beginning of the fifth *Kaliyuga* which was terrible, the war between the *Devas* and the *Asuras* took place when Bali became Indra.

16-19. Bali was the master of the ten worlds, as the seven *Pātālas* (nether worlds) and the three worlds well-known as *Bhūḥ*, *Bhuvaḥ* and *Svaḥ* were under his control. He himself resided in Heaven, enjoying pleasures not easily attainable. There *Gandharvas* led by Viśvāvasu attended on him. O

Celestial hermit ! Tilottamā and other *Apsarās* performed dance and *Yakṣas, Vidyādharas* and others played on the instruments. O Brāhmaṇa ! This Bali, the Lord of *Daityas* enjoying heavenly pleasures, mentally recalled his grandfather, Prahlāda.

20-22. Being recalled by the grandson, that *Asura*, the staunch Bhāgavata, hastily arrived in the imperishable Heaven from the nether world. Immediately on seeing him arrive, Bali got up from the throne and folding his hands, bowed to his feet. After raising the valiant Bali who had fallen on his feet, Prahlāda embraced him and sat on a grand seat.

23-26. Bali told him: "O grandfather ! By your grace, the celestials have been defeated by me and the kingdom of Indra has been snatched away by force of power.

O father, with me ! Your servant standing before you ! You enjoy this kingdom of three worlds whose best celestials have been subdued by my prowess. I would be meritorious by this much-being engaged in worshipping your feet daily and partaking of the remnants of your food. O most pious one ! A person can neither protect the kingdom nor will there be satisfaction, if one does not serve the elders, if one does not attend (on them)."

27-29. O best of the twice-born ones ! After listening to the words spoken by Bali, Prahlāda said this, conducive to the attainment of *Dharma, Artha* and *Kāma*: "O Bali ! Earlier my kingdom was made free from dangers by me and was looked after (well); my companions were honoured; liberal gifts were given; I begot sons and at present I am engaged in attaining Yoga. O my son ! I have duly received it (kingdom) and am again giving it back to you. You be always like this, intent of serving the elders."

30-33. O Brāhmaṇa ! Having said thus, he took Bali immediately by his right hand and placed him on the throne of Indra. That *Daitya*-Lord sitting on Indra's auspicious throne studded with all jewels, shone like Maghavan (Indra).

Sitting on the throne, Bali with folded hands said to Prahlāda, in a voice as deep as that of a cloud: "O father !

While protecting the three worlds, what should be done by me for (achieving) *Dharma, Artha, Kāma* and *Mokṣa*; you please direct us."

34. Simultaneously with his speech, Śukra told Prahlāda: "O valiant one ! You tell us what is proper, in reply to his question."

35-49. Listening to the words of Bali and Śukra, *Asura* Prahlāda, a *Bhāgavata,* said these excellent words in respect of *Dharma* and *Artha*: "O King ! O my son ! Take up such actions like procuring the riches beneficial to the three worlds in the long run and the wealth without violating *Dharma*; perform actions satisfying all beings and yielding the fruits of *Trivarga*; (you also do) what is salutary here and hereafter. O one of great splendour ! Now endeavour in such way that you will be applauded, that you will have fame, that there will not be any tinge of ignominy.

Men of excellence desire to accumulate riches for this purpose. Because of (such riches) these persons–persons of noble birth, those immersed in distress, friends, persons thrown out of the clan, aged ones, kinsmen, persons of character, learned men (*Vipra*)–reside in our house along with renown and glory, fully satiated. Therefore, O one of unblemished body and action ! O my son ! Endeavour in such a way that these (persons mentioned above) live with you who are (ruling) the kingdom and who are born of a noble family and that you will become glorious in the world.

Great kings achieve prosperity here in such a land which is ever adorned by Brāhmaṇas, is full of Kṣatriyas, is thickly sown (with seeds), is occupied by persons interested in serving others. Therefore, let the foremost Brāhmaṇas learned in *Vedas* and *Śāstras* help your kings to perform sacrifices; let the leading Brāhmaṇas perform divine sacrifices. By the smoke of sacrificial fire, there comes peace to the king. May the *Vipras* (Brāhmaṇas) endowed with austerity and learning be engaged in offering sacrifices and teaching and be honoured by the kṣatriyas after obtaining your permission. May the kṣatriyas be engaged in self-study and sacrifices; be liberal and live wielding the weapons; being duty-bound let them protect the people, O *Daitya*-lord ! May the Vaiśyas be engaged in study and sacrifices; be liberal; be engaged in cultivation, animal husbandry and be living on trade. May the Śūdras be always engaged in serving the Brāhmaṇas, Kṣatriyas and Vaiśyas and always carrying out your orders, O best of the *Asuras* ! O Lord of the sons of Diti ! When the Varṇas are devoted to their respective duties, then *Dharma* progresses; as there is prosperity of Dharma, there is success for the king. Hence, O Bali ! you must make the *Varṇas* attend to their respective duties. With its prosperity is your prosperity; with its failure is your failure."

50. O great sage ! After telling Bali thus, that chief of kings, the high-souled one, kept quiet. Then, Bali said: "I will do what you bid."

## CHAPTER SEVENTY-FIVE

### Jayaśrī resorts to Bali

*Pulastya said:*

1. O one rich in austerity ! After the *Devas* went over to Brahmā's abode, Bali, devoted to *Dharma* always, ruled the three worlds.

2-4. Seeing the world endowed with *Dharma* as in Kṛta-age, Kali sought refuge in Brahmā because of its character being negated. Having gone, Kali saw the Lord (Brahmā) with Indra, accompanied by the *Devas*, along with the celestials and the *Asuras*, brightening his own surroundings with his brilliance. Bowing down to Brahmā, the Overlord, Kali said to him: "O most excellent *Deva* ! My character has been destroyed by Bali."

5-8. The venerable Brahmā told him: "The character of (the entire) world, not only yours, has been taken away by that mighty one. Get up; you will see Indra, Varuṇa as well as Māruta; even Bhāskara (Sun) has been reduced to a miserable state by the might of Bali. There is no one in the three worlds who could resist his activity, except Hari with a thousand heads and a thousand feet. He will withdraw (take away) the earth, the Heaven, the Kingdom, the wealth, the glory and might (of Bali). This Bali is one who does that which comes within the ambit of *Dharma.*"

9. So told by Lord Brahmā, the imperishable Kali, having seen the miserable Indra and others, went away to Vibhītaka forest.

10-13. O Nārada ! Then Kṛta-age set in, in the three worlds (as) Kali was not there. Even among the four *Varṇas, Dharma* was having all the four feet. O Brāhmaṇa ! Austerity, non-violence, truthfulness, purity, control of senses, compassion, charity, kindness, service, sacrificial performance–all these got widely established in the worlds. The Kali-age was forcibly disturbed and changed into the Kṛta-age. The *Varṇas* were established in their respective *Dharmas.* The twice-born ones (Brāhmaṇas) were (duly) taking up the *Āśramas.* The bulls among men (Kṣatriyas) were always established in the *Dharma* of protecting the subjects.

14. O Brāhmaṇa ! When these three worlds were in the highest state of *Dharma,* Lakṣmī of the three worlds, then came to the Lord of *Dānavas.*

15. As soon as he saw Lakṣmī of Indra herself approaching, Bali questioned: "Oh (my lady)! Who are you? Please tell me; with what purpose have you come (here)?"

16-30. Having heard his words, that Lakṣmī wearing a garland of lotuses, then said: "O Bali ! Listen why (I), a queen, have been forced to come to you. Indra was forsaken by that Lord, the wielder of discus and mace and of unimaginable prowess. Therefore, I have come here to you.

"The supreme Lord created four damsels endowed with beautiful form. (One) wore white garments, had white garlands and unguents, rode on a white elephant, had a white form and was endowed with *Sattva* (*guṇa*).

"The other one (second one) was wearing red garments, had red garlands and unguents, rode a red horse, had a red form and was endowed with *Rājasa (guṇa).*

"(The third one) was wearing yellow garments, had yellow complexion, had yellow garland and unguents, rode a golden chariot and was endowed with *Tāmasa-guṇa.*

"(The fourth one) was wearing blue garments, had blue garlands, blue unguents, a complexion similar to that of a bee, rode a blue bull and was endowed with the three *Guṇas.*

"She, the white one, wearing white garments, rich in *Sattva* and seated on an elephant went over to Brahmā, Moon and the followers of Moon. She, the red one, wearing red garments, possessing *Rajas* and seated on a horse was given over to the King of *devas,* Manu and his son. The lovely one of golden complexion with yellow dress and sitting in a chariot was given to the Prajapatis, Śukra and Vaiśyas. The fourth one having blue robes, having a complexion similar to the bee and seated on a bull, went over to the *Dānavas,* *Nairṛtas,* Śūdras and *Vidyādharas.*"

Vipras (Brāhmaṇas) and others call that one of white form Sarasvatī and always extol her along with Brahmā with Mantras and so on during sacrifices. Kṣatriyas praise the red one as Jayaśrī. She is glorious along with Indra and Manu, O foremost *Asura* ! Vaiśyas as well as *Prajāpatis* always adore the yellow-robed one of yellow form as Lakṣmī. Śūdras along with *Daityas* and *Rākṣasas* glorify the one of blue form devotedly with the name Priyadevī. Thus these women were distinguished by that Discus-bearing Lord.

31-35. The imperishable treasures exist assuming the nature of these women only. *Itihāsas, Purāṇas,* the *Vedas* and their auxiliaries, the sayings (of yore), the sixty-four arts and the Mahāpadma treasure are found in the white one. Jewels, gold, silver, elephants, horses, chariots, ornaments, weapons, missiles and such material and the Padma treasure are known as the red one. Cows, she-buffaloes, asses and camels, gold-embroidered clothes, fields, herbs and animals and the Mahānīla treasure are found in the yellow one. The one class comprising all other classes and bringing together all others is the Śaṅkha treasure, the blue one.

O *Dānava* ! Learn about the characteristics of the people attached to each of these women; I will relate to you.

36-39. O *Dānava*-chief ! The people attached to Mahāpadma will be possessing truthfulness and purity and they will be engaged in sacrifices, charity and festivals. Those attached to Padma will be sacrificers, wearing garlands. They are handsome, proud, very generous and have happiness common to the people. Those attached to Mahānīla will possess truth and falsehood, will be expert (competent) in the distribution and collection (of wealth), will have expenditure, both legal and illegal. O Bali ! Those attached to Śaṅkha will be atheists, not given to purity, miserly, denied of pleasures, indulging in thefts and speaking falsehood.

40-47a. "O *Dānava* ! Thus you have been given the complete details of these women. I, Jayaśrī, by name Rāgiṇī, have come to you. O *Dānava*-Lord ! I have a vow agreeable to the pious ones. I resort to a valiant one and never to an imbecile and there is no one equal to you in being mighty in the three worlds. O King ! You have implanted a lasting attachment in me by your might, in that Devarāja (Indra) was defeated in the battle by you with valour. Therefore, having witnessed your excellent prowess exceeding the might of all, an abiding keen interest (towards you) is kindled in me, O *Dānava* ! Hence, I have come on my own to you, the valiant one, having a very high self-respect. O foremost *Dānava* ! It is no surprise that you born in the family of the *Asura*-chief, Hiraṇyakaśipu, should have accomplished such a task. O King ! You have excelled your grandfather, the son of Diti, in that you have reconquered the three worlds taken away by other (*Devas*)."

47b-50. Having said thus, the moon-faced and brightly glowing Jayaśrī, encompassing the earth, entered the

*Dānava*-chief. When she entered, bashfulness, fame, splendour, effulgence, intellect, patience, prosperity, learning, conduct, compassion, knowledge-resorted to Bali like widowed women (having none to look after). O Brāhmaṇa! The Vedic lore, *Smṛtis*, might, fame, steadfastness, *tranquillity*, activity, nourishment, contentment and other qualities associated with the resplendent *Sattva*–all taking shelter in Bali, relaxed in comfort.

51-52. This bull among the sons of Danu, Bali, was high-souled, self-restrained, a performer of sacrifices, austere, sympathetic, truthful, benevolent, a good protector, a guardian of kinsmen and was endowed with good qualities and virtuous thoughts. When the *Dānava*-chief was reigning the Heaven, there was no one afflicted with hunger, no sinner and no one miserable even among human beings. They too were born always bright and were engaged in piety.

They being self-controlled, enjoyed sensual pleasures.

## CHAPTER SEVENTY-SIX

### Aditi offered a boon

*Pulastya said:*

1-4. As the kingdom of the three worlds passed on to the *Dānavas*, Purandara, the Lord of Śacī together with the *Devas*, went to the abode of Brahmā. There he saw the Lord of *Devas*, the lotus-born Brahmā and his own father, Kaśyapa, sitting along with the sages. Then Indra, along with the groups of celestials, bowed down his head to Brahmā, Kaśyapa and all those sages, rich in penance. Indra along with the celestials told the Grandsire, the protector of *Devas*: "O Grandsire ! My kingdom was taken away by the mighty Bali."

5. Brahmā said: "O Indra ! You are experiencing the fruit of what has been done." Indra asked: "O Sir ! Please tell me, what sin was committed by me ?"

6. Kaśyapa also said: "O King of Devas ! You have killed the embryo. The embryo in the womb of Diti was forcibly cast into pieces by you."

7. Indra told his father: "O Lord ! That was due to the fault of the mother. The embryo indeed got (dissected), for she was impure."

8. At that Kaśyapa said: "It was due to the fault of the mother that the embryo was reduced to Dāsahood. Even though a slave, it was injured by your *Vajra*."

9. Hearing the words of Kaśyapa, Indra asked the Grandsire: "O Lord ! Please tell me the (means of) removal of my sin and the atonement."

10-11. Brahmā, Vasiṣṭha and Kaśyapa told the Lord of Celestials (Indra): "For the entire world and for Indra in particular, the pre-eminent *Puruṣa*, Mādhava, the wielder of conch, discus and mace (is the Lord). You take refuge in him; he will arrange everything for you."

12. Indra listening to the words of the superiors, said: "Can great prosperity be achieved in a short time?" The gods replied: "Great prosperity can be achieved in a short time on the earth."

13-18. So told by Brahmā, Kaśyapa, the son of Marīci and the son of Mitrāvaruṇa (Vasiṣṭha), Indra immediately went and stayed on earth. He stayed in the well-known holy place which was to the north of Kālañjara, to the south of Himālaya, to the east of Kuśasthala and to the west of Vasupura. The place was where *Aśvamedha* with liberal *Dakṣiṇā* was performed one hundred times and *Manuṣyamedha* one thousand times and the well-known sacrifice by name *Mahāmedha* which is difficult to perform by the gods and the *Asuras* was performed by King Gaya in the days of yore. It was the place where the venerable Murāri of auspicious shape and of unmanifest form assumed the form of a door-keeper and became well-known as Gadādhara. (The place was) where even the best of the twice-born ones (Brāhmaṇas), devoid of *Veda* and *Śāstra* learning, attain equality with the Grandsire; where by worshipping one's fathers with devotion even once with concentrated mind, people acquire the infinite fruit of the *Mahāmedha* sacrifice through the grace of the venerable Lord; where the excellent river, the foremost daughter of the celestial sage coming to Himālaya in the guise of water, made the world absolved of sin by (mere) seeing (it), drinking (the waters of the river) and taking ablution (therein).

19-21. Arriving at that spot, Indra built a hermitage on the spectacular bank of the great river for worshipping the Lord and dwelt there. Taking bath (early) in the morning, lying on the ground and eating only once a day some food got unasked for and adoring the Lord Gadādhara, Indra practised austerities. As Indra was practising austerity, restraining his senses well and keeping away lust and anger, a whole year passed.

22-23. O Nārada ! Being pleased at that, Gadādhara told Indra: "Go, I am pleased with you and now you are cleansed of your sin. O King of *Devas* ! You will get (back) your kingdom before long. I will endeavour in such a way that welfare happens to you, O Indra !"

24. So told by Gadādhara and dismissed by him, Indra took ablution in the river Manoharā. As the Lord took his bath, his sins in the form of men asked him: "Please command us."

25. Indra told those of terrible actions, the Pulindas by name: "O you who are born of my sin dwell between the principal mountains, Himālaya and Kālañjara, O Pulindas !"

26-29. So saying to the Pulindas, the King of celestials, absolved of sin and being adored by the gods, *Siddhas* and *Yakṣas,* went to the hermitage of his mother, the worthy abode of *Dharma.* Seeing Aditi, he approached her with his head bent and the folded hands kept on his head. After prostrating to her feet (shining) like the inside of a lotus, he reported to her about his (austerity). Sniffing (on the head) and embracing that lord with joy and graceful looks, she enquired him of the cause (of penance). He spoke of his defeat together with that of the hosts of *Devas* and celestials, at the hands of Bali. Soon after hearing it, knowing that her son was conquered by the sons of Diti, she was immersed in grief. She being sorrowful, took refuge in the beginningless and the laudable Lord Viṣṇu, the foremost.

*Nārada said:*

30. O sage ! Tell me in which place did that mother of the foremost celestials worship the infinite and the primordial Hṛṣīkeśa, the source of the movable and the immovable and the ultimate one.

*Pulastya said:*

31-32. Seeing the miserable Indra, subdued by the leader of *Dānavas*, the Mother of celestials, of restrained speech and noble thoughts, observing fast, waited on the refuge, the Lord of celestials, on the seventh day of the bright half when the Sun was in Makara constellation, after seeing the divine Lord of heaven rise in the eastern direction on the auspicious day.

*Aditi said:*

33-35. Victory to you, O staler of (the charm of) the divine lotus petals ! Victory to you, O axe to the tree of cycle of births and deaths ! Victory to you, O fire to the fuel of sins ! O one stopping the stream of evils ! Salutations, salutations to you. Salutation to you, O Bhāskara (sun) ! O one of divine form; O lord of the wealth of the three worlds ! Salutation to you ! You are the cause of the movable and the immovable; you are the benefactor; protect me, O one of multiform ! O Lord of the universe ! O benefactor pervading the universe! by you, Indra had the loss of his kingdom and defeat from the enemy; hence, I have surrendered to your refuge.

36-38. Saying thus, she, for the welfare of Indra, smeared the one worshipped by the celestials with red sandalpaste and worshipped with *Karavīra* flowers. Along with scented fumes and lights, she offered divine food-precious food mixed with ghee. She praised with meritorious hymns and stayed near the Lord without taking food. Then, on the second day, she prostrated and after ablution, offered worship as per prescription. Having gifted gold, sesamum and ghee to the Brāhmaṇas, she stood before (the Lord) submissively.

39-41. Then the Sun was pleased. The blazing one, emerging from the sun's orb, stood in front of her and said these words: "O Daughter of Dakṣa ! I am pleased by this your vow. You will get the object you desire, not easy to attain, through my grace, without doubt. O noble lady ! O mother of celestials ! I shall give the kingdom to your sons and destroy the *Dānavas* after taking birth in your womb."

42-45. O Brāhmaṇa ! Having heard those words of Vāsudeva, the Mother of celestials told the source of the universe, trembling again and again: "How will I be able to carry in my womb, you who cannot be borne, in whose belly the entire universe—the immovable and movable are residing. O benefactor ! Who can bear you? You are the support of the three worlds and in your belly dwell the seven seas along with the (seven) mountains. Therefore, O Janārdana ! Please act in such a way that the Lord of *Devas* ! Indra ! becomes the king of celestials (again) and I will not have any distress unnecessarily."

*Viṣṇu said:*

46-49. O fortunate one ! It is true that I cannot be borne by either the celestials or by the *Asuras.* Still I take birth from your womb, O noble lady ! Through *Yogic* power I will support myself, the world, the mountains, you along with Kaśyapa; O noble lady ! Do not feel sad unnecessarily. O Daughter of Dakṣa ! When I take birth from your womb, the *Daityas* will undoubtedly become lustreless.

O Brāhmaṇa ! So saying, the venerable Lord, the subduer of enemies again entered her body and her womb through his power for the welfare of Indra.

## CHAPTER SEVENTY-SEVEN

### Bali admonished

*Pulastya said:*

1-2. When the Lord in the form of a dwarf stayed in the womb of the Mother of *Devas*, the *Asuras* became lustreless as said by the Lord, the source of the universe. Seeing the *Asuras* lustreless, Bali, the tiger among *Dānavas* said these words to Prahlāda, the Lord of *Dānavas*.

*Bali said:*

3. O father ! What is the cause of the *Daityas* having become lustreless. You please tell me. You are the supreme knower, O one expert in (knowing) good and evil !

*Pulastya said:*

4-5. Hearing the words of his grandson, Prahlāda took to meditation for a while to know about the cause, by which there was loss of splendour (of *Asuras*) and from whom (had it been effected). Knowing that an unsurmountable threat to the *Daityas* had been posed by Vāsudeva, the contemplating one thought as to where Viṣṇu stayed at that time.

6-9. O Nārada ! The restrained one, mentally visualised the earth in the form of a lotus; the seven nether worlds below the central point and the *Bhūḥ* and other worlds above the centre as well as the lotus-like golden Meru mountain full of great treasure in its (of earth) middle part. Above that (he saw) the great abodes and the eight guardians of the universe. Over that he saw *Vairāja*, the abode of Brahmā. Below that he saw the most holy hermitage of the Mother of *Devas*, honoured by the celestials and flocked by groups of beasts and birds.

10-14. O sage ! Having seen that Mother of *Devas*, even more resplendent than all, the *Dānava*-lord entered (her body) to search for Madhusūdana. In the womb of the Mother of *Devas*, he then saw Mādhava, the benefactor of the universe, the one benevolent to all beings in the shape of a dwarf. Having seen the Lotus-eyed Viṣṇu without conch and discus, whose form was pervaded everywhere by all the groups of celestials and *Asuras*, who took away the splendour of *Daityas* and who had assumed dwarfhood by his own supreme power, he (Prahlāda) returned to the normal state. Then, Prahlāda of great wisdom said to Bali, the son of Virocana, these pleasing words after saluting Madhusūdana.

*Prahlāda said:*

15-18. O *Daitya*-chief ! Listen, I will relate to you in detail the source from which you have threat, the cause due to which the *Daityas* have become lustreless. The Devas including Indra, Rudra, the Sun and the Fire defeated by you, took refuge in Lord Hari, the overlord of the three worlds. That Lord of the universe, the mighty Hari, having assured security to Indra and others has descended into the womb of Aditi. O Bali ! My thinking is that your lustre has been taken away by him. O Bali ! Darkness is not able to withstand sunrise.

*Pulastya said:*

19. Hearing the words of Prahlāda, Bali instigated by the Destiny, told Prahlāda with his lips quivering due to rage—

*Bali said:*

20-24. O father ! Who is this Hari by whom we are threatened? I have hundreds of *Daityas* who are stronger than Vāsudeva, by whom the *Devas*, including Indra, Rudra, Agni and Maruts were defeated a thousand times and made to quit heaven, their pride being shattered on the battlefield. That mighty Vipracitti who forcibly pulled the fast-moving wheel from the chariot of the Sun is the leader of my army. Ayaḥśaṅku, Śivi, Śaṅku, Asiloma, Virūpadhṛk, Triśiras, Makarākṣa, Vṛṣaparva, Asitekṣaṇa—all these and others are there who are mighty and are experts in wielding various weapons, to even the sixteenth part of any one of whom Viṣṇu cannot be a match.

*Pulastya said:*

25-37. Hearing these words of his son, Prahlāda was mad with fury. He said to Bali who spoke ill of Viṣṇu: "Fie! Fie upon you! Fie upon you of evil conduct ! O wicked-minded one ! O you simpleton ! How is it that your tongue does not fall down while you are abusing Hari? O evil-minded one ! you are to be deplored and condemned by the pious, for, O one of evil thoughts ! You condemn Viṣṇu, the Lord of the three worlds. There is no doubt, your father too is to be deplored of whom you were born, a cruel son who derides the Lord! You indeed know, and so also these great *Asuras*, that there is no one dear to me than that Janārdana. Knowing fully well, how did you condemn my dearest Lord Janārdana, the overlord of everything ? A superior person is to be honoured; of them, father is to be honoured; I am elderly even to him (your father); the venerable preceptor is to be honoured even by me; Hari is the most superior in the universe. O silly one ! You condemn the worshipful preceptor of your father's father, the one venerable to the most venerable. O sinful one ! How is it that you have not fallen down ? By you, these *Dānavas* are made deplorable and to have evil ways, of whom you are the king, a cruel one and a vilifier of Vāsudeva. Because the honourable and the adorable Hari has been condemned by you, O one of evil conductly ! May you have the loss of kingdom. As there is nothing dearer. to me than Keśava, either mentally or physically or orally, you fall down, thrown out of the kingdom. As there exists nothing excelling him in the entire fourteen worlds, may you, therefore, fall, losing your kingdom. As there is no other resort for all the beings in the world, may I find you displaced from the kingdom."

*Pulastya said:*

38-42. O Brāhmaṇa ! When these words were uttered, that Bali, immediately got down from his seat and folding his hands and prostrating with his head said: "O Lord ! Please be gracious to me. Parents do forgive the younger ones who have committed errors. O Dānava-Lord ! It is good that I was cursed by you. I am neither afraid of the enemies nor of the loss of realm. O Lord ! I am not sad that I am thrown out of the realm; that I offended you gives me great grief. Therefore, O father ! Please forgive me who have offended (you); I am an ignoramus; I am worthless and an evil-minded one; parents do forgive their children who have committed faults if they resort to humility."

*Pulastya said:*

43. When he said so, the high-souled devotee of Hari's feet, who, free from delusions, thought for a long time and spoke to his son thus in sweet and wondrous words.

*Prahlāda said:*

44-52. Now my perception and my intellect were obscured by infatuation, because of which I cursed you, though knowing Viṣṇu to be everywhere. Really, it is non-discrimination by which (I cursed) you, O *Dānava* ! O valiant one ! My wisdom too was blocked. Therefore, O king ! It is better, you do not have passion for the realm. Events that are inevitable do never stop. A wise person should never get perturbed by the gain or the loss of children, friends, wives or realms, pleasures and wealth. O *Daitya*-chief ! Human beings should bear pleasure or pain as it occur; in accordance with one's actions in earlier births. A restrained person should neither feel dejected at the sight of calamity that may occur nor should he become one of unbalanced mind on getting enormous wealth. Those who are neither dejected at the loss of wealth nor get elated at the gain of wealth and are steadfast in their activity, are the men of highest order. O *Daitya*-chief ! Considering thus, it is proper for you not to entertain even slight dejection. A scholar, a learned man never gets disheartened. So also, O valiant one! Listen to another thing which is significant and beneficial to you and others as well. Having heard it, you practice it.

53-56. O *Dānava* ! Surrender to that excellent *Puruṣa* who is the refuge. He will be your saviour from this threat. Those persons who surrender unto Hari, the lord without a beginning or middle, Viṣṇu, the preceptor of the movable and the immovable world, the controller, the helping hand to one fallen in the pit of Saṁsāra, do not indeed get afflicted in this world. O best of *Dānavas* ! Now you set your mind on him; be his devotee; that Janārdana will do good to you. I, on my part will propitiate the Lord and (go on) a pilgrimage for the expiation of my sin. I will be absolved of sin, when *Acyuta*, Nṛsiṁha, the lord of the world (blesses).

*Pulastya said:*

57. So consoling Bali, the noble one recalling Viṣṇu, the overlord of *Yoga*, and bidding farewell to the commanders of *Dānavas*, undertook the holy pilgrimage.

# CHAPTER SEVENTY-EIGHT

## Defeat of Dhundhu

*Nārada said:*

1. O Brāhmaṇa-chief ! Which were the holy places to which Prahlāda went ? You please relate to me in detail the pilgrimage of Prahlāda.

*Pulastya said:*

2. Listen, I will tell you about the pilgrimage of Prahlāda which cleanses one of the mud of sin and destroys all sins.

3-9. Leaving Meru, the golden mountain, he proceeded to the merit-giving holy place known on the earth as Mānasa, which is flocked by hosts of immortals and where the Lord of celestials assuming the form of fish is established. Having taken ablution in that excellent pond, he propitiated the *Pitṛs* and the *Devas* and worshipped *Acyuta*, the benefactor of the universe, together with the *Vedas*. After observing fast and worshipping the *Devas*, sages, *Pitṛs* and human beings again, he proceeded to visit the sin-destroying *Kacchapa* (tortoise incarnation) on Kauśikī (river). Having taken bath in that great river, he worshipped the Lord of the universe. After observing fast, he purified himself and gave gifts to the Brāhmaṇas. After prostrating the benefactor of the universe in the form of tortoise, he proceeded to visit the Horse-faced Lord on Kṛṣṇā (river).

Taking ablution there in the divine pond, having propitiated the *Pitṛs* and the celestials and having worshipped Hayaśīrṣa, he went further to the place named after the elephant (Hastināpura).

There, after bath, he duly worshipped the Discuṣ-bearing Lord, Govinda, the benefactor of the universe and moved on to Yamunā river. Becoming purified after taking bath in that river and having propitiated the sages, celestials and

*Pitṛs,* he visited the Supreme Lord, the benefactor of the universe, Trivikrama.

*Nārada said:*

10-11. The overlord, the venerable Viṣṇu, the Lord of the universe will now assume a form pervading the three worlds and restrain Bali. Then, how is it that the Lord was *Trivikrama* even in the earlier age ? Whom did Viṣṇu restrain (then)? Please tell me that.

*Pulastya said:*

12. Listen, I will tell you about this one who is called *Trivikrama,* in which age he appeared and whom he deceived.

13-15. There was one known as Dhundhu, Kaśyapa's own son, born of Danu and of vast strength and prowess. O Nārada! The Asura propitiated Brahmā with penance and sought the boon of not being killed by the celestials including Indra. The Lotus-born (Brahmā), pleased with his penance, bestowed that boon. The valiant one, proceeded to Heaven.

16-19. In the beginning of the fourth Kali-age, having conquered the *Devas* together with Indra, Dhundhu assumed Indra's position when Hiraṇyakaśipu was also there. At that time, the valiant *Daitya,* Hiraṇyakaśipu associated with Dhundhu, roamed about in the Mandara mountain and the *Asuras* moved about as they liked in Heaven. The celestials staying in Brahmā's abode were distressed. Then, learning that the immortals were dwelling in the abode of Brahmā, Dhundhu spoke to the sons of Diti: "O *Daityas* ! Let us go to the abode of the First-born to conquer the celestials together with Indra."

20-25. Hearing the words of Dhundhu, those *Daityas* said: "O protector of the world ! We do not have the means by which we could reach the abode of the Grandsire; the path is too long and difficult to traverse. At a distance of several thousands of *yojanas* from here, there is the region called

Mahaḥ where dwell the great sages, by whose sudden look of the eyes turned to see, the *Daityas* get burnt down. After that, at a distance of one crore *yojanas*, there is the region called Jana where dwell Cow-mothers, whose destroyer there is no one among us, O great *Asura* ! After that, at a distance of thirty crore *yojanas* is the region having the brilliance of a thousand suns called Satya, which is the dwelling of the venerable one who offered the boon to you and listening to whose chanting of *Veda* the celestials and others become elated and the *Asuras* and those akin to them shrink. Therefore, O mighty one ! Do not entertain such thought. O Dhundhu ! The region of Vairāja is always difficult for human beings to ascend."

26-27. Hearing their words, Dhundhu, desirous of going to the abode of Brahmā to conquer the Lord, said to the *Dānavas*: "O bulls among *Dānavas* ! How and by which act can one go there? How did Indra with the *Devas* reach it?"

28. Those *Dānavas*-chiefs questioned by Dhundhu replied to their master: "We do not know that act; undoubtedly, Śukra knows it."

29. Having heard the words of the *Daityas*, he enquired Śukra, the *Purohita* (priest) of *Daityas*: "Doing what, can one reach the abode of Brahmā ?"

30-31. O Lover of Quarrels (Nārada)! Then, the honourable preceptor of *Daityas* told him the past history of Indra, the foe of Vṛtra: "O *Daitya*-chief ! Indra in the past performed one hundred *Aśvamedha* sacrifices. By that he could go to the abode of Brahmā."

32-35. Hearing the words of Śukra, the valiant *Dānava*-lord made up his good mind to perform *Aśvamedha* sacrifices. Then, inviting the *Asura*-preceptor and the top-ranking *Dānavas*, he said: "I will perform *Aśvamedha* sacrifices with profuse *Dakṣiṇā*. Hence, you all come; let us go to the earth and having conquered the kings, (we can perform) *Aśvamedha* sacrifices having the desired qualities. May the prime treasures (of Kubera) be invited; may the *Guhyakas* be ordered; may the best of the Brāhmaṇas be invited. We will proceed to the banks of Devikā (river). That excellent river is indeed considered to be holy and a bestower of all success. Going to the eastern place (i.e. bank) we will perform the horse-sacrifices."

36. Hearing the words of the foe of celestials, the *Asura*-preceptor said: "Very well." Then, he being pleased, ordered the treasures.

37-41. Afterwards, on the eastern bank of Devikā, the destroyer of sin, Dhundhu was consecrated for *Aśvamedha* by Śukra, the foremost Bhārgava. O Brāhmaṇa ! Śukra's disciples and scholars, the Brāhmaṇas of Bhārgava family were appointed as *Sadasyas* and *Ṛtviks* on the approval of Śukra. O sage ! Svarbhānu and the foremost *Asuras* were made the partakers of the offerings of the sacrifice by the *Asura*-king on the advice of Śukra. Then, the sacrifice was begun; so also the horse was sent forth. Following the horse, went the glorious, great *Asura*, Asiloma. O great sage ! Then the earth with the mountains was pervaded and the quarters and the space between the quarters were all filled with the smoke of the fire. With the strong scent that touched the skies, the wind blew in the region of Brahmā.

42-49. Smelling that scent, the celestials came to know that Dhundhu was consecrated for the horse-sacrifice and were despondent. Then, they with Indra took refuge in Janārdana, the refuge and the final resort of the universe. Prostrating themselves before Lord Padmanābha, Janārdana, the grantor of wishes, all the groups of celestials said with a voice choked with fear: "O venerable Lord ! O master of *Devas* ! O final resort of the movable and the immovable (beings)! O Viṣṇu ! O destroyer of affliction of the celestials! Please listen to our plea. The mighty *Asura*-chief by name Dhundhu, surrounded by his army, has defeated all the celestials and has captured the three worlds. Except the Pinākа-wielding Lord (Śiva), there is no protector of us. Hence, he has prospered like a disease neglected. At present, he is attempting to conquer (us), staying in the region of Brahmā. He has been consecrated to perform *Aśvamedha* sacrifice on the advice of Śukra. The great *Asura* of controlled senses, desires to ascend to *Brahmaloka* after offering one hundred sacrifices to defeat the celestials. Therefore, O preceptor of the universe ! Please think of an expedient to obstruct the sacrifice without loss of time, so that we will be free from any trouble."

50-55. Hearing the words of the celestials, the venerable, the valorous Madhusūdana assured security and sent them back. Having sent them back, considering the great *Asura* to be invincible and now feigning *Dharma*, he made up his mind to bind Dhundhu. Then, the venerable overlord assuming the form of a dwarf, threw himself without any support like a log of wood into the waters of Devikā, drowning for a moment and coming up again, with his hair let loose of its own accord. He was seen by the *Daitya*-lord, the *Daityas* and also by the sages. Then, being afflicted, the foremost Brāhmaṇas, the *Sadasyas*, the chief-sacrificer and the lustrous *Ṛtviks*, giving up their sacrificial functions, rushed to take him out. They brought out the dwarf-Brāhmaṇa who was drowning. After bringing him out, they were pleased and all of them asked: "Why did you fall here or by whom have you been pushed ? Please speak."

56-59. Hearing their words and trembling again and again, he said to Dhundhu and others: "Listen to the cause. There was a meritorious Brāhmaṇa known as Prabhāsa. He was wise and learned in all the *Śāstras*. He belonged to the family of Varuṇa. He had two sons of dull intellect and was very unhappy. Of them, the elder was my brother and I was the younger. My elder brother was known as Netrabhāsa. My father gave me the name Gatibhāsa out of curiosity. My father's residence was lovely and auspicious. It had the characteristics of heaven and (living there) was equal to living in heaven. After a long time, our father died. After performing his funeral rites, we returned home. My brother was told by me: "We will divide the house." I was told by him: "You do not have a share. There is no share in the property for hunch-backs, dwarfs, lame ones, eunuchs, lepers, insanes and blind ones. Courteous words, residence in the house, food, clothing and so on—only these are provided to them; they are not claimants of property." When I was said so, I told him: "How is it that I am not worthy of half of the property, the paternal house; for what reason ?" When told so, my brother who was stronger than me, held me by the hair and lifting me up, he threw me into the river, O *Asura*! I did not know how to come out. For me, floating in the middle of this river, a period of one year has elapsed. I, yet living, was rescued by you. Who are you who have come here like affectionate relatives ? Who is this one shining like Indra in your midst ? O ascetic ! Please tell me everything as it is; you, sympathetic towards a person like me, are comparable to great sages."

70-71. Hearing the words of Vāmana, the best of the Brāhmaṇas of Bhārgava clan said: "O Brāhmaṇa ! We are the Brāhmaṇas of the family of Bhārgavas. This great *Asura* of great splendour is Dhundhu by name. He is a donor, an enjoyer and a protector and is consecrated for the sacrificial performance."

72-73. So telling Vāmana, the Lord of *Devas*, all the Bhārgavas then spoke to the *Daitya*-lord, words benefitting Vāmana: "O *Daitya*-chief ! Give this person a beautiful house with all furnishings, female servants and various jewels."

74-75. The *Daitya*-lord after hearing the words of the Brāhmaṇas said: "O Brāhmaṇa-chief ! I will give you as much of copious wealth as you may desire, female servants, house, gold, horses, chariots, elephants, cows, land, kingdom, clothing and so on, O Lord !"

76-79. Hearing the words of the *Dānava*-chief, Lord Vāmana said to Dhundhu, the *Asura*-lord, words that would accomplish his task: "For a person whose (inherited) wealth has been snatched away by one's own brother, what is the use of riches and why, O King ! Do you give me riches only? O valiant one ! Give male and female servants, attendants, house, jewels and garments to the Brāhmaṇas capable (of receiving them). To me, however, you give (land measuring) my three steps, considering my size. O *Daitya*-lord ! This is what I ask you."

80. Laughing along with the *Ṛtviks* at the noble one who said thus and when he did not accept anything else again, the *Daitya*-lord of restrained senses, gave away three steps to the Brāhmaṇa.

81-86. Seeing that three steps were given by the great *Asura*-chief, the all-pervading Lord of infinite power like moon, assumed the form of Trivikrama consisting of three steps to stride over the three worlds. Assuming such a form, killing the sons of Diti and bowing down to the sages, he snatched away (from the *Asura*) with one step, the earth along with mountains, oceans, repositories of jewels and cities. Immediately with the second step, the lord, desirous of doing good to the *Devas*, snatched away the mid-region along with heaven, the dwelling of the celestials and the sky adorned by the stars, sun and moon. When the third step was not covered, the venerable Trivikrama with full rage, fell on the back of the bull among *Dānavas* with a body equal to Meru in size. O Nārada ! A crater in the earth measuring thirty thousand *yojanas* was created by Vāsudeva who fell on the *Dānava*. Then, lifting the *Daitya* and throwing him in it quickly, he rained with a shower of gravel and filled the crater.

87-89. Then, Indra and all the celestials regained the heaven and the three worlds without any trouble by the grace of Vāsudeva. The venerable one, on the other hand, throwing the *Daitya*-chief in the sea of gravel and assuming the form of Kālindī, became invisible there only. Thus in the past, Viṣṇu became Vāmana and Trivikrama to conquer Dhundhu in the great holy hermitage, where the son of *Daitya*-chief went, O great sage !

## CHAPTER SEVENTY-NINE

### The story of Purūravas

*Pulastya said:*

1-9. Having bathed in the waters of Kālindī and having worshipped Trivikrama, he observed fast for a night and then went to the Liṅgabheda mountain. Having duly taken bath there, having worshipped Śiva with devotion and having observed fast for a night, he proceeded to the holy place Kedāra. He duly took bath there, propitiated the Lord of the universe and having dwelt for seven days, he went over to Kubjāmra. Having gone there, the valiant one of controlled senses, keeping fast, worshipped Hṛṣīkeśa and then went to Badarikāśrama. That wise one after bathing in the waters of Sarasvatī and devotedly worshipping, propitiated Nārāyaṇa. After visiting Garuḍāsana in *Varāhatīrtha* and worshipping him, the devoted one then went to Bhadrakarṇa and adored Lord Śiva. After worship, the restrained one went towards Vipāśā. Taking ablution there and worshipping the Lord of Lords, Dvijapriya, he then visited Jagannātha Parameśvara in Irāvatī. O best of the twice-born ones ! Attending on that eternal Lord of the Universe (Jagannātha), he (*Purūravas*) attained excellent form and prosperity not easy to get in the same way as Bhṛgu afflicted with leprosy, obtained unmatched health and imperishable progeny.

*Nārada said:*

10. O most pious Dvija ! After attending on Viṣṇu, how did *Purūravas* give up his ugly form and obtain beauty along with prosperity ?

*Pulastya said:*

11. Listen, O one rich in penance ! I will relate to you the event that destroys grave sins, as it happened earlier in the beginning of *Tretāyuga.*

12-22. There was a country well-known as Madradeśa, well regarded by Brāhmaṇas. A city called Śākala was an excellent and important town (there). There was a merchant Sadharma by name pursuing the profession of trader. He was very rich, virtuous, learned in several *Śāstras* and was enjoying pleasures. Once he arranged to go to Saurāṣṭra from his country with a large caravan, having various items of merchandise intended for sale. O lover of quarrel ! While proceeding on the road in the desert at night, there occurred a fierce attack of robbers. Then, the merchant who had lost everything, roamed about like a mad man stricken by grief, without any help in the desert. O Nārada ! While roaming about in the forest afflicted with grief, he himself came across an auspicious, big *Śamī* tree. Seeing that *Śamī* tree, devoid of animals as well as birds, he being tired and seized with hunger and thirst, sat at its side. He slept and after a good rest, he woke up at noon. Then he saw a ghost surrounded by hundreds of ghosts coming. (He saw) a ghost-leader being carried by another ghost along with the tired ghosts of rough appearance running in the front. That ghost came there, after roaming about that land. Having approached, he saw the son of the merchant at the foot of the *Śamī* tree. Sitting comfortably under the shade, the ghost felt pleased and asked about his (merchant's) welfare after greeting him and then, they talked to each other.

23-24. The merchant was asked by that ghost-leader: "O friend ! Tell me, where did you come from or where will be your dwelling? How is it that you have come into this wide forest devoid of beasts or birds ? May you have welfare; you better state everything."

25. O Brāhmaṇa ! Thus questioned by the ghost–leader, the merchant related everything–his separation from his country and the (loss) of wealth in brief.

26-30. Having heard the incident, he being sad at his sadness, the master of ghosts told the son of merchant as a kinsman: "O you of good conduct ! Though you are reduced to this condition, it is not proper for you to grieve. If you are fortunate enough, you will have riches again. With the loss of luck, riches are lost and they will be there with the dawn of fortune. The body emaciated by worry cannot prosper." So saying, he called his attenders and told them: "Today this is our honourable guest, my brother and my countryman. By seeing this son of merchant (feel as though) I have visited all my kins and relatives. O ghosts ! By his arrival I have unmatched happiness."

31-33. Even as he was saying thus, a new and strong earthen vessel, full of curd and rice arrived there, as desired. So also a new and strong water-jug, full of excellent water arrived and stood before the ghosts. Having seen the water with rice arrive, the wise one said: "O merchant's son ! Get up and attend to the daily routine."

34-37. Then, both the merchant and the leader of ghosts duly performed the daily routine with the water of the water-jug. Then, giving the curd and rice sumptuously to the merchant's son and to all those ghosts, he kept down the remaining food. When all of them had their food and drank water to their full, the master of ghosts ate the excellent food. O Brāhmaṇa ! After the ghost was satisfied fully, the water-jug and rice disappeared, even as the merchant's son was seeing.

38-41. Then, seeing that wonderful incident, the restrained and thoughtful merchant asked the master of ghosts with curiosity: "O good Sir ! Whence did rice arrive in this forest bereft of human beings ? Whence did this water-jug, full of excellent water come? Still, these, your attenders are lean in their appearance. You, on the other hand, are bright and have slightly good physique too. You are wearing white garments and you are looking after so many. You tell me all this. Who are you ? What about this *Śamī* tree ?"

42-49. Hearing the words of the merchant, the leader of ghosts described everything as it occurred in the past: "In the foremost city of Śākala, I was in the past, a Brāhmaṇa known by the name Somaśarma, born of the womb of Bahulā. There was my neighbour, a wealthy and prosperous merchant. He was Somaśravā by name and a glorious devotee of Viṣṇu. But I was a silly one, a miser and a wicked one. Though I had riches, I would neither give to Brāhmaṇas nor would eat precious food. If by chance, I ate food with curds, milk and ghee, then, at night I would be beaten with sticks by three ferocious beings. The next morning, I would be having death-like terrible cholera. None of my kinsmen would stand by me then. Somehow, my life was sustained by me. Thus I lived, a most unscrupulous sinner. I was sustaining myself with bad food and with meals of sour gruel, oil-cakes of sesamum, husk, vegetables, etc. and passed my time.

50-55. O friend ! As I was passing time in this way, there arrived a good time. That was the day called *Śrāvaṇa-dvādaśī* in the month of *Bhādrapada*. Then all the citizens, Brāhmaṇas, Kṣatriyas and others went to take bath at the confluence of Irāvatī and Naḍvalā. Because of the association with my neighbour, I too followed (him). Becoming pure and keeping the vow of restraint, I observed fast on the *Ekādaśī* day. Then, to a Brāhmaṇa, who was very bright by the activity related to his birth, was given a strong and new water-jug filled with the waters of the confluence, covered with cloth along with an umbrella and (a pair of) shoes as well as an earthen vessel, full of very delicious curd-rice. O merchant's son ! In my entire life of seventy years that was the only gift given by me; I did not give anything else.

56-60. After death, I became a ghost and was given food. These are the ghosts who did not give any gifts; they live on the food given by me. This is the cause I have told you, of the arrival of food with water at noon everyday; they are what I had gifted. (The food and water) are not exhausted till I partake of them. After I eat and drink, all disappear. By the gift of umbrella, this *Śamī* tree has grown. Because I gifted a pair of shoes, a ghost is my vehicle. With this, I have told you all about my ghosthood; so also I have told you about that holy *Śrāvaṇa-dvādaśī* which enhances merit."

61. When he told so, the merchant's son said these words: "O respected Sir ! You please instruct me as to what I should do."

62-67. O Nārada ! Having heard the words of the son of merchant, the master of ghosts, then said that which would benefit him: "O dear, wise one ! I will tell you clearly what you should do for my welfare and for your and my prosperity. Having taken bath in *Gayā-tīrtha* and being pure, offer oblations in fire and offer Piṇḍa in my name. O friend ! By the offering of *Piṇḍa* there, I will be released from this ghosthood and I will be having the same region as all donors. The twelfth day in the bright half of Bhādrapada is holy. If it is conjoined with Budha (*Graha*) and *Śravaṇa* (asterism), it is still more auspicious." So speaking to the merchant, the pious master of the ghosts along with his followers felt that he had given correct information.

68-73. The merchant who was placed on the shoulder of a ghost and sent out of the desert, arrived in the beautiful country called *Śūrasena*. Having earned a lot of wealth by virtue of his good action and piety, he proceeded to the excellent *Gayā-tīrtha*. There, he performed the offering of *Piṇḍa* to the ghosts in due order and afterwards to his own relatives and fathers. The wise one offered *Mahat-śrāddha* to himself without sesamum and he performed the offering of *Piṇḍa* for those born in other families as well. When five *Piṇḍa*-offerings were made thus, the twice-born ones, released from ghosthood, went over to the region of Brahmā. The merchant's son, on the other hand, returned to his house. Observing *Śrāvaṇa-dvādaśī*, he followed the course of time (died).

74-77. Enjoying for a long time in the region of *Gandharvas*, the pleasures which are not easy to get, he obtained birth as a human being and the great one lived in the Śākala (country). He being in the profession proper for his *Dharma* and action was engaged in *Śrāvaṇa-dvādaśī.* After death, he went to the abode of *Guhyakas.* Staying there for a long time and enjoying pleasures at will, he came back to the mortal world and became the son of a King (Kṣatriya). Then also, being in the profession of Kṣatriyas, the restrained one was engaged in giving gifts and enjoyment. Having defeated the hosts of enemies engaged in capture of cows, he attained the (final) course of time. He, reaching the abode of Indra, was honoured by all the *Devas.*

78-83. Deprived (of heaven) due to diminution of merit, he became a twice-born in Śākala (country). Then, he of an ugly form but thoroughly learned in all the *Śāstras,* married a Brāhmaṇa's daughter of unequalled beauty, O Brāhmaṇa! Considering that the lady thought of her husband as ugly, though of good conduct, he became miserable. Then with disgust, the glorious one went to the great hermitage on the bank of Irāvatī and found Viṣṇu of beautiful form. Propitiating Jagannātha with the vow of *Nakṣatra-puruṣa,* he assumed beautiful form in that very birth. The restrained one became the beloved of his wife and an enjoyer of pleasures. Because of the earlier practice, he became a devotee of *Śrāvaṇa-dvādaśī.*

84. Thus in the past, the best of Brāhmaṇas who was ugly, became one like Cupid by the grace of the venerable lord. After death he was born as King Purūravas.

# CHAPTER EIGHTY

## The vow of Nakṣatra-puruṣa

*Nārada said:*

1. O best of the twice-born ! Tell me now, how Purūravas propitiated Viṣṇu with (the vow) called *Nakṣatra-puruṣa.*

*Pulastya said:*

2-9a. O Nārada ! Listen, I will speak to you about the vow of *Nakṣatra-puruṣa,* as to which asterism forms which bodily part of the Lord. The *Mūlā* asterism is in the feet of Viṣṇu; Rohiṇī in the two shanks; the two *Aśvins* in two knees of Rūpadhārī; the *Āṣāḍhā* asterism is in the buttocks; two *Phālguṇīs* in the genitals, the *Kṛttikās* are in the waist of Vāsudeva; *Anurādhā* is located in the thighs and *Dhaniṣṭhā* at the back; *Viśākhā* is in the arms and *Hasta* in the two exquisite hands; *Punarvasu* is in the fingers and in the nails, *Āśleṣā*; *Jyeṣṭhā* is in his neck; *Śravaṇa* in the ears; *Puṣya* is in the lips; *Svātī* in the teeth; *Śatabhiṣak* in the jaws; *Maghā* in the nose; in the two eyes of Rūpadhārī is *Mṛgaśiras*; (*Citrā* in the forehead; *Bharaṇī* in the head); *Ārdrā* is in the hair. These are the asterism-limbs of the body of Hari.

9b-26. O Nārada ! I will now speak about the method (of performing *Nakṣatra-puruṣa*) properly. Hari, worshipped as prescribed, will bestow one's desired things. When the Moon is in *Mūlā* asterism in the bright eighth day of *Caitra* month, then the feet of the Lord are to be worshipped as prescribed. In the *Nakṣatra-puruṣa* (vow) food is to be offered to an excellent Brāhmaṇa. (On the day) with the association of *Rohiṇī* asterism, knees are to be worshipped with devotion. Rice used for *Havis* is the desired (offering). A Brāhmaṇa is to be fed as before. (On the day when the Moon is) in the association of the two *Āṣāḍhā* asterisms, a wise one should worship the buttocks. Cold water is recommended as the desired offering. In the case of the two *Phālgunī* asterisms, the genitals are to be worshipped by wise ones. Cow's milk is the desired offering and a Brāhmaṇa is to be fed. In the *Kṛttikās*, the waist is to be worshipped by those with restrained senses and keeping fast. The desired offering to the Lord is water, made fragrant with flowers. In the two *Bhādrapada* asterisms, the sides are to be duly worshipped and jaggery prepared from rice has to be gifted as the desired offering and it brings about the satiation of the Lord. In *Revatī* asterism, the two bellies are to be worshipped and the desired offering is sweet-meats made with green-gram. In *Anurādhā* asterism, the chest is to be worshipped and the desired offering is rice grown in six months. Similarly, in *Dhaniṣṭhā*, one should worship (the back) and the desired offering is boiled rice. In *Viśākhā*, one should worship the two arms and the desired offering is excellent rice. In *Hasta*, the two hands are to be worshipped and for the desired offering barley preparation is spoken of. In *Punarvasu*, the pair of fingers are to be worshipped and the desired offering is snake-gourd. In *Āśleṣā*, the nails are to be worshipped and the meat of *Tittira* bird (partridge) is the desired offering. In *Jyeṣṭhā*, one should worship the neck and the sweat-meat made of sesamum is the desired offering. In *Śravaṇa*, the ears are to be worshipped and curd preparation is the desired offering. In *Puṣya*, the face is to be worshipped and the desired offering is ghee and milk preparation. In *Svātī*, one should worship the teeth and the desired offering is *Śaṣkuli* cakes made with sesamum. For pleasing Keśava, food is to be given to a Brāhmaṇa. In *Śatabhiṣak*, the jaws are to be earnestly worshipped. The desired offering for the killer of Madhu is a preparation of long pepper (*Priyaṅgu*). The nose is to be worshipped in *Maghā* and the desired offering is honey and ghee. In *Mṛgaśiras*, the eyes are to be worshipped and the desired offering is the meat of deer. In *Citrā*, one should worship the forehead and the desired offering is tasty food. In *Bharaṇī*, the head is to be worshipped and the desired offering is tasty food preparations. In *Ārdrā*, the learned one should worship the hair. Brāhmaṇas are to be fed with devotion and the desired offering is jaggery and ginger.

27-29. After worshipping the Lord of the Universe in the conjunctions of these asterisms, gifts are to be given to a Brāhmaṇa, learned in *Veda*. An umbrella, a pair of shoes, a pair of garments, seven kinds of grain, gold, a vessel with ghee, a milch-cow—these are to be offered to a Brāhmaṇa. At the conjunction of each of the asterisms (with the Moon), Brāhmaṇas are to be honoured. Separate gifts are to be given to a Brāhmaṇa who is an astronomer.

30-34. The vow called *Nakṣatra-puruṣa* is the best of vows. This vow, the destroyer of all sins was observed by Bhṛgu. O divine sage ! All the major and minor limbs of the Lord are to be worshipped. One gets beautiful form in each of those limbs. The sin that might have been committed since seven births or the one that might have been due to quarrels (Kali) or the one transmitted from the father or mother—all these are destroyed by Keśava. One attains all welfare and excellent physical health. Janārdana, having asterisms as his body, when adored, bestows infinite mental pleasure, very attractive beauty, sweetness in speech, complexion and anything else wished for.

35-38. O Nārada ! Observing fast in these asterisms in order, Arundhatī of great fortune attained highest glory. Adoring *Nakṣatra*-limbed Govinda, Janārdana, for the sake of a son, Āditya got a son in *Raivata*. Rambhā obtained beauty and sweet voice. Tilottamā obtained exquisite complexion like that of the Moon and King Purūravas got the kingdom. O Brāhmaṇa ! In this way, all those who worshipped Rūpadhārī Janārdana of *Nakṣatra*-body have fulfilled their wishes.

39. Thus is the best method of performing the vow of *Nakṣatra-puruṣa* which is sacred and bestower of welfare, glory and health to people. Now listen to the meritorious pilgrimage.

# CHAPTER EIGHTY-ONE

## The killing of Jalodbhava

*Pulastya said:*

1-17. Approaching Irāvatī, the holy daughter of a sage and having taken bath there, Prahlāda worshipped Janārdana on the eighth day of *Caitra* month. The *Dānava*-chief, Prahlāda performed the merit-giving, pious vow of *Nakṣatra-puruṣa* and then proceeded to Kurukṣetra. O sage ! Calling out the pretty *Cakra-tīrtha* with the *Airāvata-mantra*, he took bath in accordance with Vedic precepts. Keeping fast for a night, he worshipped Kurudhvaja with devotion. After purification, he proceeded to visit Nṛsiṁha. After taking bath in Devikā, he worshipped Nṛsiṁha. Keeping fast for a night, the *Dānava* visited Gokarṇa. Taking bath in the eastern part there and adoring Lord Viśvakāraka, the *Daitya* went to the other side to visit Kāmeśvara. Having taken bath there, he visited and worshipped Śaṅkara. Further, Prahlāda went to Mahāmbhas to visit Puṇḍarīka. Taking bath in Mahāmbhas and satiating the *Pitṛs*, he worshipped Puṇḍarīka and kept fast for three days. Afterwards, he visited Lord Ajita in Viśākhayūpa. Further, taking bath in *Kṛṣṇa-tīrtha*, he stayed there for three nights. Later, he visited Haṁsa in Haṁsapāda and worshipped Lord Śiva. Then, he proceeded to Payoṣṇī to visit *Akhaṇḍa-Acyuta*. After taking bath in the waters of Payoṣṇī and worshipping Akhaṇḍa, the Lord of the Universe, the wise one went to Vitastā to visit Kumārila. He (Prahlāda), attended upon by the Vālakhilyas and Marīcis, having taken bath there, worshipped Lord of *Devas* and had all his sins absolved. (Next he came to) Devahrada, where Surabhīdevī gave birth to her elegant daughter Kapilā, for pleasing the *Devas* as well as for the welfare of the universe. Taking ablution there and devotedly worshipping Śambhu according to the precepts in order, he went to Maṇiman. Having taken bath in the foremost *Tīrtha* of Prajāpati, the wise one visited Śambhu, Brahmā and Prajāpati, the Lord of *Devas.* O one rich in austerities ! Adoring these *Devas* according to the precepts, he stayed there for six nights and then left for Madhunandinī. The foremost son of Danu took bath in the waters of Madhu and visited Hara, wielding a discus and Govinda, wielding a trident.

*Nārada said:*

18. Why did the venerable Śambhu hold Sudarśana (discus) and Vāsudeva, the trident. Please tell me; I ask you.

*Pulastya said:*

19. Listen, I will relate to you this ancient story which Viṣṇu told the celestials adding, "I will take incarnation on the earth."

20. A great *Asura*-chief by name Jalodbhava of terrific powers, propitiated Brahmā by performing severe austerity. Very soon, Brahmā was pleased and offered him boons.

21-22. This enemy was invincible by the *Devas* and the *Asuras* in a battle, inviolable by any of the immortals with their weapons, unquellable by the curses of Brāhmaṇas and unsurpassable to others. With these powers, that bull among the *Dānavas* roamed on the earth, harassing the *Devas,* the great sages and the entire (group of) kings. He, with a fierce stance, impeded all rites.

23-24. Then, the immortals, sitting at the edge of the earth, went to the refuge of the overlord Hari. That venerable one along with them went to Himālaya, where Hara of three eyes was. Consulting with each other about the task to be undertaken, for the welfare of the *Devas* and sages and making up their minds for killing the foe, the two Lords of *Devas* of dreadful action, exchanged their weapons.

25-26. Then, that *Dānava,* feeling that the two Lords of the celestials, Viṣṇu and *Śiva* (Śarva) who had come intent on killing (him) were invincible by the enemies (though) of terrible form, entered into the river due to fear. Learning that the enemy of the Lord of Heaven had entered into the river Viśālā, full of birds and fish, the two Lords who came to the bank of the river, immediately concealed their forms.

27-29. Looking up at the sky with tremulous eyes, the *Dānava* at once entered the Himālaya, difficult to traverse. Viṣṇu and Śambhu saw their enemy roaming on the top of the mountain. Both of them armed, Viṣṇu with the trident and Śiva with the discus, chased him fast. He was seen by the two foremost *Devas*. His body of golden hue, torn by the discus and the trident, fell from the mountain, like a bright star falling from the sky. Thus Viṣṇu wielded the trident and Śiva wielded the discus for killing the foe.

30-33. (Prahlāda came to that place) where Jalodbhava left the water thinking that, Śaṅkara and Vāsudeva had gone away, but fell on earth from the lofty mountain because of the wound caused by the striking trident. Having arrived at that *Tīrtha,* the Lord of the *Daityas* offered worship to the two overlords of the celestials and kept fast for his own purification. After fasting with devotion, he came to Himālaya, to Śiva-Viṣṇu-*mārga* to visit Śiva. After worshipping him according to the precepts and offering gifts to Brāhmaṇas, he went over to Bhṛgutuṅga (near the confluence) in Vitastā in Himavatī, where Lord Īśvara, the noble Śaṅkara, knowing the power of the missile, gave the exquisite weapon, the discus to Viṣṇu, the foremost *Deva,* by which weapon (Viṣṇu) pierced the enemy force.

# CHAPTER EIGHTY-TWO

## The story of Śrīdāma

*Nārada said:*

1. O venerable Sir ! Why did the Lord-with-Three-Eyes give the weapon, discus, respected by all the worlds to Viṣṇu, the benefactor of the universe ?

*Pulastya said:*

2-7. Listen attentively to this ancient story concerning the gift of the discus and adding to Śiva's greatness. There was a Brāhmaṇa, a blessed householder, Vītamanyu by name, who was well-read in *Veda* and *Vedāṅga.* His wife Ātreyī was virtuous, of approved conduct, devoted to her husband, who regarded her husband as her life and was well-known as of pious conduct. To that sage who met his wife at regular periods but had no children (for a long time), a glorious son by name Upamanyu was born. O tiger among sages ! Because of penury, the mother nourished the boy giving water with rice-paste saying, "it is milk". The boy not knowing the taste of milk, took the water with rice-paste itself to be milk.

8-13. One day, he ate rice with milk which nourishes the beings, in the house of a Brāhmaṇa along with his father. The young son of the sage (now) knowing the excellence of the taste of milk, did not accept the paste solution given by his mother, the next day. Because of childhood, he cried (for milk), as Cātaka would do for water.

The mother told the crying boy with her voice choked with tears: "When Śaṅkara, Umā's spouse, Paśupati, the one wielding the trident, Virūpākṣa is not gracious, how can one have food with milk ? O son ! If you want to partake of milk which gives instant strength, then propitiate Lord Virūpākṣa, i. e. wielder of the trident. If he, the creator of the universe and the bestower of all welfare is pleased, one can even enjoy nectar; what to speak of partaking of milk."

14. Hearing the words of the mother, the son of Vītamanyu said: "Who is this Virūpākṣa whom you asked me to propitiate?"

15-23. Then, the mother of pious conduct, spoke to her son, words which were endowed with *Dharma*: "Listen to who this Virūpākṣa is; I will tell you about him. There was a great *Asura*-king, well-known as Śrīdāma, by which wicked person the whole universe was roamed about in the past like Viṣṇu and the three worlds were made wealthless. The great *Asura* desired to carry away the Śrīvatsa of Vāsudeva. Learning about his evil intentions, the venerable Janārdana, desirous of killing him, approached Maheśvara. In the meanwhile, the imperishable Śambhu, assuming *Yoga* form was on the Himālayan plateau characterised by evenness. Then, Jagannātha, Hari, approached the thousand-headed Lord and personally adored his own self by himself. He stood on his beg toe for a thousand years, praising in his own words the primeval, indefinable Brahman, the object of meditation of the *Yogīs*. Then, the Lord being pleased, gave Viṣṇu a supreme status and a divine discus, Sudarśana endowed with visible effulgence.

24-30. Having given the discus which was like the wheel of time to the Lord of the *Devas*, Lord Śaṅkara, the embodiment of all beings, spoke to Viṣṇu: "O Lord of *Devas*! Sudarśana is the foremost weapon and the destroyer of all other weapons. It has twelve spokes, six navels and is as swift as a bird. In the spokes reside the *Devas*, months and constellations (*zodiac*) and for the protection of the pious, the six seasons reside there. Agni, Ṣoma, Mitra, Varuṇa, Indra, Indrāgni, Viśvedevas, Prajāpatis, the mighty Vāyu, divine physician *Dhanvantari*, *Tapasya* and *Tapas*, the terrible—these twelve are established therein. The (lunar) months from *Caitra* to *Phālguna* are established therein. Therefore, O omnipresent one ! Taking this weapon, discus, kill the enemy of the celestials; do not hesitate; this is unfailing and respected by the king of immortals; I had kept it with me in the form of a mantra because of the strength of austerity."

31-32. So told by Śambhu, Viṣṇu said these words: "O Śambhu ! How will I know if it is unfailing or failing ? O omnipresent one ! To know that it is unfailing and unmatched, I will hurl the discus at you; you receive it."

33-36. Hearing those words of Vāsudeva, the wielder of Pināka said with least hesitation: "If so, hurl it." Hearing the words of Maheśa, Viṣṇu, desirous of knowing its power, hurled the Sudarśana at Śaṅkara with all force. The discus left by the hands of Murāri, approached the Trident-bearer and made the Lord of the universe, the Lord of sacrifice and the sacrificer into three parts. Seeing Hara cut into three parts, the long-armed Hari with his body immersed in shame, immediately prostrated himself.

37-41. Seeing Dāmodara fallen at the feet, the glorious one pleased with him said, "get up", again and again. (Śaṅkara said): "O virtuous one ! This is only the transformation of my physical form that is cut and not my real form, which cannot indeed be cut or burnt. O Keśava ! the three parts cut here by the discus shall become holy; there is no doubt. This is Hiraṇyākṣa; the other one is Suvarṇākṣa and the third one is Viśvarūpākṣa—all these three parts of my body are givers of holiness to human beings. O omnipresent one ! Get up and go to kill my foe. Learning Śrīdāma to be dead, the Devas will rejoice."

42-44. So told by Hara, the venerable Garuḍa-bannered Lord went to the plateau of the mountain of the celestials and saw Śrīdāma. Seeing that *Daitya* who had set at nought the pride of the *Devas*, Hari, the best of the *Devas*, the omnipresent one, hurled the swift discus saying, "you are killed." Then the head of the *Daitya* was severed by that discus that has no equal. The *Daitya* with his head severed, fell down from the mountain, like the peak of the mountain cut by *Vajra*.

45. After the death of the foe of *Devas*, Murāri propitiated Īśa with three eyes. Lord Viṣṇu, obtaining the exquisite weapon, the discus, went to his abode, the Ocean.

46. O my son ! It is that Virūpākṣa, the Lord of Lords, Maheśvara. If you desire a meal with milk, propitiate him, O pious one !"

47. Hearing those words of the mother, the mighty son of Vītamanyu, propitiated Virūpākṣa and obtained a meal with milk.

48. This I have told you, the highly sacred (story of) Murāri which cuts down the tree of sin. The *Tīrtha* is there only. The great Asura went there for earning merit.

## CHAPTER EIGHTY-THREE

### Prahlāda's pilgrimage

*Pulastya said:*

1-11. Having bathed in that excellent *Tīrtha*, having visited the Three-eyed Lord and worshipping Suvarṇākṣa, he proceeded to Naimiṣa from there. There are in the midst of Gomatī, Kāñcanākṣī and Śubhadā, thirty thousand *Tīrthas*, cleansing the sins. Having taken bath in them, he worshipped the Yellow-robed Lord of Lords, *Acyuta*, as well as the sages residing in the Naimiṣa forest. Then, duly worshipping the Lord of Lords, Īśāna, the great *Asura* went forth to Gayā to visit Gopati. Having taken bath in the Brahma-taḍāga and circumambulating it, he performed the holy job of offering rice-balls (*Piṇḍa*) to the *Pitṛs*. Taking bath in the pond, the restrained one worshipped the *Pitṛs* there. Then, he adored Gadāpāni and Śaṅkara, Gopati. He took bath in *Indra-tīrtha* and propitiated *Pitṛs* and *Devas*. After bathing in the waters of Mahānadī, he proceeded to Sarayū. After taking bath there and worshipping Gopratāra, Kuśeśaya, he observed fast for a night and went further, bending low with modesty. Having taken bath in *Rajas-tīrtha* and having offered *Piṇḍa* (*rice-balls*) to the *Pitṛs*, the glorious one went to visit Ajita Puruṣottama. After visiting the imperishable Puṇḍarīkākṣa, the pure one, observed fast for six nights and proceeded to South Mahendra. Visiting there, white coloured Hara with half of his body as female (*Ardhanārisvara*), the foremost of the *Devas*, he went to North Mahendra after worshipping the *Pitṛs*.

12-18. He visited the supreme god Śambhu-Gopāla adorned by the Moon. He took bath in *Soma-tīrtha* and arrived at Sahyācala. Having taken bath in Mahodakī, he worshipped Vaikuṇṭha with devotion and propitiated the celestials and *Pitṛs*, before leaving for Pāriyātragiri. He took bath in Lāṅgalinī and worshipped Aparājita. Then, arriving in Kaśeru country, he visited Viśvarūpa. There, the supreme god, Śambhu, the lord of *Yoga*, revealed his all-encompassing form, well-respected by the *Gaṇas*. Taking bath there in the waters of Maṅkuṇarikā and worshipping Maheśvara, Prahlāda proceeded to the ever-fragrant Malaya mountain. There he took bath in the big pond and adored Śaṅkara. Next Prahlāda, endowed with *Yoga*, went to visit Sadāśiva in the Vindhyas. Then, he bathed in the waters of Vipāśā and worshipped Sadāśiva. He observed fast for three nights before going to Avantī city.

19-32. He bathed there in the waters of Śiprā and worshipped Viṣṇu with devotion. He then visited Śiva in the form of Mahākāla, a dweller of cremation ground. Śaṅkara, the restrained one, assuming the *Tāmasa*-form brings about the annihilation of all beings. The Lord of the celestials staying there, rescued King Śvetaki by name, by burning Yama (Antaka) who takes away (the life of) all beings. Bhava (Śiva) whose form is adored by the celestials dwells there, always much pleased and surrounded by crores of *Pramathas*. After visiting and adoring that Mahākāla, Śambhu, the destroyer of the fierce God of Death, the restrainer of Yama, the death of Death, the multi-formed one, the dweller in crematorium, the benefactor of beings, the Lord of the Universe, the trident-bearer, he went towards Niṣadha country. Visiting and adoring Amareśvara there with devotion, he arrived in Mahodaya and visited Hayagrīva. Having taken bath in *Aśva-tīrtha*, he visited the Horse-faced Lord. After worshipping the all-pervading Lord, Śrīdhara, he proceeded to Pāñcāla country. He visited there Pāñcālika, the son of Kubera, endowed with the qualities of a lord.

Then, the restrained one went over to Prayāga. In the world-famous *Prayāga-tīrtha*, the giver of blessedness in the Yamunā region, he visited *Vaṭeśvara-Rudra* and *Yogaśāyī-Mādhava*. The great *Asura* worshipped the two deities who are to be adored with devotion. He observed fast for a month in *Māgha* and then moved to Vārāṇasī. This city is indeed a destroyer of sins. Arriving in this holy place, he took bath separately in each of the *Tīrthas* and worshipped the *Pitṛs* and *Devas*. He circumambulated the city, worshipped Avimukta and Keśava, visited Lola-Divākara and then went to Madhuvana. The most pious of the *Asuras* saw there Lord Svāyambhuva. After worshipping the deity, the lustrous one came to the Puṣkara grove. He bathed in all the three *Tīrthas* and adored the *Devas* and *Pitṛs*.

33. This most sanctifying ancient story was also told by the great sage Agastya. It bestows wealth and glory and destroys many sins by reciting it or by listening to it or by remembering it.

## CHAPTER EIGHTY-FOUR

### Prahlāda's Pilgrimage (Continued)

*Pulastya said:*

1-9. O sage ! After the *Dānava*-chief, Prahlāda proceeded on pilgrimage, Vairocana (Bali) came to visit Kurukṣetra. In that most pious *Tīrtha*, the Bhārgava, Śukra, the bull among Brāhmaṇas, invited all leading Brāhmaṇas. Having come to know of the invitation by Bhṛgu, the learned sages—Ātreyas, Gautamas, Kauśikas and Āṅgirasas, left Kurujāṅgala. They went towards northern direction along the river Śatadravī. Having taken bath in the waters of Śatadravī, they then proceeded to Vipāśā. Having performed ablution there and having worshipped *Devas* and *Pitṛs*, they reached the holy Kiraṇā river which emerged from the rays of the sun. O divine sage ! All those great sages proceeded to Īśvarī after bathing in the holy waters of Airāvatī. The hermits had their ablutions in the waters of Devikā. Later, the hermits, Ātreyas and others descended into the river Payoṣṇī for bathing, O sage ! O best of Brāhmaṇas ! When they plunged, they saw their reflection under water which caused great wonder. Rising up, they again saw and were surprised. Then, all the sages came out after bath.

10-28a. They worshipped Puṣkarākṣa, Ayogandhi and Brahmā. Then, again in *Koṭi-tīrtha*, a *Tīrtha* in Sarasvatī, famous in the three worlds, they saw the Bull-bannered Rudrakoṭi.

The foremost Brāhmaṇas from Naimiṣa, Magadha, Sindhu, Dharmāraṇya, Puṣkara, Daṇḍakāraṇya, Campā, Tārakaccha and *Devikā-tīrtha* came over there to visit Śaṅkara. O sage ! The Brāhmaṇas who had success in austerities came there in crores and were anxious to see Hara. They were vying with one another to be first (to see Hara), O sage ! Seeing those agitated great sages, whose sins had been burnt down, Hara (Śiva) out of pity assumed crores of forms. Then all the sages were very much pleased. They created *Tīrthas* separately and stayed there worshipping Maheśvara. Thus Śambhu came to be called by the name Rudrakoṭi. The glorious, self-controlled devotee, Prahlāda saw Rudrakoṭi. After bathing in the *Koṭi-tīrtha*, he propitiated the *Vasus* and the *Pitṛs* and worshipped Rudrakoṭi.

Next he went to Kurujāṅgala. Then, he saw the foremost deity, Sthāṇu, Śaṅkara, the beloved of Pārvatī and the one respected by the celestials, immersed in the waters of Sarasvatī. Having taken bath in the waters of Sarasvatī, he worshipped Sthāṇu with devotion. Next he bathed in Daśāśvamedha and adored the celestials and *Pitṛs.*

He being pure after a bath in the pond there, worshipped Sahasra-liṅga. After prostrating himself before the preceptor, Śukra, he went over to *Soma-tīrtha.* He bathed there and worshipped the *Pitṛs* and *Soma* with devotion. Going over to Kṣīrikāvāsa, the wise one took his bath. Circumambulating the tree and adoring Varuṇa, the wise one went to Padmākṣī city after visiting Kurudhvaja again. Adoring there, *Mitrāvaruṇa* and the *Bhāskaras* who are honoured by one and all, the restrained one came to Kumāradhārā and saw Svāmi. Having bathed in Kapiladhārā, he propitiated the *Pitṛs* and celestials. After visiting and adoring Skanda, he went to Narmadā. Having taken bath there and having worshipped Vāsudeva, the spouse of Lakṣmī, he proceeded to see the sustainer of earth, the discus-bearing Varāha. Taking bath in *Kokamukha-tīrtha* and worshipping the sustainer of earth, he went to Madhu country (to visit) Trisauvarṇa, Mahādeva. Then, having bathed in Nārīhrada, he worshipped Śaṅkara. From there, he arrived at Kālañjara and visited Nīlakaṇṭha. Taking bath in the waters of *Nīla-tīrtha,* he worshipped Śiva.

28b-33. Then, he proceeded to Prabhāsa in the region near the sea, to visit Iśvara. Having taken bath at the confluence of the river Sarasvatī with the ocean, he saw the Lord of the Universe, Someśvara with matted hair. Moon, the Lord of stars emaciated and condemned by the curse of Dakṣa was rejuvinated by Viṣṇu and Śaṅkara of matted hair. Having adored these two deities, he went to Mahālaya. Having worshipped Rudra there, he proceeded towards Uttara Kuru country. After worshipping Padmanābha there, he went to Sapta-godāvara. He bathed there and adored the Lord of gods, Bhīma, bowed to by the three worlds. Going to Dāruvana, the glorious one visited Śrīliṅga. After worshippng there, he went to Brāhmaṇī, bathed there and adored

Tridaśeśvara (The Lord of thirty-three (30 tridaśa-30 being the round number) Gods.

34-41. Going to Plakṣāvataraṇa, he worshipped Śrīnivāsa. Next he went to Kuṇḍina, where he worshipped Prāṇatṛptida. After duly worshipping four-armed Śūrpāraka, he arrived at Māgadhāraṇya and visited Vasudhādipa. After worshipping the Lord of the Universe, he went to Prajāsukha. Having taken bath in the great *Tīrtha,* he prostrated himself before Vāsudeva. Arriving in Śoṇa and worshipping Īśvara, Rukmadharma, he went with devotion to visit Mahādeva called Haṁsa in Mahākośī. Having worshipped Jagannātha, he proceeded to the excellent Saindhavāraṇya. After visiting and worshipping Hari, he went to *Kanakhala-tīrtha.* There, the *Dānava* worshipped Bhadrakālīśa, Virabhadra, Dhanādhipa and Mervarka. Later he went to Girivraja. Having duly worshipped Lord Paśupati, Maheśvara, the benefactor of the universe there, he went forth to Kāmarūpa. After worshipping the foremost god of three eyes and of moon's complexion together with Mṛḍānī, he went to the excellent *Tīrtha* called Mahā, where he adored Mahādeva.

42-45. Then, he went to Trikūṭa mountain, the son of the mountain (Sumeru), to visit Cakrapāṇi. Worshipping with devotion the Lord who rescued the elephant, he recited the hymn which is highly sanctifying. The son of the Lord of *Dānavas* reverently dwelt there for three months, subsisting on roots, fruits and water. Gifting gold to excellent Brāhmaṇas, he went to the dreadful Daṇḍaka forest. There he saw Puṇḍarīkākṣa, assuming the form of a divine tree with numerous branches that kept away the large beasts of prey. The *Asura,* an ardent devotee, stayed under that tree for three nights, sleeping on the bare ground and reciting the *Sārasvata* hymn.

46-49. The learned *Dānava* proceeded from there to the important *Tīrtha, Sarvapāpapranāśana,* to visit Hari, the destroyer of all sins. Before Hari, he recited the two hymns that destroy all sins and which were instructed in the past by the venerable Janārdana in the form of a hog (Kroḍa). From there, the Lord of *Daityas* went to Śālagrāma of great merit, where Viṣṇu is established in pillars and other immovables. O sage ! The mighty ardent devotee liked that place, knowing Viṣṇu to be all-pervading there and worshipped the feet of the Lord.

50. This I have told you, the highly sanctifying pilgrimage of Prahlāda associated with hosts of sages, by reciting, listening to or making a gift of which people become freed from sins.

## CHAPTER EIGHTY-FIVE

### The release of the King-Elephant

*Nārada said:*

1. You please relate to me the four (hymns): The release of the King Elephant and others, worthy of recitation, which Prahlāda, the *Dānava,* recited with devotion before the Lord.

*Pulastya said:*

2. O one rich in penance ! Listen, I will relate to you those hymns. The evil dreams of those who recite, recall or listen to them get destroyed.

3. First you listen to the Release of the King Elephant; after that *Sārasvata* hymn and then the two holy *Pāpapraśamana* hymns.

4-5. The glorious mountain Trikūṭa by name, the son of the Mountain-chief Sumeru, having the effulgence of the Sun and full of jewels, sprung up by breaking through the ocean. Its rock-surfaces were washed clean by the waves of the waters of the Milk-ocean and it was resorted to by hosts of *Devas* and sages.

6-9. The elegant mountain with many a cascade was thronged by *Apsarās, Gandharvas, Kinnaras, Yakṣas, Siddhas, Cāraṇas, Guhyakas* and *Vidyādharas* along with their spouses and by self-controlled hermits. It looked great with wolves, leopards and huge elephants. It was adorned everywhere with varieties of trees like *Punnāga, Karṇikāra, Bilva, Āmalaka, Pāṭala, Cūta* (mango), *Nīpa, Kadamba, Candana* (sandal), *Agaru, Campaka, Śāla, Tāla, Tamāla, Sarala, Arjuna, Parpaṭa* and others.

10-15. From its peaks dotted with minerals, torrents issued forth. It was made beautiful by the charming plateaus and three wide peaks. The peaks were full of deer, monkeys, lions and elephants which were always in rut. They were filled with the noises of *Cakora* and peacocks and the crying of *Jīvañjīvakas.* One of its peaks was golden served by the Sun. It was strewn with varieties of flowers and scented with varieties of perfumes. The second was a silver peak served by the Moon. It had the shining of grey cloud and was comparable to a collection of jewels. It brightened the quarters with lusters of diamond, sapphire and *Lapis Lazuli.* The third peak was the abode of Brahmā and was excellent and the best. Neither the ungrateful nor the cruel nor *Rākṣasas* nor those who have not performed austerities in the world nor the people who have committed sins could see it.

16-18. On one side of that mountain was a lake with golden lotuses. It was full of *Kāraṇḍavas* and was adorned by *Rājahaṁsas.* It was beautified with *Kumudas, Utpalas, Kalhāras, Puṇḍarīkas* and adorned by *Kamalas* and golden *Śatapatras.* The lake was surrounded on all sides by leaves shining like emeralds, by flowers appearing golden and by the bushes of bamboo.

19-21. In that lake there was a mighty, wicked crocodile hiding under the water, unbeatable even by the huge elephants. Then, there was the chief elephant of the herd, whose body with elegant tusks appeared like a walking-mountain. It was oozing ichor and was desirous of water.

That elephant having the shine of collyrium was comparable to *Airāvata.* He perfumed the mountain with the aroma of ichor and his eyes reeled due to infatuation.

22-31. Once, he being thirsty and desirous of having bath, entered the waters of that lake. While he moved into the lotus grove majestically, surrounded by the herd, he was caught by that ferocious crocodile whose form was not visible. Even as the female elephants were looking on and were piteously crying, (the leader) was being dragged by the very powerful crocodile into the lotus grove. As the elephant was pulling towards the bank, the crocodile was pulling into the water. The wonderful, fierce duel between the two, took one thousand years. The elephant was made unable to move, being entangled by the aquatic creepers. Being tied round by the strong and tight nooses and caught by the terrible one, the elephant who struggled to his best and trumpeted loudly was at grief and breathless. Being in such profound calamity, he thought of Hari. That excellent elephant devoted to Nārāyaṇa, fully surrendered then to that divine being only. With a single mind, with self-control and with purity of inner-self, he was devoted to the *Garuḍa*-bannered Lord because of practice in the earlier births. He adored the primordial Lord, the great Lord Keśava as white as the foam of churned nectar, the wielder of conch, discus and mace, the one having a thousand auspicious names, the all-pervading one, the birthless one and the first of the gods. Holding a golden lotus in the tip of his trunk and seeking release from the calamity, the elephant recited a hymn.

*The King-elephant said:*

32-44. OM. Salutation to the primary source, to the invincible one, to the magnanimous one, to the lord who is not subordinate; salutation to you, to the desireless one; salutation to the first one, to the lovely one, to the ancient one, to the founder; salutation to the one without a second, to the unmanifest one; salutation to the mysterious one, to the hidden one, to the virtue, to the one abiding in virtue; salutation to the inconceivable one, to the inestimable one, to the unmatched one; salutation to Śiva, to the peaceful one, to the undisturbed (unfretting) one, to the glorious one; salutation to the primeval one, to the first one, to the ancient one; salutation to that god who is beyond attributes and is endowed with attributes; salutation to the basis of the universe, to Govinda; salutation to Padmanābha (having lotus in the navel), to the source of *Sāṅkhya* and *Yoga*; salutation to the overlord of the universe, to Lord Śiva, to Hari; salutation to Nārāyaṇa, to the universal one, to the supreme soul; salutation, salutation to the dwarf physically, to Nārāyaṇa of limitless prowess, to the one who bears *Śrī, Śārṅga,* discus, sword and mace; salutaton to that *Puruṣa* par excellence; salutation to the mysterious one, to the abode of *Veda,* to the great serpent, to the lion, to the killer of the *Daityas,* to the one with four arms, to the one praised by Brahmā, Indra, Rudra, sages, *Cāraṇas,* to the best of gods, to the perfect one, to the imperishable one; salutation to one reclining on the expanded hoods of the Chief of serpents, to the most-liked one, to the one comparable to cow's milk, gold, parrot and dark cloud, to the yellow-robed one, to the destroyer of Madhu and Kaiṭabha, to the universe, to the one with charming diadem, to the indestructible one; salutation to the one in whose navel is grown a lotus on which sits Brahmā, to the glorious one dwelling in the Milk-ocean, to the one decorated with many varieties of golden armlets, to the master of all, to the giver of boons and to the excellent one; salutation to the one pleased by devotion, to the one having the best glowing Sudarśana, to the one whose prowess is intent on clearing the impediments of Indra, to the one with wide and bright eyes like a full-blown lotus, to the overlord of *Yoga,* to the boon-giver and to the excellent one; salutation to the abode of Brahmā, to the abode of the immortals, to the abode of the universe, to the abode of one's own welfare, to Nārāyaṇa,to the self-evolving one, to the great boar; salutations.

45-50. I take refuge in the unchangeable one, in the unmanifest one, in the one of inconceivable form, in Nārāyaṇa, in the primeval divine cause, in the ancient *Puruṣa,* in that lord of gods who alone remains at the end of the *Yuga.* I take refuge in the Lord of *Yoga,* in the one having wonderfully charming diadem, in the one beyond comprehension, in the exquisite one, in the one beyond *Prakṛti,* in the inner-self, in the self-born, in the supreme Vāsudeva. I take refuge in the mysterious lord, in the imperceptible one, in the unmanifest one, in the inconceivable one, in the imperishable one, in the one whose form is Veda, in the eternal one whom the great speak of as *Puruṣa,* the eternal one. I resort to that eternal Lord Viṣṇu, the final resort who is satiated by excellent virtues, who is spoken of as imperishable, all-pervading Brahmā and learning about whom one is rescued from the jaws of death. I take refuge in Viṣṇu, Janārdana, the lord of the celestials, the treasure of *Veda,* the almighty, the one with lotus in the navel (Padmanābha), the one with gold in the navel (Hiraṇyanābha), the ungaugeable one, the one who is the result, the action and the cause. I resort to Keśava whose entire body is adorned with jewels, with diadem, with armlets and very valuable necklaces, who is yellow-robed, who is wonderful with golden embellishments and who is wearing garlands.

51-56. I surrender to the master, to the primeval Acyuta, to the one arisen from the high-note, to the most worthy among the masters of the *Veda,* to the most worthy among those engaged in *Yoga* and the experts in *Sāṅkhya,* to the one having the splendour of Āditya, Rudra, the Aśvins and the Vasus. I surrender to the one marked by Śrīvatsa, to Mahādeva, to the mysterious one, to the attractive one, to the subtle one, to the matchless one, to the most distinguished one, to the giver of security. I surrender to the origin of all beings, to the attributeless one, to the supreme lord, to the final resort of ascetics who have renounced all attachments. I devotedly surrender to the venerable one, to the presiding one of *Guṇas*, to the indestructible one, to the one with lotus-like eyes, to the refuge, to the one who is affectionate to the devotees. I surrender to Janārdana, to the one with three strides, to the Lord of the three worlds, to the Grandsire of all, to the one engaged in *Yoga*, to the magnanimous one. I surrender to the primordial deity, to the unborn one, to Śambhu, to the manifest and the unmanifest one, to the eternal one, to Nārāyaṇa, to the one of atomic form, to the one who is fond of the Brāhmaṇas.

57-60. Salutation to the god Hara and salutation to the light of all; I surrender to the lord of god of gods and to the one who is always minuter than the minutest; salutation to the single principle of the world, to the supreme soul beyond; salutation to the thousand-headed one, to the infinite one, to the magnanimous one. All the sages, the masters of the *Vedas* speak of you as the refuge and the final resort of Brahmā and others. Salutation to you, O lotus-eyed one ! O giver of security to the devotees ! Salutation to you, O Subrahmaṇya ! Save me; I have surrendered unto you.

*Pulastya said:*

61-68. Considering the devotion of that elephant, Viṣṇu, the wielder of conch, discus and mace, whose birth was not in vain, became pleased. O one rich in penance ! Sitting on Garuḍa, Keśava, the lord of the universe and the basis of the universe, made the occasion for his presence in that lake. Madhusūdana of inconceivable nature brought out of the lake quickly, the King Elephant caught by the crocodile, as well as that crocodile. Mādhava severed the crocodile in the water with his discus and released the King Elephant who had surrendered to him from the nooses. Thus the most pious *Gandharva*, Hūhū who had to take the form of the crocodile due to the curse of a *Deva* and being released by Kṛṣṇa, went to heaven. The elephant too, being touched by Viṣṇu, became a person of divine form. The elephant and the most pious *Gandharva* were simultaneously freed from sin. The lotus-eyed lord of gods, fond of those who surrender, being worshipped by both of them became pleased. O tiger among sages ! The venerable *Yogī*, Madhusūdana spoke in a sweet voice to the King Elephant who had surrendered himself.

*The venerable one said:*

69-73. The evil-dreams of those persons who being pure and who with a fixed mind remember me, you, this lake, this slaying of crocodile, the bushes of *Kīcakareṇu*, the form of the son of Meru, the *Aśvattha* (peepul) tree, *Bhāskara*, Gaṅgā, as well as the Naimiṣa grove and of those who with a vow of purity recite and listen with devotion (to this anecdote)—will get destroyed and they will have good dreams. Those persons who getting up in the morning recall to their mind the Fish, Tortoise, Boar, Dwarf and Narasiṁha (incarnations of Viṣṇu), Garuḍa, the King Elephant and the cause of the creation and destruction, become absolved of all sins and attain meritorious worlds.

*Pulastya said:*

74-75. So saying to the King Elephant, the *Garuḍa*-bannered Hṛṣīkeśa, touched both the elephant and the *Gandharva* with his hand. Then, assuming a divine form, the King Elephant with his mind set on Nārāyaṇa, took refuge in Viṣṇu, Madhusūdana.

76-77. Releasing the best of the elephants from the bondage of sins and the crocodile from the curse, the venerable and glorious Nārāyaṇa, Viṣṇu, the master of the wonderful act, being adored by the sages who had fixed their minds on the mysterious god assumed a movement which is hard to comprehend.

78-79. Observing the release of the King Elephant, the *Devas* led by Indra bowed to the magnanimous master, Hari, Nārāyaṇa. After observing the release of the King of elephants, the exalted sages and the *Cāraṇas* with their eyes wide due to wonder, glorified Janārdana.

80-84. Brahmā, the master of the Prajāpatis, seeing the release of the King Elephant performed by the Discus-bearer, said these words: "Persons who listen to this, getting up every morning, will attain exalted success and their evil dreams are destroyed. O one rich in austerity ! The (episode of) the release of the King Elephant, whether recited, recalled or listened to, will be the destroyer of all sins. This account of Murāri is sanctifying, supremely holy and worthy of being recited, by reciting which one attains release from the bondage of all sins just as the elephant was (released). I bow down to that unborn one, to the exalted one, to the one having unique lotus in the navel, to Nārāyaṇa, to the treasure of *Veda*, to the lord of celestials, to the mysterious deity, to the primeval *Puruṣa*, to the exalted master of the universe."

## CHAPTER EIGHTY-SIX

### The Sārasvata hymn

*Pulastya said:*

1-6. There was a greedy Kṣatriya, an ill-wisher of the Brāhmaṇas, fond of troubling others, mean and unscrupulous by nature. He never paid respect to the *Pitṛs* or *Devas* or Brāhmaṇas. After the end of his life, he was born as a fierce *Rākṣasa.* The foremost of sinners lived by cruel acts due to the evil results of his own action and more so because of his *Rākṣasa* nature. As he was thus engaged in evil ways, one hundred years elapsed. Because of that very blemish of his acts, he was not interested in any other types of livelihood. Whatever animal that the *Rākṣasa* would see and was within the reach of his arms, that *Rākṣasa* of fierce acts would grab and eat. While thus he, the most wicked one was carrying on the killing of animals, a large stretch of time passed and the age too, matured.

7-26. Once on the bank of a river, he saw a distinguished, pure ascetic, an adept preceptor of *Yoga*, performing austerity with his arms raised like a child, with his senses controlled properly and solely directed towards Vāsudeva. O Brāhmaṇa ! He was guarded by this protective hymn—

"Let Viṣṇu, bearing the discus stay in the east; Viṣṇu, bearing the mace in the south; Viṣṇu, bearing the *Śārṅga* (bow) in the west; in the north, Viṣṇu, bearing the sword; let Hṛṣīkeśa stay in the corners and Janārdana in the space between them; Hari in the boar form on the earth and Hari of man-lion form above me in the sky; (May) this stainless Sudarśana discus with razor-like edges, whirling, and having dazzling beams, kill the spirits and the *Rākṣasas;* may this mace with a thousand rays, kill the wolves above and be the destroyer of *Rākṣasas, Bhūtas, Piśācas* and *Ḍākinīs*; may Vāsudeva's *Śārṅga,* making a loud twang, kill completely my enemies—animals, human beings, *Kūṣmāṇḍas,* spirits and so on; may those my shaken enemies be instantly made humbler by the sword with the blade having the lustre of moon-light, like the snakes (humbled) by *Garuḍa*; the Kūṣmāṇḍas, *Daityas, Yakṣas, Rākṣasas,* the spirits, Vināyakas, cruel human beings, Jṛmbhakas, birds, lions and other animals, reptiles like snakes–may these be humbled, being struck by the trumpet of the conch of Viṣṇu; may those *Kūṣmāṇḍas* who hamper mental faculty, those persons who destroy memory, those who bring down the strength and energy, those who destroy the shadows, those who impede the pleasures, those who distort the lucky marks—get lost, being struck by the force of Viṣṇu's discus; may I have intellectual health, mental health and health of the sense-organs through adoring the Lord of Lords, Vāsudeva; may Hari, Janārdana be at my back, in my front, on the south, on the north and at the corners. Having adored the Lord, the infinite, the imperishable Janārdana, the lord of life, one does not sink down. As Hari is the supreme Brahman, so also Keśava in the form of the universe. By singing the name of Acyuta with that eternal truth (in mind), may the three types of my evils (in auspiciousness) get destroyed."

Thus he sat creating for himself, Viṣṇu-cage for safety.

The mighty *Rākṣasa,* however, ran after him. O divine sage ! Then the speed of the *Rākṣasa* was cut short all of a sudden by the protective force set by the Brāhmaṇa and the *Rākṣasa* stood for four months, when the Brāhmaṇa completed his meditation. Then, at the end of his prayers, he saw the *Rākṣasa*—miserable, having no strength or inclination, powerless and not knowing what to do. Seeing such a *Rākṣasa,* he overcome by compassion, consoled him. He asked the reason for his coming there. He stated the facts as they happened, his nature and the crippling of his power by the protective force (when he came) to see him.

27-32. After duly stating the reason, the *Rākṣasa* being despondent with his actions, said to the Brāhmaṇa: "Please be gracious to me. I have committed a number of sins. Many a pious person has been killed by me. Many women have been made widows and childless by me. I have brought extinction of a large number of animals for none of their fault. From those sins, I would like to be absolved by your grace. To annihilate those sins, please bring about the destruction of my *Adharma.* Please impart me instruction that destroys this my sin."

Hearing those words of the *Rākṣasa,* the best of Brāhmaṇas spoke these words, which were cogent from the point of view of *Dharma* and *Artha*—

"O *Rākṣasa* ! How is it that inquisitiveness regarding the path of virtue has all of a sudden arisen in you who are not pious and are unscrupulous by nature ?"

*The Rākṣasa said:*

33-35. O Brāhmaṇa ! Today I encountered you but was forcibly thrown away by the protective force. By your contact, this despondency of high order has arisen in me. What that protective force, the contact with which, have I been made to have this good despondency is, I do not know nor do I know its effects; O knower of piety ! Please be compassionate; have sympathy for me; O respected Sir ! Please do that by which my sins are absolved.

*Pulastya said:*

36. O noble one ! So told by him, the sage replied the *Rākṣasa* after deliberating for a long time.

*The sage said:*

37-38. That you, being despondent by your actions, asked me for instruction is indeed proper. Getting rid of the sins is beneficial. But I do not instruct *Dharma* to *Rākṣasas*. O gentle one ! You ask those Brāhmaṇas who are engaged in imparting instructions.

39-41. So saying, the Brāhmaṇa went away and the *Rākṣasa* got engrossed in worry. His senses being afflicted by worry, he thought, "How will there be destruction of my sins." He did not eat any living being, though tormented by hunger. He only ate a little living being at the sixth part of the day. Once while roaming about in the vast forest overcome by hunger, he saw a *Brahmacārī* carrying fruits, coming.

42. The hermit's son caught by that *Rākṣasa*, losing all hopes of life, told the *Rākṣasa* in gentle words—

*The Brāhmaṇa said:*

43. O sinless one ! You tell me for what reason you held me; please speak; may you fare well; I am here; command me.

*The Rākṣasa said:*

44. At the sixth part of the day you have come as food for me who am hungry, hard-hearted, very sinful, unscrupulous and engaged in harming the Brāhmaṇas.

*The Brāhmaṇa said:*

45-47. O *Rākṣasa* ! If it is very necessary that you should eat me, I will immediately return to you after offering these fruits to my preceptor. Coming here, I collected the fruits for the sake of my preceptor. (It is proper) for me who am duty-bound to place the collected fruits before him. You please wait for a while till I come back here, after offering the fruits to my preceptor.

*The Rākṣasa said:*

48-49. O Brāhmaṇa ! No one, be it a god, caught at the sixth part of the day is released; that is wicked life; there is only one condition for your release; listen to that; without doubt I will let you go, if you carry it out.

*The Brāhmaṇa said:*

50. O *Rākṣasa* ! I shall carry it out, if it is not disagreeable to my preceptor, if it does not go against piety and if it does not conflict with my vow.

*The Rākṣasa said:*

51-55. O Brāhmaṇa ! Sinful acts have incessantly been committed by me naturally and due to the defect of my social status in particular, without any discriminative thought. Right from my childhood my mind is interested in doing evil deeds and not in pious (acts). You tell me that, by which I may be released from the destruction caused by those sins. Ignorantly, varieties of (sinful) acts have been committed by me after getting this evil birth. O Brāhmaṇa ! Please tell me the way out. O hermit's son ! If you tell me this in detail, then you will surely get free from me, afflicted by hunger. Otherwise, you will be consumed as food by me of wicked nature, who am hungry and thirsty. Unscrupulous and hard-hearted as I am, I eat you at the sixth part of the day.

56-60. So told by the terrible *Rākṣasa*, the hermit's son, unable to explain that, was engaged in deep thought. The Brāhmaṇa who was in a fix, after deliberating for long, took refuge in Agni to get enlightenment: "If Agni is attended upon after serving my preceptor or if the vows have been well observed by me, then, may Agni of seven flames protect me. As I have looked upon my preceptor with such respect which was not inferior to that shown to my mother or father, may Agni, the purifier, protect me. As I have not disrespected my preceptor mentally, physically or verbally, may that Agni protect me."

61-64. O sage ! Sarasvatī, at the behest of the seven-flamed Agni, appeared before him who was making such oaths mentally. She said to the hermit's son, afflicted due to the *Rākṣasa* hold: "O hermit's son ! Be not afraid; I will now liberate you from this danger. Being on the tip of your tongue, I will say all that is beneficial to the *Rākṣasa* and then, you will get liberated." Saying thus, unseen by that *Rākṣasa*, Sarasvatī disappeared. The Brāhmaṇa on his part told the *Rākṣasa*—

*The Brāhmaṇa said:*

65-73. Listen to what is beneficial for cleansing all sins and to what helps in accruing merit for you as well as for other sinners. It is to be repeatedly recited, after one gets up in the morning or at noon or in the evening. Its constant recitation will undoubtedly give the reciter, prosperity and peace: OM. I prostrate myself before Hari, Kṛṣṇa, Hṛṣīkeśa, Vāsudeva, Janārdana, Jagannātha; may he drive away my sins. I prostrate myself before the Lord of all the movable and immovable beings, the benefactor, Govinda, Śeṣaśāyī (recliner on Śeṣa), the supreme deity, may he drive away my sin. I prostrate myself before the Conch-bearer, the Discus-bearer, the Śārṅga-bearer, the one wearing necklace, the spouse of Lakṣmī; may he drive away my sin. I prostrate myself before Dāmodara, the exalted one, the lotus-eyed one, Acyuta, the one adored by the adorable; may he drive away my sin. I prostrate myself before Nārāyaṇa, Nara, Śauri, Mādhava, Madhusūdana, the support of the earth; may he drive away my sin. I prostrate myself before Keśava, the killer of Keśi, the slayer of Kaṁsa and Ariṣṭa, the mighty-armed one; may he drive my sins away. I prostrate myself before the one having Śrīvatsa on the chest, Śrīśa, Śrīdhara, Śrīniketana (abode of Śrī), the beloved of Śrī; may he drive my sin away.

74-80. I surrender to that indefinable Vāsudeva, the restrainer of all beings, the imperishable one whom the self-controlled ones meditate upon. I surrender unto the one called Vāsudeva on whom (the *Yogins*) meditate, withdrawing the movement of Manas from all mental objects. I surrender unto Vāsudeva, the supreme Brahma, the all-pervading one, the one having the form of all beings, the receptacle of all, the overlord. I surrender unto the supreme-self, the unmanifest one, the imperishable lord whom the wise ones resort to, at the cessation of Karma. I surrender unto him who is bereft of both virtue and vice, resorting to whom the *Yogins* will not have rebirth. I surrender unto Acyuta, the lord who as Brahmā creates all the universe with *Devas, Asuras* and humans. I surrender unto him from whose faces as Brahmā, emerged the form of the four *Vedas*, the highest form of the master.

81-89. I bow down to Janārdana, the lord who assumes the form of Brahmā, the source of the universe, the one engaged in creating in the world of creation. I bow down to Janārdana, to Viṣṇu, the primeval lord by whom the earth was sustained, the *Daityas* were killed and the immortals were rescued. I bow down to Janārdana, to Viṣṇu who is the embodiment of sacrifice, the lord of sacrifice, the promoter of sacrifice and the one whom the Brāhmaṇas worship with sacrifice. I bow down to Janārdana, to Rudra, to the destroyer who destroys the row of nether worlds, living beings as well as the worlds. I bow down to Janārdana who as Rudra dances, after consuming all this universe as it was created. I salute the all-pervading deity whose aspects are the Celestials, *Asuras,* hosts of *Pitṛs, Yakṣas, Gandharvas* and *Rākṣasas.* I salute the all-pervading deity of whom all the *Devas* and all types of human beings are aspects. I salute the all-pervading deity of whom the trees, bushes etc., as well as the animals and beasts are parts. I salute the omnipresent one who is all (everything), the inexhaustible one, the endless one, apart from whom there is nothing and in which magnanimous one, everything is.

90-99. As Viṣṇu is imminent in all beings like fire in wood, so may my entire lot of sins get destroyed. As everything from Brahmā onwards including the movable and the immovable and that which is comprehended by knowledge is encompassed by Viṣṇu, so may my sins get destroyed. So also may all my good and bad actions, my *Rajas, Sattva* and *Tamas* characteristics and sins committed in many births get destroyed. The sins committed by me physically or mentally or verbally, at night, in morning, at noon, in the afternoon, at twilight; whatever vice, mental or physical committed by me while standing or moving or while on bed; whether done involuntarily or voluntarily or with mind disturbed by infatuation—may all these get dissolved at once because of adoring Vāsudeva. The sin arising from greed for another's wife and other's wealth and from malice, sin committed by me while hurling blames on magnanimous ones, hurting others, those committed in respect of food, drinks, eatables, food to be sucked, food to be licked-may all these get dissolved like a vessel made of salt in water. The sin committed by me in my childhood, in boyhood, in youth and in old age as well as that committed in another birth-may all these get dissolved like a vessel made of salt in water, through the recitation of the names like Nārāyaṇa, Govinda, Hari, Kṛṣṇa.

100-104. Salutations to Viṣṇu, to Vāsudeva, to Hari, to Keśava, to Janārdana, to Kṛṣṇa; salutations, salutations once more; salutation to the one who sets at naught the impending hell, to the one who killed Kaṁsa; salutation to the one who killed the enemies of Devas—Ariṣṭa, Keśi and Cāṇūra. Who can be other than you that could deprive Bali (of greatness)? Who can be other than you that could subdue the King of Haihayas (Kārtavīrya)? Who can build a bridge across the ocean other than you? Who can kill the ten-headed Rāvaṇa along with his ministers and capital city? O Madhusūdana ! who, except you can feel pleasure in Nanda's Gokula? Who can be the restrainer or punisher of Pralamba, Pūtanā and others, other than you, O god of gods !

105-109. If this holy, excellent *Dharma* of Viṣṇu is recited by a person in favourable or unfavourable situations, voluntarily or involuntarily, the sins committed by such a person in previous seven births, major or minor sins, holy sacrifices and others, repetitive recitations, burnt offerings and vows—all of a *Yogī* get dissolved like an unbaked vessel in water. Along with reciting this and recalling Hari, if a person gives over every day, sixteen vessels full of sesamum for one full year by keeping unflinching celibacy, will attain the abode of Viṣṇu. What I have told you is the truth.

110. Thus what is factual is told by me. There is not even a little of falsehood in this. So too, may this release me, whose entire body is held by the *Rākṣasa*.

*Pulastya said:*

111. When it was uttered thus, the Brāhmaṇa was released by that *Rākṣasa*. The Brāhmaṇa having no desire, told the *Rākṣasa* again.

*The Brāhmaṇa said:*

112-116. O fortunate one ! This Sārasvata hymn of Viṣṇu, which destroys your sin has been uttered by me as said by Sarasvatī. As directed by Agni, Sarasvatī, being on the tip of my tongue uttered this hymn of Viṣṇu that gives peace to all. You worship Jagannātha, Keśava with this. When Keśava is adored, you will get the removal of the curse. O *Rākṣasa* !

by adoring Hṛṣīkeśa every day with this hymn and having firm devotion, you will be absolved of the sin. Hari, when adored shall without doubt destroy all sins. When Hari is praised with devotion, he will be the destroyer of all sins of the people.

*Pulastya said:*

117-119. Then, bowing down to that Brāhmaṇa, the mighty and distinguished *Rākṣasa* getting (what he needed), started towards *Śālagrāma* from there only for austerity. Reciting this *Sārasvata* hymn day and night and being deeply attached to divine worship, the *Rākṣasa* performed austerity. Propitiating Jagannātha, the *Puruṣa* par excellence there, and being absolved of all sins, he reached the auspicious abode of Viṣṇu.

120-121. O Brāhmaṇa ! This *Sārasvata* hymn of Viṣṇu, I have told you, the hymn which Sarasvatī sitting in the mouth of the Brāhmaṇa, recited beautifully. Any person who recites this excellent hymn of Vāsudeva will get relief from all miseries.

## CHAPTER EIGHTY-SEVEN

### The sin-allaying hymn-1

*Pulastya said:*

1-23. Salutation to you, O Lord of the Universe ! Salutation to you, O God of Gods ! O Vāsudeva ! Salutation to you; O one of multiforms ! Salutation to you ; O unique sovereign ! Salutation to you; O Vṛṣākapi ! Salutation to you; O Śrīnivāsa! Salutation to you; O promoter of beings ! Salutation to you; O Viśvaksena ! Salutation to you; O Nārāyaṇa ! Salutation to you; O bull-bannered one ! Salutation to you; O truth-bannered one ! Salutation to you; O sacrifice-bannered one! Salutation to you; O virtue-bannered one ! Salutation to you; O palm-bannered one ! Salutation to you; O Garuḍa-bannered one ! Salutation to you; O worthiest one ! O Viṣṇu! O Vaikuṇṭha ! O most excellent Puruṣa ! Salutation to you; O Jayanta ! Vijaya, Jaya, Ananta (endless), Aparājita (unconquered), Salutation to you; O Kṛtāvarta ! O Mahāvarta! O Mahādeva ! Salutation to you ! O beginningless one ! O one who is the beginning and end, O one who is the middle and end ! O beloved of the lotus-born (Lakṣmī)! Salutation to you; O conqueror of city ! Salutation to you ! O conqueror of enemy, Salutation to you ! O conqueror of wealth ! Salutation to you; O conqueror of prosperity ! Salutation to you; O one having creation as embryo ! O one of bright fame! O widely-known one ! Salutation to you; Salutation to Hiraṇyagarbha (one having gold as embryo); Salutation to Padmagarbha (one having lotus as embryo); Salutation to the lotus-eyed one; salutation to the time-eyed one; salutation to the time-navelled one; salutation to the large-navelled one; O promoter of Vṛṣṇi family ! O original source ! O original abode ! Salutation to you; O abode of virtue ! O abode of water ! O abode of Śrī (Goddess of Wealth)! salutation to you; O overseer of Dharma ! O overseer of beings! O overseer of the universe ! salutation to you; O overseer of army ! Salutation to you; O overseer of time ! Salutation to you; O bearer of mace ! O bearer of Veda ! O bearer of discus ! O bearer of Śrī (Lakṣmī) ! O wearer of garland of wild flowers ! O Hari ! O bearer of earth ! Salutation to you; O Ārṣṇisena ! O Mahāsena ! O widely-praised one ! salutation to you; O multifarious one ! O great cycle of time ! O source of imagination ! Salutation to you; O universal soul ! O omnipresent one ! O all-pervader! O creator ! O white one! O Keśava ! O blue one ! O deep-blue one ! Salutation to you; O Aniruddha ! Salutation to you; O one composed of twelve forms ! O one composed of time ! O one composed of Sāmans ! O supreme soul ! O one of the nature of the sky and sun ! O Subrahman! O subtle-natured one ! Salutation to you. O tawny-haired one ! O excellent-haired one ! O thick-haired one ! salutation to you; O yellow-haired one ! O master of sense-organs ! O benefactor of all ! salutation to you; O subtle one ! O gross one ! O most subtle one ! O terrifier ! O wearer of light-yellow garments ! O wearer of dark-blue garments ! Salutation to you; O recliner on Kuśa grass ! Salutation to you; O recliner on lotus ! O recliner on water ! O Govinda ! O one affectionate to all ! O Haṁsa ! O one fond of yellow garments ! Salutation to you; O Adhokṣaja ! Salutation to you; O Śārṅga-bannered one ! O Janārdana ! Salutation to you; O Vāmana ! Salutation to you; O Madhusūdana ! Salutation to you; salutation to the thousand-headed one, salutation to the head of Brahmā; salutation to the thousand-eyed one; salutation to the one having the eyes of sun, moon and fire; salutation to *Atharvāśiras*; salutation to the elegant-headed one; salutation to the eye of *Dharma*; salutation to the excellent-eyed one; salutation to the thousand-footed one, to the foe of thousand-armed one; salutation to the adorable boar; salutation to you, to the elegant form; salutation to you, to the universal god; O soul of the universe! O source of the universe ! O omnifarious one ! Salutation to you; this universe has emerged from you.

24-29. You are the banyan tree; you are the mighty-branched, adored with roots and flowers; salutation to you, to the trunk, leaves, sprout, creeper and foliage; salutation to you; O lord of trees ! Brāhmaṇas are your root, Kṣatriyas are your trunk; O lord ! Vaiśyas are branches and Śūdras are your bark; brāhmaṇas with Agni were born of (your) face; Kings (Kṣatriyas) with weapons from arms; Vaiśyas from sides and thighs; Śūdras were born of feet; from your eyes came into being the sun; from the feet, the earth; from the ears, the quarters; from the navel, the atmospheric region; moon from your Manas; from the breath came into being, wind; from desire, Brahmā, the Grandsire; Rudra of three eyes from anger; Dyauh (heaven) from head; Indrāgni were born of face; animals are the creations of excreta; plants are born of hair; you are Virajā (blemishless); salutation to you.

30-47a. O one with smile of a flower ! Salutation to you; O one with loud laughter ! salutation to you; you are Oṁkāra; you are *Vaṣaṭ, Vauṣaṭ* and *Svadhā* syllables; you are nectar; salutation to you, *Svāhā* syllable; salutation to you, *Hantā* syllable; O omnifarious one ! O formless one ! O form of Veda ! Salutation to you; you are the lord consisting of *Veda*; you are also the lord of all gods, of all *Tīrtha*, of all sacrifices; you are the essence; salutation to you, O *Yajña-puruṣa* (*Yajña* personified)! Salutation to you, O partaker of the sacrificial offering ! Salutation to one having thousand-edged (weapon); salutation to one having hundred-edged (weapon); salutation to one of the form of *Bhūḥ, Bhuvaḥ* and *Svaḥ*, to the giver of cow, to the giver of nectar, to the giver of riches and learning, to the sustainer of everything; salutation to you, to the lord of Brahmā, to Brahman and to the one assuming the form of Brahman; salutation to you, supreme Brahmaṇa; salutation to you, *Śabda*-Brahman (word); you are the learning; you are the form of knowledge; you are also the respectable; you are the knowledge, the known and the knower, salutation to you; you are the sacrificer, the process of offering, the oblation, the deity to whom the oblation is offered, the carrier of offering, the protector, the Brahmaṇa (one of the officiating priests at a sacrifice), the purified, the process of purification; Om. Salutation (to you); you are the killer and the killed; you are the one who is carried away; you are the carrier, the leader, the method of leading, the worshipful one, the top-ranking one, the support of the universe; you are the *Sruk* and *Sruva* ladles, the resort of the universe, the potsherds, the mortar, the pestle, the fire-churning wood pieces (*Araṇi*), the sacrificial utensils produced by *Araṇi*; you are the one having one form, three forms and many forms; you are the sacrifice; you are the principal sacrificer; you are the one invoked and the sacrificer; you are the knower, the knowable and the knowledge, the meditator and the meditated upon, the lord; you are the *Dhyāna-yoga* (path of meditation), the *Yogī*, the goal, the emancipation, steadfastness, (fortitude), pleasure and the steps of *Yoga*; you are the controller; you are the omnipresent one, salutation to you; you are Brahmā, the *Hotṛ*, the *Udgātṛ*, the *Yūpa* of *Somayāga*, the *Dakṣiṇa*; you are the consecration; you are the *Puroḍāśa*; you are the *Paśu* and you are the slayer of the *Paśu*; you are the mysterious one, the principal creator, Nara, Nārāyaṇa, the people in general, the renunciation, the one having the form of a thousand Suns and Moons; you are the wheel of time having twelve spokes, six navels, three modes, two characteristics; you are the most wise, Śambhu, Indra and Wind; you are the form of Mitrāvaruṇa, the formless one, the blemishless one, the auspicious one; you are the one having a body turned towards east, the *Bhūta* and such, the foremost *Bhūta*, Acyuta and the twice-born one; you are the high-bannered one, the upward-support, the celibate, salutation to you; you are the banisher of major sins as well as the banisher of minor sins; you are the master of ascetics, the destroyer of all sins. I have taken refuge in you.

47b-49. Thus is the excellent hymn that relieves all sins. O sage ! In olden days, it was recited by Maheśvara in Vārāṇasī before Keśava after going there and taking bath in the excellent water of the *Tīrtha*. Then Rudra became free from all sins. This hymn gives freedom from sin. O great sage ! By reciting this holy hymn revealed by the killer of Tripuras, a person becomes absolved of sins and being one of serene form, becomes adorable along with the *Siddhas*, by even the chief gods in the abode of Viṣṇu.

## CHAPTER EIGHTY-EIGHT

### The sin-allaying hymn-2

*Pulastya said:*

1. O sage ! I will relate to you another sin-removing hymn by properly learning which, one will have destruction of sins.

2-27. I prostrate myself before Lord Matsya (Fish) and Lord Kūrma (Tortoise); I prostrate myself before Lord Hayaśīrṣa (horse-headed), Bhava, Viṣṇu, Trivikrama; I prostrate myself before Mādhava and Īśāna, Hṛṣīkeśa and Kumārila; I prostrate myself before Nārāyaṇa; O Garuḍāsana! salutation to you; I prostrate myself before Jayeśa, Narasiṁha, Rūpadhāra, Kurudhvaja, Kāmapāla, Akhaṇḍa and Brāhmaṇapriya; I prostrate myself before Ajita, Viśvakarmā, Puṇḍarīka, Dvijapriya, Hari, Śambhu, Brahmā, and Prajāpati; I prostrate myself before Sūlabāhu, Lord Cakradhara, Śiva, Viṣṇu, Suvarṇākṣa, Gopati and Pītavāsas (yellow-robed); I prostrate myself before Gadāpāṇi (wielder of mace); I prostrate myself before Kuśeśaya (the recliner on Kuśa grass); I prostrate myself before Lord Ardhanārīśvara (having half female form); I prostrate myself before Pāpanāśana (the destroyer of sins); I prostrate myself before Gopāla, Vaikuṇṭha and the wielder of bow; I prostrate myself before the form of Viṣṇu and Jyeṣṭheśa as the fifth; I prostrate myself before Upasānta, Mārkaṇḍeya, Jambuka; I prostrate myself before Padmakiraṇa; I prostrate myself before Vaḍavāmukha. I prostrate myself before Kārttikeya, Bāhlika, Śaṅkhi; I prostrate myself before Padmakiraṇa; I prostrate myself before Kuśeśaya; I prostrate myself before Sthāṇu, and Anagha (the sinless); I prostrate myself before Vanamālin (the one wearing a garland of wild flowers); I prostrate myself before Lāṅgalīśa; I prostrate myself before the spouse of Śrī; I prostrate myself before Trinayana (the three-eyed lord); I prostrate myself before Agni (carrier of *Havya*); I prostrate myself before Trisauvarṇa; I prostrate myself before Dharaṇīdhara (the bearer of earth); I prostrate myself before Triṇāciketa and Brahmā; I prostrate myself before Śaśībhūṣana (the one adorned with the Moon); I prostrate myself before Kapardin and the destroyer of all diseases; I prostrate myself before Moon, Sun, Dhruva, Rudra and Mahaujas (of extraordinary energy); I prostrate myself before Padmanābha, Hiraṇyākṣa, Skanda and the imperishable one; I prostrate myself before Bhima and Haṁsa; I prostrate myself before Hāṭakeśvara; I always prostrate myself before Haṁsa; I prostrate myself before Ghrāṇatarpaṇa; I prostrate myself before Rukmakavaca (the golden-armoured), Mahāyogī and Īśvara (the overlord); I prostrate myself before Śrīnivāsa; I prostrate myself before Puruṣottama; I prostrate myself before the four-armed one; I prostrate myself before the Lord of nectar; I prostrate myself before Vanaspati (the Lord of Forests), Madhupati (the lord of honey), Manu, the imperishable one; I prostrate myself before Śrīkaṇṭha, Vāsudeva, Nīlakaṇṭha, Sadāśiva, Śarva, Anagha (blemishless), Gaurīśa (spouse of Gaurī) and Lakuḍeśvara; I prostrate myself before Manohara, Kṛṣṇeśa, Cakrapāṇi; I prostrate myself before Yaśodhana, Mahābāhu and Kuśapriya; I prostrate myself before Bhūdhara (the bearer of earth), Chāditagada (the one with concealed mace), Sunetra, the one praised by the celestials, Bhadrākṣa, Vīrabhadra and Śaṅkukarṇi; I prostrate myself before Vṛṣadhvaja (the bull-bannered), Maheśa, Viśvamitra (the one affectionate to all), Śaśīprabha (the one with Moon's splendour), Upendra, Govinda, Paṅkajapriya (the one fond of lotus); I prostrate myself before Sahasraśiras (the thousand-headed lord), Kundamalin (the one with garland of Kunda flowers); I prostrate myself before Lord Kālāgnirudra, Kṛttivāsas (the wearer of elephant's skin); I prostrate myself before Chāgalesa, Paṅkajāsana (the lotus-seated); I prostrate myself before Sahasrākṣa (the thousand-eyed one), Kokanada, Harīśaṅkara; I prostrate myself before Agastya,

Garuḍa, Viṣṇu, Kapila, the Vedic lore, the eternal Brahmā, the supreme Brahman; I prostrate myself before the inconceivable one, the four-armed one, the thousand-rayed one; I prostrate myself before *Tapomaya* (the one consisting of austerity), Dharmarāja, Lord Garuḍavāhana; I prostrate myself before the one imminent in every being, the peaceful one, the blemishless one, the one having all auspicious marks, Mahāyogī, the unmanifest one, the destroyer of sin; I prostrate myself before Nirañjana (the unsullied), Nirākāra (the formless), Nirguṇa (the attributeless), Nirmalapada (pure-footed), and the destroyer of sins; I take refuge in the refuge.

28. This holy, very ancient hymn was revealed by the great sage Agastya. It bestows wealth, glory and destroys many sins on reciting it, recalling it or hearing it.

## CHAPTER EIGHTY-NINE

### The birth of Vāmana

*Pulastya said:*

1-10. After *Dānava*-lord Prahlāda had started for pilgrimage, Bali, the son of Virocana came to visit Kurukṣetra. In that most pious *Tīrtha*, Bhārgava Śukra, the bull among Brāhmaṇas, invited all the leading Brāhmaṇas. Having come to know of the invitation by Bhṛgu, the learned sages—Ātreyas, Gautamas, Kauśikas and Aṅgirasas, left Kurujāṅgala. They went towards northern direction along the river Śatadravī. Having taken bath in the waters of Śatadravī, they then proceeded to Vipāśā. Having performed ablution there and having worshipped *Pitṛs* and *Devas*, they went to the holy Kiraṇā river which emerged from the rays of the Sun.

O divine sage ! Having bathed in that river, all those great sages proceeded to Īśvarī after a bath in the holy waters of Airāvatī. O sage ! After a bath in the waters of Devikā, the hermits, Ātreyas and others descended into the river Payoṣṇī for ablution. O best of the twice-born ! As they plunged, they saw their reflection under water which caused great wonder. Rising up, they again saw and were surprised. After the bath, all the sages came out of the river. O Brāhmaṇa ! From that place also they went away with surprise, thinking and talking with each other all along, "what is this ?"

11-16. Then, they saw at a distance a very wide thicket of trees. Being dense and as black as cloud, it removed the fatigue of birds. O Nārada ! The excellent trees were covering the sky and the great mountain, because of their height. The ground below was covered by the spreading creepers. The forest with trees having flowers and fruits like the arrows of Cupid, appeared like the sky with a multitude of stars. Having seen that forest which appeared like a forest of lotuses as it was full of lotuses, adorned with white lotuses, so also full of *Kokanada* lotuses, they had unmatched contentment and great joy. They with rejoicing heart, entered the forest, like swans (entering) a great lake. O most pious sage ! In the middle of it, they saw a holy hermitage, adored by the people of four human values which are the guardians of the universe.

17-19. O Brāhmaṇa ! The hermitage of *Dharma* faced east and was covered by *Palāśa* trees; that of *Artha* faced west and was covered by sacred trees; the south-facing one was of *Kāma*, full of plantain and Aśoka trees; that of *Mokṣa* faced north and was like pure crystal. *Mokṣa* dwells in the hermitage at the end of *Kṛta-age*; *Kāma* at the end of *Tretā-age*; *Artha* occupies the hermitage at the end of *Dvāpara-age* and *Dharma* occupies the hermitage at the end (*beginning* ?) of *Kali-age*.

20-22. Having seen the hermitage, the imperishable sages, Ātreyas, took delight in that very place Akhaṇḍa, flooded with water. Because of *Dharma* and other (*Puruṣārthas*), the venerable Viṣṇu, Jagannātha called *Akhaṇḍa*, with four forms was already established there. O Nārada ! The self-controlled and learned sages worshipped him with service, austerity and chastity.

23-26. Thus they resided there along with Bhārgava (Śukra), they were afraid of the *Asuras* and resorted to *Akhaṇḍa-parvata*. O Brāhmaṇa ! The other Brāhmaṇas, *Aśmakuṭṭas* and *Marīcipas* went southwards after taking bath in the waters of Kālindī. Reaching Avantī country, they stayed resorting to Viṣṇu. It was hard for the mighty *Asuras* to enter the country because of Viṣṇu's grace. Vālakhilyas and other celibates, helpless due to the *Dānava* threat, proceeded to the refuge of Rudrakoṭi and stayed there.

27-34. O sage ! Gautamas, Āṅgirasas and other Brāhmaṇas having thus gone away, Śukra engaged all the Bhārgavas in the sacrificial procedure. In the great sacrifice in which the Bhārgavas participated, Śukra himself duly performed consecration for sacrifice to Bali of infinite splendour. The *Daitya* clad in white garments, wearing garland of white flowers, having his body anointed, having his back covered by deer skin and appearing charming with peacock feathers, was seated in the spread-sacrifice surrounded by Sadasyas, Hayagrīva, Kṣura, Maya as well as Bāṇa and others. His wife Vindhyāvalī, daughter of a sage being the chief of a thousand wives (of Bali) was consecrated in the sacrificial performance. In the month of Caitra, a horse of white colour with auspicious marks was released by Śukra to go round the earth and Tārakākṣa followed the horse. When thus the horse was released in the long-spread sacrificial rite and three months passed by, when fire was carried (to the main altar), when the *Daityas* were being worshipped, when the Sun was in Gemini (*Mithuna*) constellation, the mother of *Devas* gave birth to Mādhava in the form of a dwarf.

35. O great sage ! As soon as the venerable Nārāyaṇa, the controller, the Lord of the universe, the primordial one was born, Brahmā arrived with the great sages and then gave expression to a hymn—

36-41. O Mādhava ! O one with Sattva body ! Salutation to you; O Sātvata ! O multifarious one ! Salutation to you; O fire to the fuel of the forest of foes ! Salutation to you; O great bonfire for sin, salutation to you ! O lotus-eyed one ! salutation to you; O cause of the universe ! Salutation to you; O support of the universe ! Salutation to you; O Puruṣa par excellence! Salutation to you; O Nārāyaṇa ! O one having universe as body ! O benefactor of the universe ! O bearer of mace ! O yellow-robed one ! O beloved of Śrī ! O Janārdana ! Salutation to you; you are the saviour, the guardian, the soul of the universe, the omnipresent one, the imperishable one, the support of all, the bearer of earth, the assumer of form, salutation to you; O thriving one ! O increaser of the entire three worlds ! O one worshipped by the celestials ! O Lord of *Devas* ! Please do wipe the tears of Indra; you are the creator, the protector, the destroyer; you are Maheśvara, Mahālaya, Mahāyogī, Yogaśāyī, salutation to you.

42. Being lauded thus, the omnifarious, the omnipresent, the venerable Jagannātha, Hari said: "O Lord ! Perform initiation to me."

43-47. Then, Bharadvāja Bārhaspatya of great splendour and the one rich in penance, performed the birth-rite and other rituals to the Lord. The learned in all *Śāstras*, completed the rites of taking the vow (of chastity) to the Lord.

Then, everyone gladly presented (gifts) in due order. Pulaha gave *Yajñopavīta*; Pulastya gave two white garments; Agastya gave deer skin; Bharadvāja gave the girdle; Marīci, the son of Brahmā, gave the *Palāśa* staff; Vasiṣṭha gave a *rosary*; Aṅgiras gave a garment of *Kuśa* grass; the Lord of Heaven (Sun) gave an umbrella; Bhṛgu gave a pair of sandals; Bṛhaspati of great splendour gave Viṣṇu, a *Kamaṇḍalu.*

48-51. Initiated thus, the venerable cause of the beings, learnt the *Vedas* with auxiliaries, being praised by the sages. O sage! He learnt from Bhāradvāja and Aṅgiras, the *Sāmaveda* with excellent accent along with *Gandharva* (*Veda*) and great legends. The venerable one, knowing the ocean of *Vedic* lore, became an expert in one month to be a model for the people's practice. Acquiring expertise in all *Śāstras*, the imperishable and the inexhaustible Lord said these words to Bharadvāja, the best of Brāhmaṇas.

*Śrī Vāmana said:*

52-53. O Brāhmaṇa ! I am going to Kurukṣetra which confers great prosperity; please permit me. There, a sacred horse-sacrifice undertaken by the *Daitya*-lord is going on. You see the powers that have approached the earth. All dispositions that enhance merit are my aspects always. Because of that, I am sure, Bali has gone to Kurukṣetra.

*Bharadvāja said:*

54-55. You stay or you go as you wish; I do not command you; O Viṣṇu ! We will go from here to the sacrifice of Bali immediately. O Lord ! Please tell me what I am going to ask you; O all-pervading Puruṣottama ! Which are those places where your presence is found; you please tell me; I would like to know clearly.

*Viṣṇu said:*

56-58. O Guru ! Listen. I will tell you those holy places where I dwell with many forms. O Bharadvāja ! The earth, the expanse of the sky, the nether—world, the oceans and heaven, the entire quarters, the mountains, the clouds—all are pervaded by my incarnations which are similar to me. O Brāhmaṇa ! The beings of heaven, of earth, the aquatic and aerial beings, the immovables, Indra, Sūrya, Candra, Yama, Vasu, Varuṇa, Agni, all protectors from Brahmā to the immovables along with the oviparous and birds, those with concrete forms and those without form-all these have been created with multifarious characteristics to fill the earth.

59. O worthy Brāhmaṇa ! These holy persons (my forms) established on the earth are worshipped by the celestials,

Siddhas and *Dānavas*, by the very sight of whom or by mentioning whom (whose names), sins at once get destroyed.

# CHAPTER NINETY

## The mention of one's own abodes

*The Venerable One said:*

1-34. First my *Fish* form is located in Mānasa pond. It cleanses all sins by mentioning it, touching it and so on. Next my *Tortoise* form which destroys sin is near Kauśikī (river). Hayaśīrṣa in Kṛṣṇā (river); Govinda in Hastināpura; Trivikrama in Kālindī (river); in Liṅgabheda all-pervading Bhava; Mādhava and Śauca in Kedāra; Kṛṣṇamūrdhaja in Kubjāmra; Nārāyaṇa in Badarī; Garuḍadhvaja in Vārāha; Jayeśa in Bhadrakarṇa; in Vipāśā, it is Dvijapriya; Rūpadhārī in Irāvatī; Kurudhvaja in Kurukṣetra; in Kṛtaśauca, Nṛsiṁha; Viśvadhāraṇa in Gokarṇa; Kāmapāla in Prācīna; Puṇḍarīka in Mahāmbhas; Ajita in Viśākhayūpa; Haṁsa in Haṁsapāda; Yamakhaṇḍa in Payoṣṇī; Kumārila in Vitastā; Śambhu in Maṇimatyāhrada; Prajāpati in Brahmaṇya; Cakradhara in Madhu river; Śūlabāhu in Himācala; O best sage ! Know that Viṣṇu is established in Auṣadhasānu; Suvarṇa in Bhṛgutuṅga; Pītavāsas in Naimiṣa; Gopatideva, Gadāpāṇi, Īśvara in Gayā; in Gopratāra, Kuśeśaya, the boon-giver, the lord of three worlds; Ardhanārīśvara in Cakra; Mahīdhara in the Southern mountain; Gopāla in the Northern mountain; Somapīthi in Mahendra; Vaikuṇṭha in Sahyādri; Aparājita in Pāriyātra; Deveśa, Viśvarūpa and Tapodhana in Kaśeru country; Saugandhi in Pralayādri; Sadāśiva in Vindhyapāda; Dhiṣṇya in Avantī country; Amareśvara in Niṣadha; Pāñcālika ever established in Pāñcāla, O Brāhmaṇa-sage ! Hayagrīva in

Mahodaya; Yogaśāyī in Prayāga; Svāyambhuva in Madhuvana; Abjagandha in Puṣkara; O worthy Brāhmaṇa ! In Vārāṇasī, Keśava; Avimukta also there, sung by the celestials and *kinnaras*; Padmakiraṇa in Pampā; Vaḍavāmukha in the ocean; Bāhlīśa in Kumāradhāra; Kārttikeya in Barhaṇa; Śamhbu and Anagha in Ojasa; Sthāṇu in Kurujāṅgala; the people living in Kiṣkindhā call me Vanamālin; Vīra, Kuvalayārūḍha, Śaṅkha-cakra-gadādhara, Śrīvatsāṅka, Udārāṅga and Śrīpati in Narmadā; Trinayana in Māhiṣmatī and Hutāśana there only; Trisauparṇa in Arbuda; Kṣmādhara in Sūkarācala; Triṇāciketa and Kapardin in Prabhāsa; a third form, *Śaśiśekhara* is also well-known there, O Brāhmaṇa-sage ! The trio of Śaśi, Sūrya and Dhruva in Udaya; Hiraṇyākṣa in Hemakūṭa; Skanda in Śaravaṇa, O sage ! Rudra is known in Mahālaya; Padmanābha, the giver of all happiness in North Kurus, O foremost sage ! The well-known Hāṭakeśvara in Sapta-godāvara and Mahāhaṁsa there only; Maheśvara in Prayāga, O Brāhmaṇa ! Rukmakavaca in Śoṇa; Ghrāṇatarpaṇa in Kuṇḍina; Mahāyoga in Bhillīvana; Puruṣottama in Mantra; Viśva and Śrīnivāsa in Plakṣāvataraṇa; Caturbāhu in Sūryāraka Sudhāpati in Magadhā, O best Brāhmaṇa ! Paśupati in Girivraja; Śrīkaṇṭha on the bank of Yamunā; the dweller in Daṇḍakāraṇya is famous as Vanaspati: Nīlakaṇṭha in Kālañjara; Anuttama in Sarayū; Haṁsayukta, destroyer of all sins in Mahākośī; Śarva in South Gokarṇa; Vāsudeva in Prajāmukha; Mahāgaura in Vindhyaśṛṅga; Madhusūdana in Kanthā; Īśvara, Cakrapāṇi in Trikūṭaśikhara; Hṛṣīkeśa in Lohadaṇḍa; Mahodaya in Kauśalā, O Brāhmaṇa! Mahāvāsa in Surāṣṭra; Yaśodhara in Navarāṣṭra; Bhūdhara in Devikā river; Kuśapriya in Videhā (river); Chāditagada in Gomatī; Śaṅkhin in Śaṅkhoddhāra; Sunetra in Saindhavāraṇya; Śūra established in Śūrapura; the form called Rudra in Hiraṇvatī; Vīrabhadra in Triviṣṭapa; Nīlābha in Śaṅkukarṇa; Bhīma in Śāla forest; Viśvāmitra in Ghaṭita; Vṛṣabhadhvaja in Kailāsa; Maheśa in Mahilāśaila; Śaśiprabha in Kāmarūpa; Gomitra in Valabhī; Brāhmaṇapriya in Kaṭāha:

Upendra in Siṁhala island; Kundamālin in (the island) called Śakra.

35-44. The famous Sahasraśiras, Kālāgni, Kapila as well as Kṛttivāsas in Rasātala, O sage ! Acala and Kūrma in Sutala; Paṅkajānana in Vitala; Guru and the famous Deveśa, Vṛṣaleśvara in Mahātala; Sahasracaraṇa, Sahasrabhuja, Īśvara called Sahasra and the form called Musalākṛṣṭadānava in Tala; the lord of Yogīs (Yogīśa), Harīśaṅkara established in Pātāla; Kokanada in Dharātala; Cakrapāṇi in Medinī; Garuḍa in Bhuvarloka; the imperishable Viṣṇu in Svarloka; Agastya in Maharloka; Kapila in Janaloka; O Brāhmaṇa ! Akhila, Vāñmaya including Satya in Tapoloka; Brahmā established simultaneously in Brahmaloka; so also Sanātana in Śaiva (region); Parabrahma in Vaiṣṇava (region); Apratarkya in Nirālamba (region); Tapomaya in Nirākāra (region); Caturbāhu in Jambu Dvīpa; Kuśeśaya in Kuśa Dvīpa; the famous Garuda Vāhana in Plakṣa Dvīpa, O foremost sage ! Padmanābha in Krauñca; Vṛṣabhadhvaja in Śālmala; Sahasrākṣa is established in Śāka; Vāmana is established in Puṣkara; similarly, I am established in Śālagrāma on the earth and in all immovable objects, in water and on land, O Brāhmaṇa-sage !

45-46. O Brāhmaṇa ! These are the holy, ancient, eternal, excellent abodes. They are bestowers of wisdom, destroyers of sins and worthy of praise, having exquisite splendour. By praising them, the sins get destroyed. By only a visit to the deities, *Devas,* human beings and *Sādhyas* as well attain *Dharma, Artha, Kāma* and *Mokṣa.*

47. O Brāhmaṇa ! I have told you these my own excellent abodes. Now get up, I will go to the sacrifice of the Asura, for the welfare of the celestials.

*Pulastya said:*

48. O great sage ! Thus, saying these words to sage Bharadvāja, the magnanimous Viṣṇu, moving sportively, proceeded to Kurujāṅgala from that great mountain.

# CHAPTER NINETY-ONE

## Dialogue between Śukra and Bali

*Pulastya said:*

1. O great sage ! Then, as Vāsudeva was proceeding, the earth shuddered; the mountains moved; the oceans were agitated; all regions in heaven appeared with reverse movements.

2. The sacrifice became very much perturbed thinking, "I do not know what the Killer of Madhu will do to me. Will Vāsudeva not burn me down as I was burnt down by Maheśvara ?"

3. The (Sacrificial) Fires of the *Asura*, which were offered oblations with *Ṛk* and *Sāma* Mantras, did not accept the shares, though offered by foremost Brāhmaṇas, because of the fear of the all-pervading Lord.

4-6. Noticing that terrible omen, the Lord of *Dānavas*, bowed down to Auśanasa Śukra and asked him with folded hands: "O preceptor ! Why did the earth with the mountains tremble like a plantain tree hit by gale? Why the fires too are not accepting the oblations offered by the *Asuras*? O Lord ! Why did the oceans agitate? Why are the stars not traversing the sky as before? Why are the quarters covered by darkness ? Whose fault is this? You tell me now, O Preceptor!"

*Pulastya said:*

7. Listening to the words uttered by the Son of Virocana, Śukra said these words, after ascertaining the cause—

*Śukra said:*

8-9. O *Daitya*-Lord ! Listen (to the reason) why these Fires are not accepting the portion from the great *Asuras*, though offered with *Mantras*. Surely, Vāsudeva is coming to the sacrifice. O Son of Diti ! unable to bear his stepping, the earth with the mountains as well as the quarters have shaken. Following the shaking of the earth, the oceans have overflown the beach.

*Pulastya said:*

10. Hearing the words of Śukra, Bali told Bhārgava, what was pious, true, beneficial and endowed with vigour and vitality.

*Bali said:*

11. O venerable Sir ! When Vāsudeva comes, tell me what I should do, so that it leads to *Dharma*, *Artha* and *Kāma*. What should be given to him—jewels, or gold, or kingdom, or earth or riches? What should I speak to him? Should I urge for my welfare or his welfare ? O Sir ! Please tell me what is true, beneficial, pleasant and leads to my prosperity. I will do that and not anything else.

*Pulastya said:*

12. O Nārada ! Hearing those elegant words uttered by the *Daitya*-king, the able Bhārgava said, after considering the past and future events.

*Śukra said:*

13-15. The *Asura*-chiefs have been made partakers of sacrifice by you. The paths revealed in the *Veda* are discarded by you. The celestials have *Veda* as authority and are the partakers of sacrificial portions. For that reason Hari is coming over here. O *Daitya* ! Listen to what you should do to him, who arrives to the sacrifice, as you have queried. O King ! Earth or gold or other things, not even a blade of grass should be given (to him) in the sacrifice. On the other hand, you should utter sweet and vain words: "O all-pervading one !

Who is indeed capable of giving a present to you, in whose belly the protectors of *Bhūḥ*, *Bhuvaḥ* and heaven and the lords of Rasātala reside for ever."

*Bali said:*

16-20. O Bhārgava ! I have told you that I am eager to give something to a suppliant who comes to me, though he is of base character. Then, what to say, when a lord of that sort comes ? O great sage ! When the Lord of the universe, Janārdana comes to me, how can I say, "I do not have" ? O Lord ! The pious ones are heard saying thus: "Brāhmaṇas are to be respected by one desirous of prosperity. O bull among Brāhmaṇas ! This appears so and true." It is clear that actions–verbal, physical and mental–happen in accordance with the practice in earlier birth, though one may be born in a different species. O best of Brāhmaṇas ! Have you not heard the ancient story of the son of Kośakāra that took place in Malaya in olden days ?

*Śukra said:*

21. O valorous one ! Tell me the holy, ancient story about the son of Kośakāra; I am very much eager.

*Bali said:*

22. O foremost one of the Bhṛgu family ! Listen; I will tell you this story in the middle of the sacrifice; it is true that (one becomes) wise through previous practice.

23-26. O Brāhmaṇa ! There was a son of sage Mudgala, Kośakāra by name, who was rich in penance and deeply learned in all sciences. His beloved, virtuous wife, the daughter of Vātsyāyana, known by the name Dharmiṣṭhā was pious, attached to *Dharma* and devoted to her husband. His son, born of her was dull by nature; like a dumb person, he could not speak; like a blind one, he could not see. That Brāhmaṇa-mother left her son, born dull, mute and blind, at the door of her house on the sixth day.

27-29. At that time, a *Rākṣasī* of evil conduct called Śūrpākṣī who takes away young babies, came there carrying her lean baby. Leaving her own son there, she took away the Brāhmaṇa's son. Carrying him, she went to Śālodara mountain to feast on him. Then, knowing her come, her blind husband Ghaṭodara asked: "O dear ! What have you brought ?"

30. She replied: "O lord ! O chief of *Rākṣasas* ! Leaving my son in the house of Brāhmaṇa, Kośakāra, I brought his son."

31-32. He said: "O good lady ! You have not done well. That very learned chief of Brāhmaṇas will curse us in anger. Therefore, O lovely one ! Immediately leave this terrible looking boy (there) and bring quickly a son of someone else."

33. So told by him, the fierce *Rākṣasī*, capable of assuming any form at will, hastily went there, flying through the sky.

34-35. O Brāhmaṇa ! The *Rākṣasa* boy left outside the house, cried loudly, keeping the thumb in the mouth. After a long time, Dharmiṣṭhā having heard the cry, told her husband: "O foremost sage ! You see for yourself; your son is endowed with voice."

36-39. Then, that pious and fearful lady, went out of the house. That foremost Brāhmaṇa too saw that baby. The baby was endowed with colour and form in the same fashion as his own son. Then, Kośakāra said to his beloved with a laugh: "O righteous one ! Now it is possible that an evil spirit has entered. Someone is lying on earth in this form to deceive us." So telling his wife, he bound that *Rākṣasa*'s son with incantations, by writing on the ground with his hand, holding *Kuśa* grass.

40-43. In the meanwhile, Śūrpākṣī arrived there and becoming invisible, she threw the Brāhmaṇa boy on the ground in the house, from afar. Kośakāra held his son who had been thrown. That *Rākṣasī* went near to take her son, but she was not capable (to do so). Losing this and that, she returned to her husband and reported the loss of his son. O

Brāhmaṇa ! After the *Rākṣasī* went away, the magnanimous Brāhmaṇa gave that *Rākṣasa* baby to his wife.

44-50. His own son was nourished by the father with a lot of curds and milk of a black cow having a calf and with sugarcane juice. The boys were reared and became seven years of age. They were named by their father as Niśākara and Divākara. The *Rākṣasa* was Niśākīrti and his own son was Divākīrti. That Brāhmaṇa, duly performed the initiation ceremony to both of them. After the initiation, that Divākara learnt *Veda*. Niśākara, because of his dull-mind did not learn; so we hear. The relatives, his own parents, mother, brother, preceptor as well as other people dwelling in Malaya—all condemned him. Then, he was pushed into a waterless well by his angry father and he placed a big boulder on it. So pushed in the well, he stayed there for several years. A cluster of *Āmalakī* trees bore fruits for his nourishment.

51-52. O Bhārgava ! After the lapse of ten years, his mother came there and saw the well, covered by a boulder. Seeing a hill like boulder placed on the well, she queried with a loud voice: "Who is it, that placed this boulder on the well ?"

53. Hearing the voice of his mother, the son Niśākara who was inside the well, said: "O mother ! This boulder was indeed placed on the well by the father."

54. She being terrified, said: "Who are you with a wonderful voice staying in the well ?" He in turn replied: "I am your son known as Niśākara."

55. She said: "I have a son well-known as Divākara and I do not have any son by name Niśākara."

56. That son, however, related the past events completely as they occurred, to his mother.

57-60. After hearing that, the lady of fine eyebrows, picking up the boulder, threw it elsewhere. He, coming up from the well, bowed down to his mother's feet. Seeing her son resembling herself, Dharmiṣṭhā took him in front of her relatives and approached her husband. She told all the actions of her son.

Then that Brāhmaṇa asked: 'What is the cause of this fall (sin)? I am very curious to know about what you said, 'it happened earlier.'

Hearing those words, the wise son told wonderful words to the excellent Brāhmaṇa, Kośakāra, his father and mother as well.

*Niśākara said:*

61. O sinless father ! Listen to the reason why I assumed muteness, dullness and blindness of my eyes.

62-67. Previously, I was the son of the eminent Vṛṣākapi, born of the womb of Mālā in the Brāhmaṇa family of Vṛndāraka. Then, my father taught me *Śāstras* leading to *Dharma, Artha* and *Kāma*, as well as the path leading to *Mokṣa*, along with *Veda* and *Itihāsa*, O father ! O father ! such a one, I, a deeply learned one and a scholar in both lower and higher (planes of knowledge), became blind with pride. Due to that I was inclined to do evil acts; pride led to greed and by that my skill was lost; I lost discrimination; my pride turned into stupidity; because of stupidity, I was involved in sins. My mind always thought of other's wives and property of others. Because of my intercourse with other's wives and because of stealing other's wealth, I died by hanging and I was put in Raurava hell.

68-70. At the end of a thousand years, as there was a remnant of (the results of) the sin, I, a sinner from the hell, was born as the king of animals, killing animals in forest. O Brāhmaṇa ! Being in the form of a tiger, I was caught, put in a cage and taken to the city by a powerful king. Though I was a tiger, bound and put in a cage, the *Dharma-Artha-Kāma śāstras* were completely manifest in me.

71-74. Then one day, the tiger-among-kings, wearing a single garment and holding a mace, went out of the city. His wife by name Ajitā, unmatched on earth in beauty, came near me, after her husband departed. Looking at her, my eros was roused in my mind because of earlier practice and

I spoke to her as in *Kāma-śāstra*: "O princess ! O most auspicious one ! O one endowed with fresh youthfulness, O timid one ! You captivate my heart as a cuckoo (does) with its voice."

75. Hearing my words, the thin-waisted one, said: "O tiger! how can sexual intercourse be possible between us ?"

76. O father ! then I told the princess of attractive waist: "Open the door now; I will come out quickly."

77. She, however, said: "O tiger ! During day time the people will see. I will open at night and then we will have sexual intercourse at will."

78. I told her: "I cannot bear to postpone. Therefore, open the door and release me from the bondage."

79-83. Afterwards, she of fine hips, opened the door slowly. After the door was opened, I came out in a moment. The chain and other things as well as the ropes were shattered by me with force. Then, the king's wife was held by me, desirous of her union. Then, I, spotted by the servants of the king of unmatched prowess, was surrounded on all sides by them with weapons in their hand. I was struck by clubs and was bound by strong ropes and fetters. I told them: "It is not proper for you to strike me like that." O one rich in penance ! Hearing my words, (thinking that) I was a goblin, they tied me to a banyan tree and killed me.

84-94. From there again, I went to hell, because of my association with another's wife. At the end of a thousand years, I was born as a white ass, in the house of Agniveśya, a Brāhmaṇa who had many wives. In that state too, all learning was manifest in me. I was made a vehicle by the wives of the Brāhmaṇa with attachment. Once a wife of that Brāhmaṇa, known by the name Vimatī belonging to Navarāṣṭra (country), desired to go to her father's house. The husband told her: "Go riding this ass; you come back after a month; you should not stay beyond that."

So told by the husband, the frail lady untying the ass and riding on it, proceeded fast, O sage ! Then, on half the way, the frail lady got down from my back and descended into the river for bath. Seeing her in wet clothes having graceful features in all the limbs, I ran towards her. I carried her up at once and felled her on the ground. Being over-anxious, O father ! I fell on her. I was seen then by a person who was following her. Lifting up a staff, he hastily ran after me. Afraid of him, I left her and hurried towards south. When I was gallopping speedily, O sage ! The string of my rein got stuck up in a thicket, the destroyer of my life. As I was stuck up there, in six days there was loss of my life.

95-102. Again I went to hell and released from there, I became a parrot, in a dense forest. I was caught by an evil-minded hunter. Keeping me in a cage, he sold me to a merchant's son who had (riches). He in turn, placed me near the youthful ladies in the magnificent harem, considering me to be a knower of all *Śāstras* and as a destroyer of defects (evils). Those young ladies were nourishing me who was there, with cooked rice, fruits and so on as well as ripe pomegranate fruits, every day.

Once, the beloved, elegant daughter of the merchant, of lotus petal like eyes, of dark complexion, of heavy breasts, of well-shaped hips, of slender waist, by name Candrāvalī held the cage. The lady of charming limbs and of charming smile took me in her hands and placed me on her stout breasts. Then I felt attached to her and leapt with a view to sport with her. While leaping, I, a sinner, was caught in the garland (-like) trap for monkeys and later died. Wicked-minded as I was, I again reached terrible hell.

103-106. From that (birth), I assumed the form of an ox in the house of a *Cāṇḍāla.* Once, that powerful one, yoked me to a cart, caused his wife to mount it and made up his mind to go to the forest. The *Cāṇḍāla* proceeded first and she followed him from behind. She was singing as she proceeded. Hearing that, I became one with distressed senses. Looking behind, I jumped in the reverse direction. Due to the momentary amorous movement, I fell on the ground in a moment. I was tied up by the rope of the cart. Soon I died.

107-111. Again I was immersed in the hell for a thousand years. O father ! I am now born in your house, remembering my births. I remember all those my births in order. Because of my previous practice, the lines of *Śāstras* are known to me. Now that I have attained knowledge, I shall not commit on any account, terrible sins mentally, physically or verbally. Good or bad, study, earning livelihood according to *Śāstra*, bondage or death—all these happen in accordance with previous practice. O father ! When a person recalls the earlier births, he will refrain from committing such sins. Therefore, O sage ! I will go to the forest to enhance my merit and clear off the sin. You set this good son Divākīrti to take up a householder's duty.

*Bali said:*

112. O great sage ! Speaking thus, that Niśākara bowed down to his parents and proceeded to the holy abode of Murāri, the first one of the lord, the famous Badarikāśrama.

113-114. Thus, gifts, study and other things come to a person who is engaged in previous practice. Therefore, O worthy Brāhmaṇa ! These have been practised by me earlier, I am telling you. O great sage ! Gifts, austerity, study, thieving, major sin, arson and wisdom as well as *Dharma*, *Artha* and fame-all these come about in accordance with the practice (done) earlier, not otherwise.

115. So telling his preceptor and master Śukra, the mighty Lord of the *Daityas* remained meditating on Nārāyaṇa, the foe of Madhu-Kaiṭabha, the bearer of discus, mace and sword.

# CHAPTER NINETY-TWO

## Bali restrained

*Pulastya said:*

1-2. In the meanwhile, the venerable one in the dwarf-from approached the enclosure of the sacrifice and said these words loudly: "The *Vedas* beginning with *Om* syllable exist in this sacrifice in the form of ascetics, rich in penance. *Aśvamedha* sacrifice is the most distinguished of the sacrifices. O benefactor of *Daityas* ! Act in such a way that is befitting (to the performance)."

3-4. Hearing such words, the leader of the *Dānavas* of restrained senses, reached the place where the Lord stood along with vessels of worship. After duly worshipping the Lord of lords, he said: "O venerable one ! O proud one ! Tell me, what can I give you ?"

5-7. Then the imperishable Foe of Madhu told the *Daitya*-king after laughing for a long time and eyeing Bharadvāja: "(There is) a preceptor of my preceptor. He has maintained fires and he does not want to establish fire on a ground that belongs to others. For his sake, here is my plea, O King of *Dānavas* ! O King ! Give three paces corresponding to the size of my body."

8-11. Listening to the words of Murāri, Bali said after looking at his wife and eyeing Bāṇa, his son: "This person is a dwarf not only in size (of the body) but also fond of trivial things, for, he is begging for, but three paces even from a person of my sort. Perhaps the creator, like this Viṣṇu of tremendous efforts does not give profuse wealth and other things to dull-witted persons kept away from divine merits. Providence does not bestow (anything) to him whose fortune has reversed, for, here is one who is begging for three paces when I am the donor !"

12-14. So saying, the magnanimous foe of the celestials spoke to Hari again: "O Viṣṇu ! Ask for elephants, horses, land, maid-servants, gold or anything you wish for. O Viṣṇu ! you are the suppliant. I, the Lord of the universe, am the donor. Is it not a matter of shame for me to bestow three paces ? O Vāmana ! Which of these shall I give you—Rasātala or the earth or the Mid-region or the Heaven ? You ask freely."

*Vāmana said:*

15. O king ! Give elephants, horses, land, gold and such things to those who seek them. I am seeking this much only; give me three paces.

16. When these words were expressed by magnanimous Vāmana, Bali brought the golden pitcher and gave three paces to Viṣṇu.

17-27. As the waters fell on the hand, he assumed the divine invincible form, composed of the universe, to traverse the three worlds. The earth was the feet; the sky was the shanks; the Satya and the Tapas regions adored by the three worlds were his two knees; Meru and Mandara mountains were his thighs; Viśvedevas were in the waist; Maruts in the two heads of pelvis; Cupid was in the penis and Prajāpati in the scrotum; the seven seas were in the abdomen and the worlds in the belly; the rivers were in the three folds (at the belly) and sacrifice was in the stomach; all *Mantras* and deeds–religious, social and such others–were established (there); Vasu deities were in the back and *Rudras* were established in the shoulders; all the quarters were the arms; the eight *Vasus* were the hands; Brahmā was established in the heart and *Vajra* in heart bones (i.e. ribs); the thousands of Lakṣmī were in the middle of chest; Moon was established in Manas; Aditi, mother of gods, was in the neck and the *Vidyās* were established in the neckline; the Brāhmaṇas with fires were in the mouth; the sacraments together with

*Dharma-Artha-Kāma-Mokṣa* and *Śāstras* were the lips; Lakṣmī was established in the forehead and *Aśvins* were in the ears; Mātariśvan was in the breath; *Maruts* in all joints; all the hymns were the teeth; goddess Sarasvatī was the tongue; Sun and Moon were the eyes; Kṛttikās and others were in the eyelashes; Viśākhā had settled in the middle of the eyebrows of the Lord of Lords; the stars were the hair roots; the great sages were the hairs.

28-34. The venerable promoter of the beings became all-embracing by his *Guṇas* and occupied the world of movables and immovables by one pace. Of the gigantic form expanding upwards, Moon was on the right side and Sun on the left.

In the second pace, Svaḥ, Mahaḥ, Jana and Tapas regions were covered by one half and both Vairāja and the sky covered by the other half. O Brāhmaṇa ! Viṣṇu, further growing, pierced the shell of Brahmā through the space on the right and reached the region, bereft of light. As the cauldron (of the universe) was pierced by the world-wide pace, the agitated Kuṭilā river flowed forth from the sky, from Viṣṇu's feet. Therefore, the hermits eulogise that river as Viṣṇupadī.

The venerable all-pervading one, as the third pace remained incomplete, approached Bali and told him with his lips quivering a little: "O *Daitya*-chief ! You are in debt. Punishment (for default) is awful. You complete my third pace or else you accept my bondage."

35. Hearing those words of Murāri, Bāṇa, the son of Bali with a laugh, spoke to the Lord of the immortals, these words endowed with reason–

*Bāṇāsura said:*

36-38. O Lord of the universe ! How can you, the creator of the lords of the universe, having made the earth smaller, ask Bali for a wider world without you making it wide enough beforehand ? O omnipresent one ! The earth as much as it was created by you, together with the intermediate space has been given over to you by my father. Then, why is it he is being pressurised by deceitful speech ? O Murāri ! This Lord of *Daityas* is able to honour you with that capacity by which he (was expected) by you earlier. Please be gracious; please do not order his bondage.

39-44. O Lord ! It has been spoken by you in the *Veda* that the gift to a proper donee in a proper place and so also in a holy time leads to happiness. All these are seen fully in the Bearer of Discus. The gift is of land; the donee is you, the lord of lords, the bestower of all wishes and the self-controlled one. Time is when the Moon is in conjunction with *Jyeṣṭhā* and *Mūla*. The place Kurukṣetra is holy and well-known. You yourself are the first creator of even the *Vedas* and are found in the universe consisting of the real and the unreal. What can the unintelligent people like me teach you as to what is proper and what is improper ? Making your size small yourself, you asked for three paces. How can you take it (i.e., measure it) with a form respected by the world ? O omnipresent one ! O magnanimous one ? It is no surprise that the entire universe was today covered, but your three paces are not yet complete. O benefactor of the world! Are you not capable of traversing the entire earth (universe) with a single pace ? O Mādhava ! O Padmanābha ! O Viṣṇu ! Making the earth small in size yourself, how do you restrain Bali? You are the almighty; you do what you like.

*Pulastya said:*

45. When the mighty son of Bali said so, the venerable Janārdana, the first creator, said these words—

*Trivikrama said:*

46-51. O son of Bali ! Listen to my reasonable reply to the utterances you have made now: "Your father was told by me beforehand: 'O King ! Give me three paces after my measurement' and that has been done. Does not your father, the *Asura* Bali know my size, for he gave away without hesitation three paces after my measurement ? True, I can traverse *Bhuḥ, Bhuvaḥ* and other regions in a single pace. It is in the interest of Bali that these two paces were taken. Thus, O son of Bali ! That your father poured the water significantly, his life will consequently be till the *Kalpa.*"

Telling this to Bāṇa, the son of Bali, Lord Trivikrama turned to Bali and spoke these pleasing words—

*The venerable one said:*

52. O King ! Because you have fulfilled (the payment of) *Dakṣiṇā,* (you will get) the magnificent reward. You go to the nether world called Sutala and live there free from afflictions.

*Bali said:*

53. O benefactor ! While I live in Sutala, how will my enjoyments be inexhaustible, so that I shall live there free from afflictions ?

*Trivikrama said:*

54-58. O *Daitya*-chief ! I will relate to you in detail, those exquisite enjoyments you are going to have now, being in Sutala: "The gifts not duly given, *Śrāddhas* in which the learned in *Vedic* lore do not participate and the studies (of the *Veda*) done by those not keeping the vow—these give you their merit. Similarly, another sacred festival called *Dīpa-pradāna,* occurring after *Śakramahotsava* is over, is going to be of great merriment to you. At that time, well-adorned tigers-among-men, gay and strong, will worship you sincerely by offering flowers and lamps. That festival will be the most prominent one and marked in the world in your name. As it is now in your kingdom, so will it be called Kaumudī in future too."

59-60. So saying, the Madhu-killer, bade farewell to the *Daitya*-lord along with his son and wife. Taking hold of the earth, he left immediately, being resorted to by the groups of immortals including Indra and Brahmā. Handing over the heaven to Indra and making the *Devas* enjoy the shares of sacrifices, Madhu-killer, the Lord of the universe, the great Lord disappeared before the very eyes of the leaders of celestials.

61. As the creator, Vāsudeva, returned to heaven, Śālva together with a large force of *Asuras*, built a city famous as Saubha and then roamed at will in the aerial region.

62. The great Maya along with Tāraka, Vaidyuta as well as his wife and companions resorted freely to the gold, copper and iron (fortresses) called Tripura furnished with all pleasures.

63. After the Lord returned to Heaven and the restrained Bali went to Rasātala, Bāṇa found on earth, a well-protected city called, Soṇita by name and lived there with the *Dānava*-chiefs.

64. Thus in olden days, Bali was restrained by Viṣṇu, the discus-bearer, assuming dwarf-form, for pleasing Indra, for accomplishing the task of the celestials and for the welfare of the bulls among Brāhmaṇas, cows and the twice-born ones.

65. O great sage ! I have related to you the holy, pure and sin-destroying (story of) incarnation of Vāmana, which, when heard, recited or remembered, sin gets cleansed and one attains merit.

66. Thus I have related to you, O Brāhmaṇa ! The story of Vāmana and how Bali of meritorious fame was restrained. If you are desirous of listening to anything else, O Brāhmaṇa ! Please ask; I will tell you completely.

# CHAPTER NINETY-THREE

## Brahmā's hymn

*Nārada said:*

1-2. I have heard how Bali was restrained by the magnanimous Lord. After listening to it, what else is there to ask. (Still) please tell me now: O father ! Where did the venerable Viṣṇu, the imminent in all go, who disappeared after handing over heaven to the King of gods ? Please tell me.

*(Pulastya said:)*

3. After attending on Hari with worship in the prescribed mode, Brahmā asked: "Why have you returned after a long time ?"

4. Then the Lord of the universe replied him: "O Svayambhū ! I have carried out a great task of restraining Bali, for the purpose of the celestials getting their share in sacrifices."

5. Hearing those words, the Grandsire with a delighted heart said: "How ? How was it ? Will you please show me ?"

6-7. The venerable *Garuḍa-dhvaja* (*Garuḍa*-bannered One), so told (by Brahmā), immediately revealed that form consisting of all gods. Seeing Puṇḍarīkākṣa, having a width of a *yojana* and the same measure of height, he prostrated.

8. After exclaiming, "Well! Well done! Excellent! Very nice, very nice the Lotus-born (Brahmā) engrossed in devotion uttered this hymn to Mahādeva—

(Prose) Om. Salutation to you, O supreme lord of gods ! O Vāsudeva ! O only peak ! O multifarious one ! O Vṛṣākapi! O promoter of beings ! O foremost among the celestials and *Asuras* ! O subduer of the celestials and *Asuras* ! O abode of the Lord of celestials ! O creator of the celestials ! O one free from obstacles ! O Kapila ! O great Kapila ! O Viśvaksena!

O Nārāyaṇa ! O Dhruva-bannered one ! O Fire-bannered one ! O Vaikuṇṭha ! O Puruṣa-par-excellence ! O worthiest one ! O Viṣṇu ! O unconquered one ! O Jaya ! O Jayanta ! O Vijaya ! O Kṛtāvarta ! O Mahādeva ! O beginningless one ! O endless one ! O one without beginning, end, middle and extinction ! O conqueror of City ! O Dhanañjaya ! O one praised by celestials ! O wide-famed one ! O pṛṣṇigarbha ! O Hiraṇyagarbha ! O Kamalagarbha ! O one with lotus-like wide eyes ! O beloved of Lakṣmī (residing in lotus) ! O source of Vṛṣṇi ! O abode of beings ! O supervisor of groups ! O bearer of mace ! O bearer of Śrī ! O wearer of garland of wild flowers! O bearer of Lakṣmī ! O carrier of earth ! O lotus-navelled one ! O creator ! O Arṣṇisena ! O Mahāsena ! O commander of the army ! O one praised by one and all ! O multifarious one ! O one of supreme form ! O one of highest imagination ! O unchecked one ! O all-pervader ! O imminent one ! O twelve-fold one ! O one of Śarva form ! O one of Soma form! O one of time form ! O creature-formed one ! O one of Lakṣmī (Ramā) form ! O eternal one ! O one with Muñja-like hair ! O yellow-haired one ! O master of sense-organs ! O conqueror of sleep ! O bannered one ! O blue one ! O subtle one ! O gross one ! O yellow one ! O red one ! O white one ! O abode of white (colour) ! O One fond of red garment ! O pleasing one ! O abode of love ! O Swan ! O plough-bannered one ! O abode of blue (colour) ! O support of all worlds ! O recliner on Kuśa ! O Adhokṣaja ! O Govinda! O Janārdana ! O Madhusūdana ! O Vāmana ! Salutations to you.

Om. You are the thousand-headed one; you are the thousand-eyed one; you are the thousand-footed one; you are with a downward face; you are the supreme *Puruṣa*; you are the thousand-armed one; you are the one of thousand shapes; *Vedas* speak of you as thousand-faced, salutation to you, salutation to you.

Om. Salutation to you, O lord of all gods ! O nourisher of all ! O soul of all ! O multifarious one ! O cause of all ! This universe has come out of you; Brāhmaṇas were (born of) your face; Kṣatriyas (arose from) the arms; from the two thighs came out Vaiśyas; Śūdras emerged from the lotus-feet; from the navel was formed the aerial region; from the lotus face, Indra and Agni; from the mind was born Moon and I, by your grace; from anger was born Tryambaka; from breath was born *Mātariśvan*; from the head was born *Dyaus*; the quarters from the ears, O Svayambhū ! This earth adorned with mountains was born from the feet; you are the sky; you are the star; you are those born of sweat–the plants and oviparious; corporeal and incorporeal–all were evolved out of you. Hence, you are the world-formed one, the first one.

Om. Salutation to you. You are the smile of a flower; you are the supreme one; you are the great laughter; you are *Oṁkāra*, you are *Vaṣaṭkāra*; you are *Svāhākāra*; you are *Mātariśvan*; you are the one moving in the sacrifice; you are the one having the three treasures; you are the *Hotṛ*; you are the sacrifice; you are the sacrificed; you are the protector; you are the reciter; you are the killer; you are the killed; you are the path of right conduct; you are *Medhā* (intellect); you are the Fire; you are the light of the world; you are the worshipful one; you are the highest abode; you are *Sruk* and other utensils; you are the *Araṇi* (fire-churning sticks); you are the one produced by *Araṇi*; you are the form of consciousness; you are the meditation; you are the meditated upon; you are the sacrifice; you are the one adored in a sacrifice; you are the sacrificer; you are the gift; you are the *Paśu*; you are the adorable one; you are the worshipful one; you are the *Hotṛ*; you are the one sung of; you are the *Udgātṛ*; you are the principal sacrificer; you are the one having movement; you are the wisdom of the wise; you are the *Yoga* of *Yogins*; you are the *Mokṣa* of those seeking *Mokṣa*; you are the wealth of the wealthy; you are the domestic one; you are the creator; you are the supreme one; you are *Soma*; you are *Sūrya*; you are *Dakṣiṇā*; you are the consecrated one; you are Nara; you are the triple-eyed one; you are the one having effulgence of Āditya; you are the purity; you are the bright one; you are the *Jyeṣṭha* month; you are the *Āṣāḍha* month; you are the sacrifice; you are the *Śrāvaṇa* month; you are the *Bhādrapada* month; you are the *Puṣya* month; you are the *Māgha* month; you are the *Phālguna* month; you are the *Caitra* month; you are the *Vaiśākha* month; you are the time; you are the change of equinoxes; you are the valour; you are the prowess; you are the horse-necked one; you are the great intellect; you are Śaṅkara; you are Hari, Īśvara; you are *Sattva*; you are *Brahmacārī* (celibate student); you are *Svara*; you are *Mitravaruṇa*; you are the light of *Prāgvaṁśa*; you are the first of beings; you are the great element; you are the doer of lofty deeds; you are the pervaded one; you are the deliverer from all sins; you are Trivikrama, salutation to you.

*Pulastya said:*

9. Thus eulogised by the Grandsire, Viṣṇu who always does wonderful deeds, told this to the Grandsire: "O one being in pure *Sattva* ! Choose a boon."

10. The gladdened Grandsire told him: "O omnipresent Murāri ! Bestow this boon on me now. You please stay in my house with this sacred all-pervading form."

11-12. When thus the worthy boon was asked for, the imperishable soul, beyond thought, stayed with the dwarf-form, being worshipped in the abode of *Svayambhū*. The group of *Apsaras* dance there; the ladies of the celestial-chief sing songs; Vidyādharas play the *Tūrya* instrument; the groups of *Devas, Asuras* and *Siddhas* eulogise.

13-14. Then by worshipping the all-pervading Murāri, the Grandsire became very pure through the cleansing away of sins. (Indra) brought Viṣṇu to heaven from the holy abode of Brahmā and offered worship. In Heaven measuring thousands of *yojanas*, Viṣṇu was only a dwarf. O great sage ! Indra offered him worship on the same scale as that of Brahmā.

15. O Brāhmaṇa ! This I have told you, as to what the magnanimous Trivikrama did for the benefit of the *Devas*,

by making the son of Diti stay in Rasātala. This I have related to you today.

# CHAPTER NINETY-FOUR

## The Lord eulogised

*Pulastya said:*

1-4. The *Daitya* having gone to Rasātala, got constructed a city studded with varieties of precious jewels and steps of pure crystals. In the middle of it a large palace with several balconies and doors and lattices of pearls was constructed by Viśvakarmā. There he resided enjoying various divine and human pleasures. His wife Vindhyāvalī by name was his beloved. She was the chief of a thousand ladies and was an adornment of conduct. That mighty son of Virocana sported with her, O sage !

5-7. As the *Daitya* was living attached to pleasures in Sutala, the *Sudarśana* (discus) that takes away the splendour of *Daityas* entered Pātāla. When the discus entered Pātāla, terror gripped the *Dānavas.* There was great hallooing like that of an agitated sea. Hearing that loud noise, Bali held the sword in hand and the bull among *Asuras* enquired: "Oh ! What is this ?"

8-10. Then Vindhyāvalī, the virtuous wife of pure vows, put the sword into the sheath and told pacifying her husband. She said to the *Daitya*-king in pleasing and very firm words: "This is the discus of the venerable one that brings extinction of the circle of *Daityas.* O *Daitya*-chief ! It is of magnanimous Vāmana and is to be worshipped." So saying, the charming-limbed one, purified herself and went out.

11. By then, Viṣṇu's discus, *Sudarśana* of a thousand spokes, arrived. Then, O sage ! The *Asura*-king held his hand in suppliance and after duly worshipping the discus, uttered this prayer.

*Bali said:*

12-18. I bow down to Hari's discus, *Sudarśana* of thousand rays, of thousand colours, of thousand edges that cuts down the circle of *Daityas.* I bow down to Hari's discus in whose hub is the Grandsire, in the tip of which is Śarva holding the trident and at the root of the spokes, the great mountains. In the spokes are found the *Devas,* including Indra, Arka and Fire. *Vāyu, Apaḥ, Agni, Pṛthivī* and *Ākāśa* (five great elements) are found in the speed. In the spoke joints, clouds, lightning, constellations and stars are found. On the outside reside the sages, Vālakhilyas and others. I bow down to that foremost divine weapon of Vāsudeva with devotion: "O Viṣṇu's discus ! O *Sudarśana* of glowing rays ! Burn down my three types of sins—physical, verbal and mental; rid me quickly of those sins related to Kali and sins that are related to my father and my mother; salutation to you, O Acyuta's weapon! May my difficulties get destroyed; may my diseases get cleared off; by reciting your name, O discus ! May my evils have extinction."

19-21. So saying, the wise one worshipped the discus with devotion and remembered Puṇḍarīkākṣa who destroys all sins. O sage ! The discus adored by Bali, made the *Asuras* splendourless and went out of Pātāla on the day of southern equinox. After the departure of the discus, Bali was afflicted. Being in great difficulties, he remembered his grandfather.

22-26. That great *Dānava*-chief too arrived in Sutala as soon as he was remembered. Seeing the eminent one, Bali of great radiance, waited with vessels of worship. After duly worshipping the Lord, his father's father, he said these words folding his hands: "You have come here the moment I remembered you with much depressed mind. Therefore, you are my welfare; you are the one congenial to me; you are my prosperity and my auspiciousness. O father ! What should a person living in this world do and by doing which, one does not get bound ? It behoves you to explain to me as to what ferries the people of less-intellect drowned in the ocean of cycle of births and deaths."

*Pulastya said:*

27. Hearing the query of his grandson, the *Dānava*-chief pondered over and said these words which are most beneficial in the worldly life.

*Prahlāda said:*

28. It is excellent, O tiger among *Dānavas* ! That this thought occurred to you. I will tell you what is beneficial to you as well as to other people.

29-30. For those persons fallen in the ocean of worldly life, struck by the gale of pains of opposites, pressed down by the weight of looking after the son, daughter and wife, sinking without a raft in the agitated waters of pleasures, the only refuge is the raft Viṣṇu. Those persons of fortitude who resort to Hari, the infinite one, the blameless one, the primordial Nārāyaṇa, the Lord of celestials, the giver of welfare, the worthiest one, the pure one, the one moving on the King of birds, the Lord of Lakṣmī, do not enter the abode of Dharmarāja (Yama).

31. Yama, seeing his servant with noose in hand, whispers in his ear: "Avoid those who have surrendered themselves to Madhusūdana. I have power over other people and not over the devotees of Viṣṇu."

32. Similarly, there is another statement truly made by the most pious and devoted Ikṣvāku: "Those persons who are the devotees of Viṣṇu on the earth will be outside the jurisdiction of Yama."

33-35. That is the worthy tongue that praises him; that is the worthy mind that surrenders to him; those are the two hands worthy of praise that are engaged in his worship. Really, those two hands which are unable to worship the two lotus-feet of Hari, are considered as foliage at the tip of the branch of a tree. Surely that tongue that does not speak of the attributes of Hari, is only a frog in the throat or *Uvala* or some other disease and not the tongue.

36-37. The relatives should lament over a person who does not devotedly worship the lotus-feet of Viṣṇu; he is dead, though living. Those persons who are ever engaged in the worship of Vāsudeva are not to be deplored, though dead. It is the truth; it is the truth I am saying.

38-40. The physical, mental, verbal, corporeal, incorporeal, movable, immovable, visible, tangible, invisible—all these have the form of Keśava. He who worships the venerable Trivikrama in all the four modes, is deemed to have worshipped the three worlds with the immortals and *Dānavas.* There is no doubt. O my son ! Just as the jewels in the ocean cannot be counted, so are the attributes of the Lord, the Wielder of Discus, not countable.

41-48. Those who take shelter under the Wielder of conch, discus and lotus, the wielder of *Śārṅga,* the one having the banner of the King of birds, the giver of boons, the Lord of Śrī, do not become grief-stricken and do not fall again into the pit of *Saṁsāra.* Those in whose mind Govinda becomes a constant dweller, neither undergo humiliation nor are they agitated at death. Those who have surrendered to Lord Viṣṇu, the wielder of *Śārṅga,* the refuge, neither go to any *Yamaloka* nor do they have adode in hell. O tiger among *Dānavas* ! The devotees of Viṣṇu attain the same course of the pious ones, which those who are deeply learned in *Veda* and *Śāstras* attain. O tiger among *Daityas* ! The best of the men and the devotees of Viṣṇu reach a higher destination than the one reached by those killed in a warfare. That destination which is of those engaged in pious deeds, of those endowed with *Sattva-guṇa,* of the magnanimous, is also spoken of, for the devotees of the venerable ! O *Daitya*! The holy magnanimous ones can see clearly Vāsudeva, the abode of all, the subtle and the unmanifest form and the one who cuts off the worldly existence. By prostrating oneself before him according to the *Śāstra* prescription, one does not come into the worldly existence again. He dwells in the

*Kṛta-age* and such a person of infinite lustre will be ever playful.

49-55. Those who are liked by Viṣṇu and those who are ever fond of Viṣṇu, do not get attached to *Karma*, though being in any physical body. They who are his devotees, who are attached to him, who meditate on Dāmodara, who adore him bent with devotion, are not born again. O *Dānava*-chief! those who devotedly remember Madhusūdana, getting up in the morning, do not sink in the mire of worldly existence. Those who hear and those who make others hear (the hymns in his praise), cross over the impassable. O Bali ! Those whose mind is highly delighted by drinking the nectar of the song of Hari in the ear-cups, surmount the impassable. Those whose devotion to the Wielder of discus and mace is unflinching, go certainly to that place where *Yogīśvara* Hari is. That supreme destination which is attained by those engaged in the worship of Viṣṇu, cannot be attained through austerities in a thousand births.

56-58. What is the use of the *Mantras* repeated, of austerities or of being in *Āśramas*, if one does not have deep devotion ever to Madhusūdana? Sacrifice is in vain; gift is in vain; piety is in vain; exertion is in vain; austerity is in vain and fame is in vain, if one hates Madhusūdana. What should one do with many a Mantra, if one has no devotion to Janārdana ? The one Mantra '*namo nārāyaṇāya*' will accomplish everything.

59-62. In whose heart dwells Viṣṇu, Janārdana who is blue, like Indīvara lotus, it is only success for them; whence is failure to them ? All activity should be performed after saluting Lord Nārāyaṇa, the auspicious of the auspicious, the worthiest one and the boon-giver. O great *Asura* ! Hells, portentous and other calamities that result from misconduct, get absolved by remembering the name of Viṣṇu. The thousand crore *Tīrthas* and the hundred crore *Tīrthas* are not worth the sixteenth part of the salutation to Nārāyaṇa.

63-69. By reciting the names of Viṣṇu one attains the merit of pilgrimage to all the *Tīrthas* and the holy places that are on the earth. The regions which are not reached by those keeping vows or by ascetics, are attained by those persons who are engaged in saluting Kṛṣṇa. Even a person devoted to some other deity but worships Keśava for show (pretention), goes to that excellent destination of the saints and the pious ones. The fruit one gets by intently worshipping Hṛṣīkeśa, can never be attained by persons engaged in most severe austerity. Those wise ones who remember Padmanābha during the three points of the day, attain the fruit of fasting. There is no doubt in this. O Bali ! You worship Hari through actions recommended in the *Śāstras.* By his grace, you will obtain everlasting success. O my son ! Fix your thoughts on him; be his devotee; offer sacrifice to him; bow down to him. Resorting to that Lord of gods alone, you will attain happiness.

70-76. Those persons who have no attachment, and worship the primordial one, the endless one, the ageless one, the imperishable one, the all-pervading one, the supreme Brahman, the most ancient Hari, reach the everlasting and unchangeable abode of Viṣṇu. Those who always remember Nārāyaṇa, the worthiest of the celestials, those who meditate always on Acyuta, the controller, they like swans with cleansed white feather, cross over the waters of the ocean of *Saṁsāra.* Those who meditate on the blemishless one with lotus petal-like eyes will have their sins destroyed by him. Those who sing (the greatness of) the worthy Padmanābha, the boon-giver, do not suck the breast of a mother again. Those persons who with very firm devotion listen to (the greatness of) the wielder of conch, lotus, discus, bow, mace and sword, the one called the bee in the lotus face of Lakṣmī, surely reach the abode of the killer of Madhu. Those sinners from birth (who listen) to the praise of the primordial, venerable one, get absolved of sins and become happy, like those who are satiated by drinking nectar. Therefore faithful persons should attend to meditation, remembering or recitation (of the names of) Viṣṇu or listen to the pious ones reciting the names of Viṣṇu. The gods praise this as equivalent to worship. A *Yogī* should worship Keśava, the controller, both externally and mentally. The Lord is indeed to be duly worshipped by people with flowers and leaves available in various seasons.

## CHAPTER NINETY-FIVE *

### Worship of God Viṣṇu

*Bali said:*

1-4. You have said everything; the goal one reaches by worshipping Janārdana. How should he be adored ? By what kind of worship is the pleasure of the Lord obtained? Which gifts are commended for pleasing the Lord of the universe? On which days the fasting and other actions will be most fruitful ? Which holy (actions) are commended for pleasing Viṣṇu ? What other things are to be done by the unlethargic and enthusiastic ones ? O *Daitya*-chief ! You will do good to tell them now completely.

*Prahlāda said:*

5-6. The gifts that are given by a faithful devotees in the name of Janārdana are never in vain. These very days are commended on which one worships the Lord of the universe and with one's mind lost in him, a person keeps fast.

7-9. When eminent Brāhmaṇas are worshipped, Janārdana is worshipped. A silly-minded person who hates them, goes certainly to hell. A person inclined towards Viṣṇu should devotedly adore Brāhmaṇas. Formerly Hari said: "Brāhmaṇas are my body." A Brāhmaṇa whether a scholar

* In this chapter ślokas 28-37 are shifted under the heading Phalaśruti as śloka 76-85. Hence there is a difference from the numbering of the original text.

or not, should not be disrespected. He is the divine body of Viṣṇu. Therefore, people should worship a Brāhmaṇa.

10-22a. O great *Asura* ! These are the flowers commended, the flowers which have colour and are endowed with nectar and scent for the worship of Viṣṇu. I will tell you those (flowers) which are more holy, along with the *Tithis* and gifts that are commended for pleasing Mādhava. *Jasmine*, hundred-petalled lotus, *Sumanas, Kunda, Bahupuṭa, Bāṇa, Campaka, Aśoka, Karavīra, Yūthikā, Pāribhadra, Pāṭalā, Bakula, Giriśālinī, Tilaka, Japā, Pītaka, Tagara*—these flowers and other fragrant flowers except *Ketakī* are commended for the worship of Acyuta. Leaves of *Bilva, Śamī, Bhṛṅga, Mṛgāṅka, Tamāla, Mālatī* are fit for the worship of Hari. The flowers of these are also commended in the worship of the Lord. The foliage and leaves of these are spoken of in the ritual of worship of Hari. One should worship with new leaves of creepers, *Kuśa* grass and other aquatic flowers like *Kamala* and *Indīvara.* O Bali ! One should worship with the tender foliage of trees and of *Dūrvā* grass, clean and bright and washed in water. So also Viṣṇu is to be worshipped with buds and sprouts.

Then, one should anoint carefully with *Candana* and *Kumkuma. Uśīra, Padmaka, Kālīyaka* are also useful in anointing. The dust of *Mahiṣa, Dāru* (*Devadāru*), *Silhaka, Nāgara, Śaṅkha, Jātiphala* are commended in offering pleasing incense to Śrīśa.

Barley, wheat and rice cooked with ghee, sesamum, green-gram, black-gram, *Vrīhi* (rice) are dear to Hari.

22b-35. Gifts of cow and gifts of land are sacred. Gifts of cloth, food and gold will please Madhusūdana. O *Dānava* ! in the month of *Māgha,* sesamum or sesamum with cow, as well as fuel are to be gifted saying, "may Mādhava be pleased." In the month of *Phālguna, Vrīhi* (rite) cloth, deer skin and so on are to be gifted by eminent persons for pleasing Govinda. In the *Caitra* month; colourful cloth, beds and seats are to be gifted to Brāhmaṇas for the pleasure of Viṣṇu. In the *Vaiśākha* month, fragrant scents and flowers are to be gifted to eminent Brāhmaṇas for pleasing Madhusūdana. A pitcher of water and cow, fan and sandalpaste are to be given by pious ones always for pleasing Trivikrama. In the month of *Āṣāḍha*, a pair of shoes, umbrella, salt, *myrobalan* (*Āmalaka*) fruit etc. are to be gifted by a wise person for pleasing Vāmana. In the month of *Bhādrapada*, *Pāyasa*, honey, ghee, salt and rice with jaggery are to be gifted for pleasing Hṛṣīkeśa. In the month of *Āśvayuja*, a black horse, a bull, curds, a copper vessel and the like are to be gifted by persons for pleasing Padmanābha. In the *Kārttika* month, one should gift silver, gold, lamps, jewels, pearls and the like for pleasing Dāmodara. In the *Mārgaśīrṣa* month, one should gift donkeys, camels, mules, elephants, carts, goats and sheep for pleasing Keśava. In the *Pauṣa* month, one should devotedly gift palaces, cities and the like, houses and enclosures for pleasing Vāmana. Male and female servants, ornaments, food with six flavours are to be gifted for pleasing Puruṣottama at all times. Whatever is most liked and whatever pure is there in the house should be gifted for pleasing the Lord of Lords, the Wielder of discus.

36-37. He who constructs a temple of Keśava, will attain the meritorious and everlasting regions. By gifting gardens full of fruits and flowers, one enjoys the most commendable pleasures to his satisfaction. A person who constructs a temple of Viṣṇu will emancipate eight generations before his grandfather along with his own self.

38-43. The *Yogīs*, *Pitṛs* and *Devas* sing these *Gāthās* in the presence of the exalted hermit Yadusiṁha: "Will there ever be a devotee of Viṣṇu in our family, one who of pure vows, builds a temple of Hari ? Will there be born in our progeny, a person who wipes the floor of Viṣṇu temple and a noble soul who with devotion sweeps there ? Will there ever be born in our progeny, one who offers a flag to Keśava temple and offers to the Lord of Lords, lamp, flowers and anointment ? Will there ever be found in our family, a person who keeps fast on *Ekādaśī* day which destroys all sins ? A sinner who paints the temple of Viṣṇu, even if he has committed a major or minor sin, gets absolved of the sin."

44-47. O Bali ! Hearing these words of the *Pitṛs,* the esteemed king himself constructed a temple on the earth. He got painted in five bright colours, the incarnations of Keśava on the walls of the Keśava temple by painters. O Bali! He himself duly installed in the Vāsudeva temple, gold lamps filled with oil and ghee. He placed flags of various colours painted with *Mahārajana* (safflower) and decorated with nine-coloured *Mañjiṣṭha* and *Śvetapāṭalikā.*

48-50. Varieties of captivating gardens, adorned with flowers and fruits, covered with foliage of creepers and surrounded by *Devadāru* trees were laid by him. A platform was established by adept jewellers and skilled persons, knowing *Gandharva Vidyā* and *Rāgas.* On this platform, ascetics, *Brahmacārins,* learned *Śrotrīyas,* distressed ones, blind and other handicapped persons were regularly honoured.

51-53. Thus King Jyāmagha being faithful and self-controlled, reached the abode of Viṣṇu; so we have heard in tradition. By gifting lamps with the oils of mustard, Madhuka and Atasi, the king with his wife, having crossed over the hells called Andhatamisra, reached the abode of Viṣṇu. O Bali ! Even today, esteemed persons desirous of going to the abode of Viṣṇu, follow the path carved by Jyāmagha.

54-57. O King ! You also therefore, build a temple of Hari. You strenuously worship him and the learned Brāhmaṇas. You worship especially the expounders of *Purāṇas* who are pure and have good conduct with clothes, gems, ornaments, cows, land, gold etc. When you have the means, do that which pleases the Lord, the Wielder of discus. O Bali ! To you who will thus be engaged now in the *Yoga* of action, Murāri will certainly bestow welfare. People who take refuge in the all-pervading Jagannātha, the infinite Acyuta, never get distressed.

58. That Prahlāda, having said thus, went back to his city.

*Pulastya said:*

59. The *Daitya*-chief said these true and excellent words to Vairocana and was honoured by him. All his desires being fulfilled, he devoted himself to the feet of Hari and attained release.

60-62. After the departure of the delighted grandfather, the palace of Bali shone with the brightness of the moon. Then, the well-known leading sculptor of Indra carved the image of Keśava. He himself with his wife did sweeping, wiping and such work in the temple. The magnanimous one, made excellent offering of wheat, sugar and the like to Madhusūdana. Vindhyāvalī of wide eyes herself made gifts of lamps in the Viṣṇu temple. The wise one arranged for the recitation of the sacred (Dhārmic) texts by eminent Brāhmaṇas, the expounders of Purāṇa.

63-64. For protecting Bali, the bull among *Asuras*, who was following such a pious path, the Lord of the universe, the magnanimous Janārdana of divine form stood forth. Standing at the gate of the house of Bali and subduing the wicked kings, the Lord holding a pestle shining like a million suns, did not give entrance to wicked ones into the palace protected by enclosures.

65-66. As the creator and sustainer Nārāyaṇa, endowed with all graceful qualities stood at the gate, Bali worshipped Hari, the controller and the chief of the celestials and sages inside the palace. Bali, the king of *Asuras* was thus worshipping the lotus-feet of Hari. He always remembered the words spoken by Hari and that itself was the restrainer of his conduct.

67-73. That valiant *Daitya*-king recalling the auspicious, true and excellent words beneficial here and hereafter, uttered by the preceptor grandfather, equal to Indra, recited this episode. Even after hearing an Ill-advice earlier, those who later follow the affectionate advice of the elders become pure like butter and get delighted. There is no doubt here. A person stung by the wasp of adversity who does not know the *Mantra,* is made free from the poison by the drug known as the counsel of elders. Will the contentment that arises in people after drinking the nectar of the instructions of the elders and accepting their advice, occur after drinking *Soma*? Those, who fallen in adversity do not find elderly persons as advisers are to be mourned by their relatives, for they are as good as dead, though living. For those caught by the crocodile of adversity, because they will not have peace of mind, the deliverers are the elderly ones and not scholars. For those sinking in the waters of adversity and being carried away by the waves of miseries, certainly there is no succour of any sort except the advice of elderly ones.

*Pulastya said:*

74. Therefore, a person who listens to or acts according to the advice of the elders, obtains success immediately as did Bali, the son of Virocana.

*Here ends "The account of Trivikrama" in Vāmana Purāṇa.*

## PHALAŚRUTI

*Pulastya said:*

75. O Nārada ! This is the holiest *Purāṇa,* I have related to you as such. Hearing it, a person endowed with fame and supreme devotion, reaches the abode of Viṣṇu.

76-77. He who is always in Viṣṇu and he who duly worshipping with devotion, bows down to Viṣṇu and hears (to the *Purāṇa*), will always be united with children, wife and wealth. Such a person, absolved of sins will as well obtain the entire fruits of *Aśvamedha* with *Dakṣiṇā* and also the fruits of the gifts of gold, land, steed, cow, elephant and chariot.

78-81. A man or a woman listening to even a quarter of the *Purāṇa,* becomes pure and most holy in the world. Such a person attains the merit spoken of as accruing by going to and taking bath in an excellent *Tīrtha*, in the very holy Gaṅgā waters, in Naimiṣa or Puṣkara or in Kokamukha or in Prayāga during *Māgha* month, Brāhmaṇas say. After attaining such merit, reciting this with a concentrated mind, one does attain the abode of Vāmana. O Nārada ! I have told you today, (the *Purāṇa*) which bestows the fruits of *Rājasūya*. The entire supreme happiness one attains on the earth and in the celestial region through the performance of *Sautrāmaṇi* is attained by listening to this, O great sage ! I have no doubt here. The fruit of gifting jewels or of the gift during the eclipse of Sun or Moon (is attained by listening to this *Purāṇa*).

82-83. The fruit that is spoken of by the *Devas* for the gift of food to the hungry, to a worthy one coming with (sacrificial) fire, to one whose wife and children are distressed by famine, to a relative engaged in looking after the family, to the one who is looking after the deities, fire, Brāhmaṇas and sages, to a son or an elder brother who is looking after his parents is attained by reciting this.

84-87. O Nārada ! This eminent *Purāṇa* of Vāmana is said to be the fourteenth, by hearing which, heaps of sins, howsoever great, get destroyed at once. I have no doubt in this. O Brāhmaṇa ! By reciting, hearing or relating Vāmana's (*Purāṇa*), all the sins of any person are destroyed, O sage ! Just as the sins are cleansed by an ablution in the waters of Gaṅgā, so the evils are destroyed by hearing this *Purāṇa*. O Brāhmaṇa ! Neither disease nor poison nor witchcraft will have any effect on the body of a person or on any one of the family of a person who listens to *Vāmana Purāṇa*.

88. This is the utmost secret passed on to you which should not be revealed to one devoid of devotion to Hari, or to one who takes pleasure in censuring or in disrespecting a Brāhmaṇa or to one accepting sinful life on his own reasons.

89-90. "Salutation, salutation to the most powerful Nārāyaṇa who had the dwarf-form for a purpose, to the wielder of Śrī, *Śārṅga*, discus, sword and mace; salutation to that *Puruṣa* par excellence." To a person, with his mind fixed on Kṛṣṇa, who utters thus regularly, Viṣṇu, adored by the celestials, bestows the state of emancipation.

91. The expounder (of the *Purāṇa*) should be presented with cow, land and gold ornaments. Fraud against wealth should not be committed. If committed, that destroys the merit of listening to (the *Purāṇa*).

92. O Brāhmaṇa ! A person devoid of jealousy, reciting or listening (to the *Purāṇa*) at the three *Sandhya* points of the day gets absolved of sins and is bestowed with all prosperity.

## NOTES

(Numbers refer to Ślokas)

### CHAPTER FORTY-SIX

11. Read *Rudra-kara*. cf. 45. 30.

26. The reading *khareṇa pūjitaṁ* for *pūrve pūrṇeritam* may be correct because of the mention of Dūṣaṇa and Triśiras in the next verse. Khara, Dūṣaṇa and Triśiras were the generals of Rāvaṇa who led a massive army against Rāma who fought them single-handed in Janasthāna.

34. Read *Siddhaiḥ* for *siddham*.

46. The sentence has no verb.

### CHAPTER FORTY-SEVEN

3. Better read *nābhyā samudbhūtaḥ* for *nābhi-samudbhūtaḥ*.

4. Order of creation is given: from Viṣṇu was born Brahmā from whom Marīci came. His offspring was Kaśyapa who begot Bhāsvān. His son was Manu.

7. *Kṣutta* : the son of Manu was called so because he was born when Manu sneezed (see 5 above).

19. Niṣādas wereso called because they were the descendents of the one produced out of the right hand of Vena and was asked to sit (ni-ṣīda).

24. The second half gives incidentally, the etymology of the word *rājā*. It is associated with *rañjana*, delighting.

29. Sentence incomplete.

32. The reading *sthāṇoḥ* is better than *snātaḥ*.

33 & 38. Reading doubtful.

59. Vena patted the dog. His son Vainya was not there then. cf. 48. 26.

67. For ab cf. Nirukta.

69. Soma is the Moon as well as the Vedic deity Soma.

77. *Saṅkrandana*: name of Kṛṣṇa, literally, one who makes (people) cry.

79. Kaṭakaṭa-Kaṭaṅkaṭa ? cf. 86 below.

80. *Kṛśanāśa* is interpreted as *Kṛśana*-(pearls)-*āśa* (enjoyer). The reading *Kṛśa-nāśa* means one with a small nose.

85. b: reading appears doubtful. d: *tumbī-vīṇā*, a lute for which dried shell of gourd is used.

86. b: reading appears doubtful. cd: onamatopoeic words. cf. 79 above. Kaṭaṅkaṭa appears as a name of Gaṇapati also. See Gaṇeśa-sahasranāma in *Gaṇeśa-purāṇa*.

93. Apte notes Śṛgāla-rūpa as an epithet of Śiva.

95. Tuṇḍin is the name of bull of Śiva.

97. *-gotre* can not be dative; the masc. word has *-gotrāya*.

98. *Muñja* is a kind of grass. Six-fold duties: *svādhyāya* (study), *pravacana* (teaching), *yajana* (offering sacrifice), *yājana* (officiating in a sacrifice), *dāna* (gift), and *pratigraha* (receiving gift). There are also other sets. Three-fold duty: Kāyika (physical), Vācika (verbal) and Mānasika (mental); or Nitya (compulsory), Naimittika (occasional) and Kāmya (optional).

103. *mahā-megha-dhara* may also be interpreted as 'a big mountain'.

105. Viviparous and other forms of beings are all evolved from Śiva; hence they are all forms of Śiva.

107. The philosophers (*brahma-vādinaḥ*) speak of the supreme being (Brahma) as *haṁsa* (swan), as the peepal tree (*aśvattha* tree) and as a bee (*madhukara*).

108. *Śreṣṭhaka:Bhūri-śreṣṭhak,* name of a place near Banaras.

110. *Saṁvatsara* etc., terms for division of time. 2 *truṭis* are one *lava*; 2 *lavas* make 1 *nimeṣa*. 5 *nimeṣas* make 1 *Kāṣṭhā*; 30 *kāṣṭhās* make 1 *kalā*; 40 *kalās* make 1 *nālikā*; 2 *nālikās* make 1 *muhūrta*; 15 *muhūrtas* make 1 day/night. In another computation, 30 *Kṣaṇas* make 1 *nimeṣa*.

115. The ten characteristics of Dharma: *dhṛti* (steadfastness), *kṣamā* (perseverance), *dāma* (discipline), *asteya* (not stealing), *śauca* (cleanliness), *indriya-nigraha* (control of senses), *dhīḥ* (intelligence), *vidyā* (learning), *satya* (truthfulness) and *akrodha* (giving up anger).

119. Read *citra* for *tatra*.

126. *saṁvartaka* is cloud of deluge.

130. See ch. 5 above.

131. cd. identical with Viṣṇu-sahasranāma; see 847th and 848th names.

142. Ājya is clarified butter.

144. a: Upendravajrā. b: Indravajrā. c: ta bha ta ga ga. d: Layagrāhi.

145. a:? ma ta ja ga ga; bd: Indravajrā c: Śālinī. d: Upendravajrā c:? ya bna ta ga ga.

154. *pibate*, anological form. The root *pā* is *parasmaipadī*.

## CHAPTER FORTY-EIGHT

5. Arbuda was a *rākṣasa* killed by Indra.

## CHAPTER FORTY-NINE

7. The object of *pratiṣṭhāpya* is missing.
17. *Sthāṇve*: peculiar form, should rather be *sthāṇave*.
18. Phaṇīndra is Ādiśeṣa. Bhāskara is sun, the effulgent.
27. Reading doubtful.
37. Caturmukha is the name of Śiva cf. 43 below.
39. *tasya*, i.e. of the liṅga established by Brahmā.

## CHAPTER FIFTY

1. *bhaviṣyate* : anomalous form; it should be *bhaviṣyati*. acd: Upendravajrā; b: Indravajrā.
5. Read *śrutvā* for *dṛṣṭvā*.
6. Reading doubtful.
8. d: *vaḥ* is unsuitable.
11. ab: reading doubtful.
12. Read *pramadām* for pramādāt.
13. a: Vaṁśastha. bd: Indravajrā. c: Upendravajrā.

## CHAPTER FIFTY-ONE

17. Rāgavatī is Rāgiṇī.
19. Read *bhaviṣyasi* for *bhaviṣyati*.
22. pitṛ-śruta-is it *pitṛ-sutā* ?
31. Nirāśraya-name of a vow in which a person does not stay at any one place for more than a night.
36. Perhaps we should rather understand thus:
"Having seen her 'as if' his beloved Satī..." 63. acd: Upendravajrā; b: Indravajrā.
64. Mṛgāri, a lion or a tiger. ab: Upendravajrā;
c: Indravaṁśa; d: Vaṁśastha.

67. Śaśiprabhā is same as Somaprabhā.

68. *Varadā* is a maiden.

69. 'for your sake' i.e. 'for the sake of your marriage'.

74. ab: Vaṁśastha; c: Indravaṁśa; d: Upendravajrā.

75. Śārdūla-vikrīḍita. Verse 35 ff. have close similarity with *Kumāra-sambhava* of Kālidāsa, sarg 5.

## CHAPTER FIFTY-TWO

7. *arghya*: Part of ceremonial reception.

9. Kaśyapa and others are the seven sages.

16. Read *parvataiḥ* for *pārvatī*.

30. Read *bhṛtyaiś ca* for *bhṛtyena*.

40. When Śiva prostrates at the feet of Himavān, the father-in-law, latter's feet get covered by ashes.

42. cf. *Kumārasambhava*, 6. 83.

52. 'passing over you' i.e. 'without consulting you.'

55. cf. ch. 50.

59. Sentence incomplete; has no finite verb.

60. cf. *Kumārasambhava*, 7. 1.

62. '....' hold the hand.......' i.e. marries.

68. ab: Upendravajrā; cd: Indravajrā.

*Vandya*, form not accepted grammatically.

69. Śiva compared to a tree. Many of the lines in this chapter are similar to those of *Kumārasambhava*, sarga 6. ab: Indravajrā; cd: Upendravajrā.

## CHAPTER FIFTY-THREE

5. Surabhi and Suramā:Mother goddesses.

6. Mahasthi, a head ornament.

17. *Vasūn*, should have been in genitive case.

18. *Ṛṣisattamah* should have been in genitive case.

23. ff. *Buddhacarita* and *Kumārasambhava* have similar descriptions.

30. a: Upendravajrā; bcd: Indravajrā.

31. a: Vaṁśastha; b: Indravajrā; cd: Upendravajrā.

32. Upendravajrā.

33. Sragdharā.

34. Śārdūla-vikrīḍita. Read *ayate* for *ayati*.

35. ab: Vaṁśastha; cd: Indravaṁśa.

36. ab: Vaṁśastha; cd: Indravajrā.

37. Does the description suggest 'holi'? Sragdharā.

38. A different platform on the southern side spread out for religious observances.

40. *Śākri* : associated with Śakra, Indra, i.e. east.

42. *Pulahāgraje*. It is not clear what this means.

44. Upendravajrā.

45. a: Indravaṁśa; bd: Upendravajrā; c: Indravajrā.

46. abd : Upendravajrā; c: Indravajrā.

'ha' at the end of d to be omitted.

49. *dṛṣṭeti* should be *dṛṣṭam iti*.

61. ad: Upendravajrā; bc: Indravajrā.

62. abc: Upendravajrā; d: Indravajrā.

## CHAPTER FIFTY-FOUR

8. a: ta bha ta ga ga; b: Indravajrā; cd: Vaṁśastha.

24. Vāsava, Indra, desired to take Kauśikī, devī born of sheath, as *dakṣiṇā*.

25. Kauśika is an epithet of Indra.

30. *aindram padam*, Indra-hood.

36. *Balaghātin*, Indra the killer of Bala-asura.

42. *Kapardin* : one having braided and matted hair, an epithet of Śiva.

58-9. Text not clear.

60. *Bhadrāsana* : a type of seat.

68. *Nandim* : form not accepted grammatically; it should be *nandinam*.

72. 'Smelling head' is a mode of expressing one's affection towards younger ones.

77. Read *mandare* for *mandire* in b and *Vibhoḥ* for *vibho* in d.

78. acd: Indravajrā; b: Upendravajrā.

## CHAPTER FIFTY-FIVE

1. *Danu* : one of the wives of Kaśyapa. Those born of her are called *dānavas*.

8. Namuci felt like testing Indra's assurance. Foam being neither weapon nor missile should hurt (touch) him.

10. Namuci died because Indra embedded *Vajra* inside the foam. Thus Indra went against the agreement and was caught by sin. Perhaps, we should read *samaye tu* for *samayena*.

29. *Daitya* is the son of Diti, a wife of Kaśyapa.

cf. note 1 above.

30. *Niśumbha-Śumbhau* is an abnormal compound; *Śumbha-Niśuṁbhau* is normal.

52. Read *samāśrayan* for *samāśrayam*.

54. *cakāra* is another form of *cakre* and hence redundant.

55. Read-*mūrdha-srajam* for *-mūrdhnā srajam*.

*Khaṭvāṅga*: a weapon having two heads back to back at the tip. ac: Indravajrā; bd: Upendravajrā.

60. *caṇḍī* for *caṇḍa* in d would be better.

72. Karkoṭaka is a serpent. See 74.

77. Gharghara: girdle with small bells.

79. Perhaps *caṇḍī tv ādaya caṇḍam ca* is better for *caṇḍam* etc., in a.

80. Text not clear.

83. Read *dhārayase* for *dhārayate* in b.
84. abc: Indravajrā; d: Upendravajrā.
85. a: Indravajrā; bcd: Upendravajrā.
86. acd: Upendravajrā; b: Indravajrā.

ITI SHRI